—

THIS IS A REVOLUTIONARY BOOK
ABOUT THE AMERICAN REVOLUTION

WHY WE FOUGHT

E. G. RUTTLEDGE

ISBN 978-1-66780-244-2 eBook 978-1-66780-245-9

ACKNOWLEDGEMENTS

First and foremost a very big thank you to Mary who typed up my rough handwritten manuscripts which, at times looked more akin to Chinese Writing or Egyptian hieroglyphs, than a piece of written English text. Each page was liberally littered with coloured circles, arrows going across the page or indeed thru many pages to reach their final destination, 10 or 12 pages on or back. Block inserts would litter each page with boxes of new information to insert into the narrative. So, I can assure you all, each handing in of a chapter was with a full debriefing of colours, blocks inserts and bits of inserts and new directions for new pieces. It was a task in itself to decipher each page never mind type it up. So well-done Mary. Big thanks too to Aaron Roma, and Kyle for help with the machine i.e., the computer! With word counts, opening and saving files, emails, pictures, word counts and other such like mysteries of the modern age. A nice thank you to Irish Writers Union for encouragement and contractual advice. Writing can be a solitary enterprise so it's always nice to have people who have been there before you. All improper grammar is my fault, and is their thru fault or design. lastly, I would like to thank Madg who has been an inspiration and guiding light, and hidden hand. thru out this entire process from beginning to end.

DEDICATIONS

This work is dedicated to a little English fella, who on seeing my son and me, playing football on Princess Park, Irlam, Manchester, came running over with great excitement.

"Can I play with you" he asked. "Sure" I said. So, for three evening i took my son to the park and sure enough this nice little English Fella, would come running up with great excitement to join in. This little fella was called Drew. Full of life, friendly open and honest. A credit to his family and nation. The last night in the park I said to my son "I'll have to give Drew something for playing with you. I had four English coins in my pocket. That final night, no Drew.

By far, most English people are friendly, open, welcoming, a good laugh and morally decent. *When reading colonial history and especially Irish history one needs to keep that to the forefront of one's mind always. British people today have absolutely nothing to do with past wrongs, centuries ago.*

A generation born today have no hold of what generations did before one was born. You cannot and must not deliver the sins of the fathers onto their sons. That would be grossly immoral and a travesty of justice. English people today, had no say in American taxes, stamp duties, or conduct of the war, over two hundred years ago before they were ever born! Indeed, they have as much responsibility for what happened two hundred years ago as Pinkie and Perky, Mr. M Mouse. Mr. D. Duck. or Scooby-Doo and Shaggy.

This needs to be kept in the forefront of your mind, especially with regards to Irish History. Which one old English gentleman historian of English history, a man who wrote the Everyman History of England; when he turned his attention to Irish History this well-respected, and much read English Historian had to give up! It was too *dreadful*, he just could not go on with the catalogue of English, abuse, misuse, torture hangings, mass starvation programmes and enormous ethnic cleansing programs. It was all just too appalling to research never mind publish. This poor old man was sickened to the core. Also, this book is not only dedicated to that little English chap, this little book is dedicated to all the children of the world who are starting on their collective journeys of life. Life can be very tough for some of our little human people. Death and destruction haunt the middle East like an ugly cancer Spreading its tentacles of sectarianism, hatred, and intolerance. In many cases carefully fostered and promoted for geopolitical reasons to destabilise and destroy their countries from within. The work of Mr. fork tongue himself. The mad man in the furnaces, with every intention of stoking the flames of intolerance, within people's hearts and heads. This book is dedicated to all the poor kids in Palestine in the Gaza strip whose daily life is a struggle. Whose only schools are run by the United Nations. They deserve better.

The American dream was one small step for mankind, but potentially a giant leap for humanity. We all deserve to have, a little, liberty, freedom, and justice. For in the final analysis, we all breathe the same air, we all inhabit this same earth. ..."This generation of Americans has already had enough, more than enough of war and hate and oppression...We shall also do our part to build a world of peace were the weak are safe" *... 2000 thousand years ago a man called Jesus walked the hills, streets, pastures of Jerusalem, Bethlehem, Judea and Galilee preaching peace. He sure is needed now.

WHY WE FOUGHT

The middle eastern peoples are sick to death of violence. Sick to the core. All peoples of all places. Mothers, Fathers, Sisters and Brothers, aunts and uncles of all creeds all races are sick of this violent sickness, and wars dementedness and human contrived insanity.

America and its people have much good to offer the world. Far more than detention without trial for a lifetime, or much more than arresting journalists for telling the truth! This last observance, telling the truth, used to be an American virtue and not how it is today, a vice or crime to be punished. For in the final analysis, Americas hard won freedoms of speech are the envy of the rest of the world; as are its freedom of information acts, which hold the powerful to public inspection. These hard-fought rights will go, if not protected from the rich and powerful; and in doing, if they are lost, a little piece of the American dream dies, and is lost within it. The American dream, could die of a thousand and one tiny cuts to its freedoms, each cut just slicing a little more off its healthy body, social and politic. Till eventually only a grotesque caricature of plastic surgery is all that is left to view and behold. A highly ugly and contorted lady of liberty, to grotesque to even look upon or stare at! America's soul too will be damaged, if these freedoms are mitigated against; if not indeed lost or surrendered, *forever*.

America is coming out of its two decades in the valley of darkness, and re-emerging into the broad sunlit uplands, flowing green pastures, and sparkling fresh springs and streams, of its green and pleasant land.

Has it gone astray, like a lost sheep? Has It betrayed its very founders and its glorious Declaration for humanity? America and its peoples have much more to offer the world, as regards individual freedoms and liberties for all. America needs to stand up for its own good principles, which have served it well in the past, and will serve it well, into the future.

America and Americans must not throw out the baby with the bath water when it comes to cherished freedoms the envy of all mankind.

Power must be checked and come with its in built freedoms, civil liberties, rights and responsibilities for those, and from those who wield and exercise power. President Eisenhower, the slayer of the demonic dragon called Nazism, with its in- built hierarchy of humanity, personally, warned the American people before he left the highest office, to be on their ever-watchful guard, "against the acquisition of unwarranted influence ...by the military industrial complex {today we would call it the military industrial mass surveillance complex} he went on to warn Americans before he left office... "The potential for the disastrous rise of misplaced power exists" {then} and will continue to exist and persist. ** That's quite some warning from a departing American president to his peoples and public. A human man who had led American young men on a crusade to slay demonic overarching power Today Americans should take heed of President Eisenhower's final warning; especially congressmen, congresswomen, senators, vice-Presidents, serving and past speakers and serving and past Presidents.

What is happening today is a direct threat to fundamental freedoms of the press. Americas papers, and T. V. channels, need to be on their guard against the unwarranted acquisition of power by the unelected, including themselves!

The Freedoms Washington fought so valiantly for and the freedoms enshrined in the founding documents of America, the freedoms many Americans have died for. Do not let them, to have died in vain, those now gone, resting in their individual graves, in blessed repose, under perpetual light, shining upon their souls.

WHY WE FOUGHT

If you travelled to Normandy, France, just above the golden sandy beaches, are to be found the graves of young American boys and men all neatly lined up, in their well cared for beds of eternal rest. This was as far as they got, all the way from America to die along the shore and sand on the edge of the French coastline. Just a few feet in! Some never even got to set their booted feet onto French soil. They died in the water wading and swimming for land. The water turned *red* with their young blood.

That some sacrifice to make; and make it they did in their thousands. You can run your fingers along their etched names on their white bleached tombstones. These were real genuine living breathing people, with real emotions. They were as alive as you are now, with their thousand and one worries and thoughts. Within minutes they would be dead. Many taking their last breath upon this Earth, this very same Earth you are now upon. They sacrificed it all for you and me, that we may live in a world without hidden camps, and other such hidden evils. American families paid a high price for liberty, and common decency.

The flame of Americas rights and individual freedoms, has been success-fully passed down from one generation to the next generation, for years, decades, nay centuries. An ever-watchful American population, must guard against infringements, breaches of contractual faith, or transgres-sions, whenever American freedoms are trampled upon or disrespected. These collective freedoms are your freedoms, they are hard won, with blood. A constant ever watchful vigil by American Citizenry is needed to protect these rightfully cherished civic and individual rights and freedoms. President Eisenhower was so right to warn the American public as his last duty of the highest office in the land, to warn about the threats unelected powerful elites can have, or acquire, in American civic functioning and political representation. These much-loved rights are the envy of the rest of the world, they have served you and your community well in the past since the Revolution, and they will serve you and your family and the community well into the coming future.

In God we Trust

I commit this work to the general reader for
their consideration and approvement.

*Speech by President J.F. Kennedy of the United States of America, delivered at American University, Washington D.C. June 10th 1963

**President Dwight D. Eisenhower farewell televised address and warning to the American population and citizenry made on January 17th 1961

WHY WE FOUGHT

"One of the greatest mysteries of American history has revolved around the intriguing question of how General George Washington and his revolutionaries, could have possibly prevailed over the mighty British Empire. Many explanations have been offered to explain, this enduring mystery. Can a more accurate and *correct* answer be found at this late date, to better explain how and why England lost its thirteen colonies?

For more than two centuries now, what has been forgotten"? What part of the story has been lost? *.. What indeed?

*Historian Philip Thomas Tucker Author "How the Irish Won the American Revolution". Skyhorse pub. Taken from an extract in www SALON.com "The Irish have become the forgotten players of Americas struggle for Independence "March 17th, 2020

Major Jason Palmer, Assistant prof: of History at the United States Military Academy…. West Point.

"One of the primary jobs of American historians is to be MYTH, BUSTERS"

THE IRISH AT THE CUTTING EDGE OF AMERICAN FREEDOM:

To you the reader; what you are about to embark upon, is a journey back in time, to the real revolution. That your descendants or fellow countrymen experienced, and in some cases died for, to enable it to come true. What you are about to read is no Walt Disney version of these times and happenings. No neat smart uniforms will be on show.

The continental army regulars were rough, tough, scruffy, diseased, starved, and ill shod. But they could shoot and use tomahawks and knifes and bayonets up close and personal, to kill their enemy. Down south a mean guerrilla war was waging with all its internecine violence and atrocities. The American Revolution was tough, very tough, and a very close-run thing. This book I hope brings some of that reality to the smoke-filled pages. Blood and guts abounded, much of it innocent. The violence could be visceral, destroying mind and body. You are about to read the truth, the whole truth, and nothing but the truth... So, help me God.

IN GOD WE TRUST

WHY WE FOUGHT

Very IMPORTANT NOTICE, thru out book, when New Englanders are mentioned, the author is not referring to the geographical place, or its general inhabitants but to the landed gentry, who at that time in the American Revolution cared more for their British heritage than American Independence, and more IMPORTANTLY who subsequently have made themselves out to be the true patriots, when history shows that not to be the case at all! They created a legacy which in my humble opinion may be misplaced, for when one puts the American Revolution under the historical microscope a very different outcome and analysis clearly comes into view. It is one thing to have misplaced loyalties, many did, and honourably held too. But it is a totally different matter to steal the show and legacy from its true heirs, the American poor, the American Army foot-sloggers and its Southern Partisans, and those communities and heroic individuals which struggled long and very hard under extreme physical and mental hardships, that would have wrecked most people. To them rightly goes the victory laurels. AND very hard they were won too, very hard.

CONTENTS

George Washington the leader of the Revolution. No George Washington, no Revolution. For seven long years he carried America's cross all alone, on the battle front.

The real founding fathers of the United States of America, the ragged poor who would not lie down and be beaten. Who fought shoeless, in rags, full of disease and could bear any burden, under the most extreme circumstances, under which no other army could have endured over 7 long torturous years, to a final victory on American soil. The very first American Army to take to the field under the Stars n stripes. circa 1777. Who gave as good as they got!

CHAPTER 1

Brothers In Arms

......A brave New World - in tatters and torn.

"There is no gloomier period in our American Revolution than that which marked the retreat of Washington's skeleton army across New Jersey. None more cheering and important than that which witnessed the capture of the Hessians and the repulse of Cornwallis. Now known as the two battles of Trenton". (F.n. lifted from preface to some antiquarian book I have misplaced... and found again!" Battles of Trenton & Princeton Pub. 1871.by C. C. Haven) Benjamin franklin visited the Irish House of Parliament prior to 1776 (in 1769 & 1771). The Irish Parliamentarians insisted Benjamin Franklin be sat amongst them. A privilege and requirement, strictly according to parliamentary protocol, only applicable to representatives of other countries and sovereign states. Visitors were only allowed to sit in the Gallery. This showed to the world for all to see that with regards to the American 13 colonies, Irish parliamentarians considered them a country in their own right. This was the first time anyone had declared such an outrageous proposition or entity. To the Irish, Benjamin Franklin was no mere visitor, he was the Representative, representing America. A country in Irish eyes separate to Britain. And what's more they did not care two hoots for anyone's sensibilities or political peevishness. So, make no mistake about it, Ireland and the Irish people were the first ones to recognise Americas rights as a separate nation equal to; Spain, France, Portugal, or Britain, the old European countries at that time.

The Americans were interested in how the Irish Parliament operated within British Sovereignty. Ireland was a separate legal and parliamentary body with its own laws and taxation policy (it wasn't part of the Blessed Union then; 1801 Act of Union) Benjamin Franklin, was impressed with the Irish set up, most Americans at that time were not pushing for full independence or even a fight with H.M.G.

Later on, after Benjamin Franklin's visit... just prior to 1776... his Majesties government forced through laws on Irish Taxation without Irish representation i.e., they did not discuss this matter with the Irish Representative parliament. From now on H.M.G. stated it did not need Irish Parliamentary approval to raise taxes in Ireland. The Americans were shocked at this affront to representative democracy, and H.M.G.s willingness to assert such an undemocratic abuse of power over an established and sitting parliament The American Masons took note of this shocking action; the die was set, though not stated in public. From that moment on, the movers and shakers the hidden hand of history were quietly at work, every day and into the wee small hours of night, feverishly working away, organising Rebellion and talking sedition in America. The sands of time were running out of the British historical timepiece, as far as America, s rule was concerned. The countdown to rebellion had begun!

To the clever men, the vanguard of the American Revolution, the die was cast, only the people needed to be aroused. The vanguard would await and fabricate if need be; the spark that would set America alight and set it onto a new journey. To boldly go where no government or country had ever trod before, into the pursuit of freedom, liberty, and happiness, as a stated, countries aim, purpose, and governmental pursuit.

The book, "A case for Ireland" pub; 1698, by William Molyneux, the American Masonic inner circle of revolutionaries, ensured that this little book was widely distributed throughout the 13 colonies, pre- revolution. It was just as popular as Thomas Paine's, "Common sense", and his "The American crisis" which would be published later on. William Molyneux's little book showed up British corrupt rule in Ireland, its abuse of pension lists, and questioned the rights of any British sovereign to rule over the Irish people or bring in legislation in which the Irish had not been consulted upon, nor voted its consent upon. etc this little book was widely distributed with other pro revolution tracts. H.M.G. was so scared of Mr. Molyneux little book, they took the outrageous step of officially publicly burning the little book, like a convicted witch! They ordered the Public Hangman to officially burn this book! This little book was duly burnt in public by the hooded man. It was given no representation nor legal trial; the book was found guilty of having *uncomfortable* ideas by H.M.G. And duly burnt at the royal stake.

The poor little book took its sentence well. With stoic fortitude it went to its death admirably, without letting out a righteous yelp or whispering a screech, it faced down the hooded villain, as he turned its little uncomfortable pages to ashes. It may burn the book, but it cannot put out the flames of freedom and fairness to all that it so eloquently told its readers all about.

The noble human rights this little book espoused and promoted, freedom of conscience, human civic rights and the noble pursuit of happiness, an equitable and fair tax system. Such talk as the little book spoke, was all treachery to the British elite. Such dangerous ideas needed to be stamped upon thoroughly,, given absolutely no chance to grow, they needed to be

rooted out! Common democracy, human equality was going too far...
Equality and democracy!

The British elite had no intention of letting these pollical pursuits and
human freedoms or any other freedoms for that matter develop on the
American continent; and it had no intention of letting America go lightly.
If these dangerous ideas of human freedom or liberty; as a bad example,
to all; if they ever took root into the American soil, or its mind, then they
would be answered with British cold steel, and fiery cannons, if needs be.

Britain regarded the whole continent of America as British. German king
George over 3000 miles away in his dickied up palace had no intention to
give in to American wishes. If the Americans wanted freedom, then by
God they would have to take the gun from the clasping hands of the British
soldiers, from their dying hands the gun would have to be snatched and
placed into the hands of freedom. The fight of the titans was about to begin.
Soon militias would be formed trained, drilled, and organised. If America
were ever to win its freedom it might have to take to the field in arms. It was
one thing to talk about Democracy and human freedoms and rights in the
Taverns of New England; another completely different spectacle to endure
and prosecute resistance over many hard years of toil, and deep, deep suffering to bring to fruition their Progressive laws, deliberations, and enact-
ments. *All* could possibly be settled on the bloody battlefields of America!

Another gent, Thomas Paine, was stating truths too, to all that would listen.
He too promoted equality before the law and representative government
of the people, by the people, for the people. As Americans would find out,
Thomas Paine's ideas came at a terrible cost. And that cost was written in
blood and sacrifices. Soon time would tell, those who were determined to
stay and fight. Those who fought, and those who fled.

...TIME & PLACE.... The very first official year of battle for independence...early December 1776, New Jersey

Washington's Army had just taken numerous beatings one after the other, off the Mighty British Expeditionary force sent over in a vast Armada to teach these American upstarts a lesson in the affairs of war and the display of real power; that delivered from the barrel of British guns and cannons. This was the largest ever amphibious Armada ever to set sail in the history of the world.*. This large task force must have, to the American Public and its armed boys and men, intimidated, impressed, and horrified all at the same time. These American patriots, would soon find out, that the regular professional soldiers of the British Army were well trained very well equipped and knew how to fight and subdue a population, with uppity ideas, above and beyond their stations. They would soon be brought to heel and learn how to be good and loyal subjects of their esteemed king. Americans had to be taken down, a peg or two. And that my friends is what duly happened, that long hot summer of 1776. The British Army and their hired guns, the much-feared Hessians, had duly kicked Washington's army out of the important loyal harbour and port town of New York. Long, Island too had been overrun by the British and their mercenaries, just guns for hire, brought over to teach these Americans upstarts humility and obedience to their betters.

The American Army was a shambles and on the retreat. Both Fort Washington, and Fort Lee had been overrun and successfully captured. Unfortunately, both were lost with their well stacked hordes of vital equipment. All was lost militarily. Washington's patriots, 90% of them saw the writing on the wall and fled, tout sweet. Back to their warm homestead's nice hot fires, farms, and families. American Independence was a busted flush, a veritable pipe dream. The vast majority had fled the field whilst they still could, get out alive! General Washington had confessed to a relative in a letter; that he thought the game was up!

Only the die-hards remained around the American flag. The Die-Hards were mostly the Irish and they to a man were going nowhere fast. To the Die-Hards or the American Freedom fighters; for one could no longer call it an Army. The Army had up and left: Only the real hard core stayed fast and stuck to the spot. They had nailed their colours, to the mast of Freedom and Liberty, come what may; either hell or high water. They had every intention to fight the British. And whilst they could still muster a few thousand, in their Irish eyes, the game was most definitely still on. That hard core was 100% Irish or as near as 100% can be. What in the name of God was going on? Let me explain my little children, all gather round, to hear the tale of how America, won its freedom from the British. Those who stayed, those who fought. And more importantly Why they fought?

When the most glorious revolution happened in Britain in 1688. Orange William had fought with James 2, his father-in-law, on behalf of his wife the daughter of the opponent. This is a typical, British royalty, family Squabble. Fathers fighting sons, brother killing each other, murders of dads, sons, daughters, wives etc. this murderous tittle tattle by royal chavs who deserved a bloody good kick up the bum and definitely not worshipping or glorifying or bowing down to. This royal, definitely non-Christian, heathen white trailer trash; constantly killing their own kin, good God! (More akin to the Jeremy kyle show or the American Jerry Springer show) Anyway, on victory, low life Just Williams, apartheid laws were introduced into America, Catholics lost all rights and liberties with one stroke of his royal feather tipped pen.

Flatitious, flagitious, decadent lord William himself, had pronounced religious Apartheid was king. Unchristian sectarianism was heavily promoted in law and deeds. Certain longstanding Christians, minding their own business, had become with one stroke of the heathen royal pen, "nonpersons" people with no rights in America. Freedom of religion was banned in America. British *liberties* meant tyranny for many other human beings. Taxes were increased. America was to be run; how British royalty deemed it.

A very large proportion of the population of Pennsylvania was Irish, not Anglo-Saxon. Pennsylvania was extremely pro-independence. As to a lesser extent was the great state of Virginia. Washington on his retreat from the New York debacle, was retreating towards friendly territory. Both Virginia and Pennsylvania promised the hope of new recruits. As Washington retreated across New Jersey he was extremely disappointed that the New Jersey militia did not turn out as he had so desperately hoped. The reality was, it all looked like it was over. Washington was an extremely desperate man, in treacherous times and most looked like they would be joining a defeated Army on the run. A shambolic Army: if one could call this rabble an Army? From New York and towards the Friendly territory of Pennsylvania and the relative safety of the Delaware river this pathetic Army trudged along. Washington was heartbroken. America's dream was in tatters. Washington knew the game was up and so too did congress. American Independence was a lost cause, a spent force, a veritable busted flush. All that Britain had to do was clean up these last remnants and parade itself ticker tape style, thru loyalist New York. As the triumphant Army! Maybe even, march some American P.O.W.s at bayonet point thru the streets of New York, for all to laugh and jeer at.

An army of fools with a dejected George Washington at the front; for people to jar and spit at. Such a stupid man. Not on his high horse now! For that was how it looked all November 1776. The war was over and mass desertions were rife. A full 90% had fled. Brave though they had struggled; the professional British Army, along with the tough nuts of Europe, the Hessians, had thoroughly beaten every continental regiment, battalion, and platoon into the ground. Now they were fleeing, and good riddance to them and their blasted seditious pamphlets. They had all run home to their safe armchairs and warm fires. And would swear blind that they had not partaken in open treachery against their esteemed king. Their venerated and anointed sovereign who duly demanded their rightful obedience, to him, in all matters including personal matters of one's religion.

Religion decided whether one got fed or not, or if one had the legal right to farm their own land. Hundreds of thousands of starving Catholics in Ireland had, had their land confiscated, just for praying in the old-fashioned way. A way the kings' own descendant had adhered to for nigh on more than a thousand years. Ten long centuries, and more.

Anyone who refused to accept the latest king as master in all matters of private religion, was a traitorous fiend, a malcontent, a very religious miscreant who needed close observation, torture, or expulsion. These were the laws just William introduced into Britain, America and Ireland, and anyone who prayed in the old-fashioned way the way they had done for century upon century for over a thousand years straight from the apostle's times, anyone who refused to pray in the new way as dictated to them by the earthly king or Queen, or refused to smash up statues, or tear down altars, and tabernacles, was to be officially derided, laughed at, or murdered. And in some obscene cases, officially tortured in a most extreme and painful way, in public in front of children too. The good-natured English people were aghast at such monstrous activity; far from welcoming the new practices, they rejected them for decades and decades. What was wrong with the old way? The reformation was a very hard sell, and could only float with much horror stories from the robber's presses, which were going at full pelt for decades even down to the twentieth century. (For a honest and true protestant history of the English reformation do not read a Catholic one, read a good protestant history, read William Cobbett's the Reformation in England and Ireland. A really good exciting history of that process)

Head-chopping now became a popular public spectacle for all those who refused to bow down to the king and his new fundamentalist so called perverted Christianity. All religious pictures were to be smashed as heathen images; all churches whitewashed. Colour was idolatrous All old-fashioned Catholics staying true to old fashioned religious practices, came in for very special "treatment". All rights were taken off them.

In Ireland they were banned from towns, had their land confiscated, and were duly cast out onto the roads in their millions. Whole families made destitute. Many starved to death, women, kid's, children too. Excuses for mass torture and slaughter, were easily fabricated and made up, more land confiscations followed, and these cycles continued thru out decades even centuries. Indeed, behind their backs, the military elite the new perverted "Christians", wrote letters to each other, joking about the mass slaughter to come the fabulous wealth to be stolen. All admitted to it, in their most private inner most thoughts in their own hand written letters. In public the people to be slaughtered where constantly derided as filth, stupid, or some other caricature of twisted reality

For this scheme to really work well and efficiently and ensure the new rich, kept their massive wealth, this new wealth had to be continuously reinforced with historical justifications for pilfering it. Scandalous stories were liberally invented and old Christians were continuously demonised, derided, and vilified; indeed, old fashioned Christianity straight from the Apostles was systematically outlawed. English history degenerated into one

9

fabulously long narrative for the justification of this robbery, and still does down to this day hold vestiges of protestant supremacy. Exaggerated stories of simony, and the selling indulgences nepotism, these *stories* must be seen as exceptions so says Britanica.com. and quiet rightly. "*These instances must be seen as exceptions, however no matter how much they were played up by polemicists. For most people, the church continued to offer spiritual comfort.* "Thank you! Britannica. com. REFORMATION.

The New Christian fundamentalists set about burning down England's Cathedrals. And most ancient monasteries. In many cases blowing them up with dynamite; their very presence an uncomfortable reminder to the robbers of what they had done in their name.

Over time all was forgotten; and only the blown-up monasteries and churches remained, like sticking out rotten teeth, craggy and barren. A culture destroyed by subterfuge and horror stories. All those left still clinging on to the apostle's creed; the public were told needed close observation and could not be trusted, unlike the true robbers who became rich viscounts' and other such snobby self-congratulatory titles they so generously bestowed so graciously upon their most deserving selves.

Old Catholic Christians from classical roman times fitted that new bill of miscreants accordingly. A neurosis of new taxes were invented to penalise them. If they wanted to remain true to their religion, the religion of their ancestors and the apostles, and their own original English Kings and Queens for well over a thousand years and more, then they would have to pay handsomely for that *religious privilege*. If that did not work, then confiscate all their land and make them homeless, babies and children too. This is what the new religion brought in.

Mass expulsions followed in Ireland. Just like the American Red Indians, the Irish sticking to the original apostle's creed were expelled en masse onto the reservation rough lands. Or indeed expelled from their own country! 17th century ethnic cleansing was practised on a massive scale.

Apartheid, Segregation, and psychops; mind control programmes, soon followed for the masses to spread hate animosity, and antagonism towards people of the old original faith and between the new Christians by the robbers. The Irish in Ireland, once the finest educators of all Europe, soon became beast's, criminals, ignoramuses, or even indeed sub-human! The dye was set. Many fled to America to escape this new governments virtue, of torture, discrimination, and a strict system of unchristian legal religious apartheid, reinforced with a liberal hate message to boot.

The reformation scam was sold so well most aren't even aware that it was a scam! Only today safe from repossession of their ill-gotten gains does the elite allow the true story to be told. Today English Christian ecumenism and toleration reign supreme as it should always have. British society today is very welcoming to all religions. And its established religion is today a very broad church both Catholic and Protestant, in belief and ceremony The Kings and Queens remain catholic church goers, not new protestant bible-bashers in sandals, dancing around an oak tree.

Priests and apostolic Bishops still reign in England, for all its faults of which there are many, it still preaches the Apostolic message of care for the poor, handicapped, widows, children, human equality before God, a shared community, shared values, a moral code of conduct and a good life worn well is a life worth living. It was to these human values that made the British reject Nazism thou on the floor and denuded, and stand up and together as a Christian community save humanity for another thousand years. A debt that cannot be repaid, only lived thru. It was to these shared true Christian values that physically handicapped paraplegic President Roosevelt and British Drunk Churchill, and their respective sailors' soldiers and chiefs of staff Prayed together in Placenta Bay. The British and Americans saved Christendom the Nazis held demonic torch lit pagan processions, built secret evil camps and introduced the Nuremberg laws. Need I say any more.

When the American Revolution broke out, all the Irish rushed en masse to expel their tormentor. To get them off their land. To this cause, they were more than willing to die for. They had joined up in their thousands, far outnumbering all others. This was *their* fight; their time had come.

Now all those hopes, and dreams seemed shattered. Everybody else had fled, eight hundred German hardcase patriots still trudged along with the Die Hard Irish. They must have been extremely tough, mentally to carry on with the struggle, at these desperate times under such in-human circumstances and chronic physical hardships, enough to break any sane man. Those left, were fleeing south, towards the mighty Delaware. They had every intention to avoid the ticker tape reception of the defeated, marched at the points of British bayonets thru New York Town.

The triumphant British for their part were in chase to finish off the dregs, the pathetic remnants of the laughable continental Army. This Army looked more like a bunch of tramps, some only half-dressed tramps! God pity their silly little souls. Deluded on Thomas Paine's, pamphlets.

Flee was all they were good for! Democracy. And. freedom! What silly nonsense!

WHY WE FOUGHT

They moved like a mass of dirty tired men, draped in a few filthy rags. Most had some sort of accoutrements on their feet, oddments of shoes with their toes cut out of, so a man could slip his larger foot into a smaller shoe. Some had pieces of cow hide wrapped and secured around their feet, others had rags tied and secured. Some poor souls had nothing, except bloody swollen pieces of raw naked feet. This is what the American Continental Army had been reduced down to, over the summer and autumn of the revolutionary year 1776. All hope seemed long gone, all dreams, desires of freedom, yearnings for a better life seemed as if they belonged to another era, a past semi- conscious-dream time experience.

Now, the Continental Army was broken asunder, all the British had to do was mop up the dregs and deliver the coup de grace. And put this Army out of its misery! Those who saw this spectre, all shivered with bleak chilly despair. This slowly crawling mass was pathetic in the extreme. It trundled Passed the warm windows and fires of New Jersey homes; people inside dare not look upon them. Washington was totally, totally despondent, he had hoped the New Jersey militia would have turned out; but it did not, and any sane man would not blame them one bit. What was the point of joining a defeated army taking its last gasps of battlefield smoke ridden air? Washington had been clutching at straws. A veritable pipedream. Hallucinations of misguided patriotism filled his very head. Along with a thousand and one other worries, all mounting up. Ceaselessly mounting up. One worry on top of another annoyance, to vex his tormented weary mind. And weary was a word which summed up this motley collection. Exhausted, fatigued, jaded, worn out to the very bone. Harassed chased and harried; the British Army bore down on them to finish them off. Washington was turning into very desperate man, and these were very, very desperate times, indeed.

In his own inner thoughts, he knew the game was up; totally. And so too did Congress. The continental Army was between a rock and a hard place, and all sides were closing in fast! Those who could, had crawled out to safety, whilst they could quickly squeeze out, past the sentries, and escape the clutching, grasping hands and arms of the British Army. Its eyes and ears were everywhere in the shape of American Loyalists, now smelling victory. Many American soldiers gave up with pain and serious injuries. Others gave up mentally, worn out to the very last breath they could summon up to breathe. They collapsed, fell prostrate and gave up by the New Jersey roadside, physically and mentally unable to tread another step.

They laid down by the verge to await the inevitable, either death or the British, or sometimes both together. Those unfortunate to survive this far; were barely hanging on. They were full of dysentery, fever, and various other communicable chronic diseases. They had been hunted down, and now only a trail of blood, sweat and tears, the dead, sick, and dying, were left in this army's wake.

A veritable Via Dolorosa, a shroud of tears and heart break, hung over the weary men. This was the way of the cross. The American Army was dripping..., bleeding its way to Golgotha. Like Jesus, it had been well and truly scourged at the pillar time and time, and time again, and had suffered and endured a baptism of fire; One quickly after another. Now it only waited its crucifixion!

The American Continental army, over the summer of 1776 had gone from a 23,000, buoyant and an eager man army, to just 3,800 diehards left, come late December. A full 90% of the Continental army had upped and left. American independence was a lame duck. Those who could evacuate or desert or just get home, had all upped and left. The dream was over; the British professional expeditionary force, had swept the raw green inexperienced Continental army off the battlefield tout sweet. The Continental army had got, more than one or two or three good kicking's. British order was righteously being restored. The American patriots had now sulked home, those still alive and not yet captured, to lick their various wounds, hide their militia uniforms, and any pamphlets of "Common Sense" by Thomas Paine. Mr. Paine's, "Common Sense" now seemed like an unbelievably bad idea. Their loyalist neighbours must have looked on smugly. Very smugly indeed.

Later on, in December 1776 New York loyalists would paint an "R" on the doors of all those they suspected of Republican ideals. Now the shoe was on the other foot. The biggest amphibious landing in the history of mankind up to then; had deposited in New York estuary up to 34,000 soldiers.

*William of Oranges Invasion of Britain was actually far larger A monstrous heavily armed Dutch army Landed in the south of England to take over the country. It vastly dwarfed the infamous Spanish armada, by some degree. This was a heavily funded invasion by the city of London, it was essentially, an organised military coup. Glorious Williams Dutch Armada consisted of an enormous 500 ships, 21,000 troops, canons, horses feed etc. It was in fact 4times larger than the infamous Spanish Armada.

William did not bring freedom to England he actually brought in the bloodiest penal code in all of Europe. See Robert Ingraham. "The modern Anglo-Dutch Empire". How anyone can claim promoting and legally enforcing Sectarianism is a step forward or somehow defending freedom. Freedom for who? It beggars any rational thinking enlightened persons thought processes. It is highly contorted gymnastics of reality, to believe he brought anything but sectarianism. Sectarianism has ruined Ireland and its peoples, for centuries, and very heavily it was promoted too. It brought nothing but a cancerous division eating away at heart of Irelands civic society, and its peoples. The *freedom* loving British Empire would soon become the world's biggest enslaver of human beings in the history of the whole wide world. Britain now saw its duty to God and society as requiring it, to submit their fellow humans, to violent punishments, distress anxiety, chained up, deprived, whipped raped and beaten, millions upon millions of brown black African children kidnapped and mass human trafficked to British plantations in America.

How any Christian country can call such activity, an advancement or bringing civilisation to people is chronic self-delusion and organised depravity. These are the thoughts of the looney bin. (Britain where ever it went it elites duly promoted sectarianism in its wake as a device of its hegemonic control. It did this in Ireland and the American thirteen colonies)

...New York, July,1776 the infamous British armada disgorges 34,000*(some say 25,000 the 34,000 is from History.com) battle hardened redcoats with their German mercenaries a full third of the army were German Hessians, hired guns, tough nuts of Europe, onto American soil to teach these upstarts a lesson they would not forget too soon. Washington with his remnants of the Revolution were being hunted and chased to ground by a much larger vastly experienced British army, and its hired thugs. The once mighty patriotic army was duly kicked out of New York, kicked out of Long Island, kicked out of forts, Lee, and fort Washington. And the continental army had lost all of its much-needed military hardware when these two forts were over run.

As they approached the mighty river Delaware, and the faint hope of some safety, any safety! Maybe they must have hoped, they might live to see another day, many already *hadn't*.

If Washington could cross the Delaware, he would be in a more secure position for the winter. Before he crossed over, he made sure the way ahead was secure and prepared with enough boats, all ready to cross the remnants of the American army over, just as soon as they began to appear and turn up, on the Delaware's banks. Washington was a great man to reconnoitre ahead; he never liked moving into territory he did not have the eyes up on.

The stragglers, the remnants of the Continental Army, had starved all the way from Hackensack to Newark and all the way from Newark to Brunswick* (this little phrase I picked up from a book, but which book I'm not sure, but I thought it captured the essence of this tragic story so well.) As they approached the mighty Delaware river, friendly encouraging voices greeted them one and all. These were Irish voices, and they were 100% full in for the Revolution. The greater mass of those still clinging on for dear life, still in the fight were Irishmen and boys. The man who owned Mc Conkeys ferry a large flat-bottomed ferry pulled on ropes or wire slung across the river, was an Irishman. Presbyterian by faith. He was a hardnosed American patriot. Washington had sent two Irishmen forward to organise the logistics of crossing the entire American army over, as quickly as possible. It would take days to achieve this initial crossing. Wexford born Captain John Barry made contact with Cavan born Paddy Calvin who actually operated the ferry. By the time the continental army started to turn up, the Irish neighbours had scoured both banks for boats, for mile after mile, helped by a forward detachment of continental soldiers. Boats had to be tied together and rowed either up or down river.

The McConkey's large ferry was able to carry; coach's cannons, and horses across the mighty Delaware river. The Irish neighbours ensured a veritable Armada of small boats awaited them when they arrived. Slowly but surely, the exhausted stragglers began to turn up in little bunches. They quickly began the hurried crossing, of what was left of the mighty continental

Army. It was travelling light, most of its equipment and stores had been lost. Over the next number of days all its cannons and horses would be safely on the far bank of the river. The Irish patriots made sure no boats were left on the British side. For tens of miles in either direction. Once over the Delaware the Continental Army was among friends. Many Irish and Scotch Irish resided in the area. Pennsylvania was full of both.

Washington noted that the Irish were his most fervent supporters, when all else had deserted him. One English traveller during the time of the American revolution notes "For whilst the Irish emigrant was fighting the battles of America by sea and land, the Irish merchants particularly in Charlestown, Baltimore and Philadelphia laboured with indefatigable zeal and at all hazards to promote the spirit of enterprise to increase the wealth and maintain the credit of the country" P/157 *A hidden Phase of American History*. Here the visitor is greatly impressed with the Irish zeal in Philadelphia to set up a bank to save the Revolution; (Bank of North America set up by merchants of Philadelphia most of them Irish in 1782) and the fact that Irish merchants supplied the Continental Army when most *American* ones refused their money or trade. But I think you will get the analogy. As the Continental Army clambered onto the Pennsylvania side of the Delaware and into thankful safety, they could thankfully give their tired bodies some much needed and desperately longed for, rest.

They were a collective mess; their own mothers and sisters would not have recognised them. Some crossing over the Delaware were extremely worn out with big shaggy beards, full of disease and lice, in rags and a few totally nude! One soldier was helped out by his comrades up the embankment on the Pennsylvania side of the river. This soldier had a very scraggy beard, was thin, half-starved to death, covered in sores, barely able to walk, he looked a mess. Once up on the embankment, the scraggy man staggered out of line and came towards an American officer. This is how that American officer described the staggering barely dressed patriot… "He had lost all his clothes. He was in an old dirty blanket jacket, his beard long and his face full of sores… which so disfigured him that he was not known by me on first sight. Only when he spoke, did I recognise my brother James". James Peale had joined the thousand strong Maryland regiment, which had fought all over New York. James along with about a hundred others, were all that was left, of that once strong fit body of men.

This was the invincible American army in winter 1776 – run to ground. Citizens would describe them as positively revolting. Charles Wilson Peale, the American officer that did not recognise his own brother. Was a true patriot Once he got over the disgusting surprise of the physical shape of James; he looked back over the mighty Delaware; It was night and General Washington had ordered large fires to be lit all along the Banks of the Delaware to aid the crossing of men and equipment. He described the scene as he saw it; as:

"It was the most hellish scene I ever beheld. All the shores were lighted up with large fires, boats continuously passing and repassing, full of men, horses, artillery, and camp equipage… The Hollowing of hundreds of men in their difficulties of getting horses and artillery out of boats, made it rather the appearance of Hell than an earthly scene". (p/175of 809 *Washington's Crossings*) *(Peale was an accomplished painter.) The army crossed with little baggage. No one viewing this awful spectacle, would ever think that this sorry and sick mess of humanity were about to trounce the hard nuts of the German army – Europe's finest within days! See (*American Revolution, Trevelyan 1905 Vol III P24 – 26, Published Longman & Green*).

The American Congress would remove itself to Baltimore a very Irish town, a little later on. Washington had already informed his cousin via a letter that the game was pretty much up. Washington stated if all else failed he would relocate the Continental army beyond the Allegheny mountains and carry on a guerrilla war from there or if it came to a last ultimate battle, he would go home to Virginia surrounded by his Irish troops and die in a gallant last stand. The American Congress must have already sent to Washington their guide or outline for a peaceful settlement with Britain. Washington had been given the green light to seek peace terms with the British if he thought it advisable and prudent course of action to follow. These are all historical facts. Congress thought the game was up and so too did Washington and the whole civilian population of America. Thomas Paine would sum up the situation well and poetically: -

> "These are the times that try men's souls. The summer soldier and the sunshine patriots will in this crisis shrink from the service of his country but he that stands by it now deserves the love and respect of his countrymen. Tyranny like hell is not easily conquered but the harder the conflict the more glorious the triumph."

This was taken from Thomas Paine's *"American Crisis"* pamphlet, which would later electrify the American public and would be published after the battles of Trenton and Princeton had taken place. This little book would warm their cockles and patriotic hearts and desires, come the new year. Washington ordered it printed immediately and read out to what was left of the American army.

In December 1776, all the sunshine patriots and summer soldiers had left. Washington was down to 3,800 diehards who did not know when they were beaten. Could this dilapidated American army be resurrected, to boldly go into the jaws of hell, one more time? We will have to wait and see, my dear friends

CHAPTER 2

Redemption

This broken-down rabble, many with no shoes, half-dressed, only the Irish could stick these types of conditions. To the Irish Catholics; being half fed, freezing with no shoe's; rags for clothes this was their normal condition under enlightened British despotism, back in Ireland, the *auld* country. Only the Irish could even think or dream of carrying on. This was the normal state of existence for the Irish under British rule. i.e., Living on a poor diet, starving for 3 months every year many living in lean-toos or mud brick cabins. Thousands upon thousands even lived-in holes in the ground and among sand dunes. They lived off an unhealthy diet of daily ridicule, racial abuse, and had, all their human rights taken away from them; they had no rights before the law. It is to the likes of these men that America owes its beloved freedom to. It is to these men, that now predominated the American army's rump ranks. Carry on they would, straight into the belly of the rough tough hired thugs, the feared German Hessians, all professional mercenaries; just hired guns; to clean out and intimidate American people. Into the Valley of death would tread the American Army, tattered banner flying high.

Those soldiers Washington's had sent forward to arrange the crossing of the Delaware had done a cracking job. It was a smooth efficient operation. The whole American Army, what was left of it, had made it out alive. Washington had specifically asked his men to get all the Durham boats available, on the river Delaware, these boats were large flat bottomed bulk carriers. Many exceptionally large indeed so large were some of them, and so small were Washington's regiments that he stated, one boat could cross over a full regiment. They must have been exhausted, well beyond the limits of human endurance.

Washington as usual got them quickly down to securing their positions on their own side of the river. Sooner or later the British Army in full pursuit would show up on the far bank.

In this tiny rump of what was left of the American Army were Irishmen one and all: Some born in Ireland, others of Irish Parents: General Wayne, General Knox (Co. Derry), General Maxwell, (Co. Tyrone) General Paddy Lamb, General John Sullivan, (Co. Cork) General William Irvine, (Co. Fermanagh) plus his 5 sons & 2 brothers, General John Shee,General Montgomery, General Edward Hand, General Walter Stewart, General Andrew Lewis,(Donegal) General Richard Butler(Dublin) plus his 4 brothers Commodore John Barry(Wexford) active duty at sea Colonel Stephen Moylan(Co. Cork) Colonel Michael Jackson plus his 5 sons & his 5 brothers, Colonel Francis Johnson, Colonel Patrick Fitzgerald Colonel Daniel Morgan (Irish or Welsh probably Welsh some say Northern Irish) These are just some the list of Irish officers goes on and on and on. Into lists of Irish Colonels', Majors, Captains, Sergeants, Militia and their own Officers as well as thousands of Irish Foot-sloggers

As you can see the vast majority of senior officers are predominately Irish. Some are not Generals yet but they will be! The vast majority of the continental officers not Irish had gone home when British General Howe offered them an amnesty after the defeats of New York. Most had landed estates and most would lose them if Britain won, as confiscated enemy booty. Most rich New Englanders changed sides and allegiances at this juncture for said reasons. See page 292 The History of the American Revolution by American politician and historian David Ramsey. Published Liberty Classics vol.1 1990, originally pub; 1789 Mr. Ramsey was one of the very first to write a history of the Revolution. Pre 19th century so it is authentic. To give due credit most actually thought all was lost including Congress. Any sensible common-sense viewpoint would back up this obvious conclusion. See also "The Unknown American Revolution" by Revolutionary Historian Professor Gary B Nash Professor Nash was President of the Organisation of American Historians, member of the American Academy of Arts and Science, served on the executive of the National Council for History Education. He states p216 Unknown Revolution quoting other American Academics "each year as a rule fewer and fewer people wanted to have anything to do with Continental service "Again page218 "only a small slither of white American males of fighting age served in the Continental Army. Page221 Professor Nash sums up well "For all his obscurity, the foot soldier was, in fact, one of the main reasons that the Americans were able to sustain a series of disheartening defeats in the first two years of the war and still continue to fight.

To be fair and honest the whole Armies enlistments ended in November, so there was not much officers could do when whole regiments went home having done their service in full.

Many, many more Irish officers littered this rump ranks, these are just the more known ones. When the news came to Ireland that America had declared its Independence the whole of Ireland was ecstatic with joy. When the news reached England, they were livid with rage.

It was a miracle of discipline and fidelity; that they had made it out alive. Those that had fallen prostrate, on the New Jersey roads, never got up again. Many wounded had to be left by the roadside and most would be dead within hours; so, their friends, relations, comrades bitterly hoped. The British could be very nasty with their bayonets. (Some British soldiers bragged of "spiking" or "spitting" the American volunteers against trees, it does not sound too good to my ears. Whatever it means?) Those volunteers that were half alive longed for some sleep, but Washington pushed them further on, they had to make it to the Delaware river come what may.

Sir George Trevelyan in his book the *American Revolution Vol I of III (P 21 Chap III)* states: - Washington's army had many sick and injured and it was extremely hard to ascertain the sick and injured from its hale and hearty!

They had taken one beating after another in the New York campaign. Many prisoners had been taken. When a detachment of surrendered American soldiers was being guarded over by an English sergeant with his squad, a very senior British Commander rode up: -

> "A British officer apparently of high rank rode up at full gal-
> lop exclaiming "What! ... Taking prisoners!... Kill every man
> of them."

Thankfully, his instruction was not carried out. These men would be spared instant killing, instead they would experience the long slow death of starvation in shackles. *(George Otto Trevelyan Vol III 1905, Chapter XXI published Longman & Green NY 1922, P21 10 IBID).*

5,000 American P.O.W.'s were taken by the British. Many were held in hulks, half-clothed, chained up and ill fed. Many, many, American soldiers died of starvation under British custody.

26th may 1808 a grand solemn funeral procession was conducted to remember and honour the 11,500 American soldier's sailors and citizens who died under British captivity, during the war of liberation.

The Revolutionary army was now in a rapid course of disintegration and dissolution, claims Trevelyan, see *(Trevelyan American Revolution Vol III P17)*. Many of the militia who made it out alive or quit the field or escaped the nasty clutches of the British redcoats returned home and infected their families with typhus fever or other such army ailments.

If the British could bring what was left of the Americans to battle, they assuredly would win handsomely indeed. Indeed, some commented that the American army had ceased to exist already. This was a popular and common assessment, and one which held much military sense. *(Trevelyan American Revolution Vol III P19)*.

(P26 FN 4). As many as 70 deaths a day occurred in Philadelphia with a typhus outbreak.

What was left of the army, that had ceased to exist! ... was now digging in on the Pennsylvania side of the river. The safe side. This was probably the first time in a long time, that deeply worried George Washington could gather his thoughts and take stock. Many of his regiments once in the hundreds were now down to double figures. Many had fallen in battle, and too many, had been taken prisoner. The assorted militia were ad hoc and not fit for purpose. What Washington needed was rough, tough battle-hardened experienced soldiers in for the long haul not a few weeks here or there. One onlooker of the Continental army described them succinctly as collectively "mouldering away" * American history professor Shy in his ... *"A people numerous and armed p/22"* states "One wonders why the whole affair did not simply collapse"? British historian Trevelyan describes the scene on the way to the Delaware; The tattered footsore group which was called a battalion were trailing wearily through ruins and mud, behind a banner of gaudy cloth. *(Trevelyan American Revolution Vol III P24).*

The American army had lost a lot of its baggage and food was in short supply. The American officers had to keep the battalions going in their dreadful and agonising march to the Delaware, on large doses of whiskey but little food. Each American soldier was issued with half a pint of whiskey! The only sustenance they had, and the only sustenance they would get. Each soldier took little sips or gulps to numb the pain, agony, or fear. thru-out those final days, of this painful trudge, towards the Delaware and some safety. At all costs they must keep going onwards towards the river. They must not stop for anyone. Like Scott of the Antarctic, they must keep going one step at a time, one step in front of the other. Never stop or rest. Just plod along as if in a semi-conscious dream state. Many rightfully claimed their own families would not have recognised them. Haggard and exhausted and starved beyond the physical limits of many and most sensible human beings. They trudged on relentlessly.

The American revolution: from such early hopes and dreams, now reduced down to such chronic despair, malnutrition, and mutilation. What a bloody awful journey, a ghoulish nightmare suffered by such high-minded individuals. All with such hope and promise, now only total despair, and utter degradation and dejection. Once over the Mighty Delaware river, they could finally slump down and give in to chronic fatigue; a consuming monster that had been clinging to every soldier's body. Draining it, of all of its bodily energy, sucking, and sapping all the life out of its marrow and bones, and wasting away it starved muscles. So bad were a large quantity of this body of men that Washington had no choice but to remove a lot of them immediately to a field hospital, which Washington had set up nearby, once over the river. Those that were left, the "healthy" ones, were in a pretty bad shape, unable to return to full duties; they carried on light duties and sentry work. Once over the Delaware, Washington had the American cannons placed opposite every available river crossing. If the mighty British army came knocking, they would get a nasty surprise, all right!

American volunteers died of exposure, wounds, fatigue, and hunger on their forced march of the defeated towards the Delaware. It looked more dire and dark than anyone could have imagined, loyalist New Yorkers had spiked a lot of the Continental army's cannons by ramming down stones into their barrels. Trevelyan estimates that several hundred cannons had been spiked this way which seems such an astronomical figure. See (*Wikipedia, Battle Trenton Princeton, Trevelyan American Revolution Vol II P341*). In New York bands of American loyalists were going around singing good King George songs.

Not only did loyalists in New Yorkers spike cannons and damage Whig property i.e., patriot farms, houses etc., they produced their own pamphlet and it stated: -

> "Let us clear ourselves of the general imputation; we never consented to Congress or committees. We detest the destruction of private property we abhor the proceedings of riotous and disorderly people and finally we wish to live and die the same loyal subjects that we have been to his most sacred majesty King George III."

To the Irish there was certainly nothing good or sacred about king George or any other British King or Queen they had only brought slaughter to their land. Sometimes on a monstrous scale.

The American Revolution was really not only a war for liberation but in many cases, it was a civil war between loyalists and patriots. Very much, the Irish, American patriots, and southern Hillbillys versus the rest. An over statement I know, but it essentially holds more than a kernel of truth and accuracy For Washington's part, the patriotic militia did not cut the mustard when it came to taking on Europe's best drilled soldiers. One southern commander tells Washington that the militia are only good for sniping from behind a wall. He reckons that the northern generals do not train them hard enough, he states: -

> "They train them to run away and make themselves believe they can never be safe unless under cover of an entrenchment which they would rather extend from the North Pole to the South Pole than risk an engagement."

This unfortunately was exactly what George Washington found for himself as regards New Englanders. Shoot they would from behind a hedge or wall but don, t ever ask them to cover open ground.

As the Americans fled the crafty boys amongst them destroyed bridges and chopped down any large heavy trees that would straggle the road. Two or three heavy ones together, would cause a severe bottle neck for British wagons. Anything and everything was done to slow the advancing British down. Washington picked four Irish regiments for this difficult rear-guard task. * All commanded by; Colonel, Hand, Morgan, Shea, and Haslet. (p/176 *A hidden phase*) To successfully play a good rear-guard action, takes much will power to stay close to the enemy as the rest retreat as quickly as they can. Washington always chose Irish regiments for this task if they were available. British Commander Cornwallis wanted to run the Americans down like a trapped fox and then tear it to pieces. General Howe, his immediate commander informed Cornwallis to slow down and not to proceed until he arrived. Howe promised Cornwallis he would arrive as quick as he could; all haste was being made. Howe arrived one week later! *(Trevelyan American Revolution Vol III P20)* *

---

*Certain historians seem to think Howe was letting the Americans off the hook-on purpose. He was a Whig and a mason and had voted against military force to solve the American problem. His behaviour on the battlefield at times is incomprehensible. He regarded his orders as to settle this matter amicably.

Howe did not approve of the British government's policy of declaring martial law in America. Howe favoured a cordial settlement with allegiance to King George with an American assembly. Howe must have concluded that the game was up for the Revolution. Like Hitler in World War two at Dunkirk. Hitler had got down to writing his acceptable peace terms and good and generous the peace terms were too. How could the British possible refuse such a magnanimous offer? he thought to himself. Howes's thoughts must have sensibly been along the same lines. All that needed to be done was settle up peace terms with the colonials as from a military perspective the Continental Army has all but ceased to exist or function in any meaningful way. Howe cannot be castigated in hindsight; the revolution looked to be a busted flush. Without an army... it was over! Howe was also well aware that the vast majority of those left in the Continental army, their time of enlistment duration was up in late December. They had only signed on for a year and that year ended in a few days' time. The whole American Army would disband soon! So, he hoped and rightfully expected.

At this same time Washington was across the Delaware. In a much better situation; but still a very dire one. Most observers still felt the cause was lost, and in that group were General Washington himself and the entire American Congress, British generals, and pretty much the entire population of the 13 colonies, pretty much all concluded the war was over. But not all... Significantly, and essentially the Irish Populous of America were still all in. Both Catholics and Presbyterians had not hung up their guns yet, not by a long shot. The fight was still strong in most. The Irish Catholics and hot-headed Presbyterians, who both were behind the Revolution and had worked so hard over the last number of years, even into the wee small hours, while all else were soundly asleep; to bring it to fruition. Both in, political organisations, writing committees, producing political pamphlets and committees of public safety, and generally promoting the revolutionary ideals. To the Irish both Catholic and Presbyterian the American revolution was sweet music to their ears; and always had been from its conception, and inception years previously. The Irish Catholics and Irish Presbyterians one British General in the Southern sector of operations stated of them. "It is those two elements "that hold the whole war together. (f.n. page 102/445 *How the Irish won the American Revolution.*)

The small body of selected, very enlightened Masonic Men who controlled the Revolution were dyed in the wool revolutionaries. They could neither deliver the American Revolution nor fight for it in any meaningful way shape or form. What was needed was a large body of men fanatical to the cause, men willing to lay down their lives in a hard struggle, against British rule in America. Come December 1776 the Congress and the Masons all thought it was over. They had failed to alter the historical course of events, and America's destiny. They had now come down to accept the inevitable and consider opening and seeking peace terms.

On December 7th, 1776, Howe finally closes in on the Delaware. He orders all ferry crossings to be taken and all boats to be seized. ... No so fast my English friends, the Americans have beaten you to the punch. All boats were on the far side of the river. 12,000 British redcoats were now quickly forced marched up and down the Delaware for mile after mile, 12 long miles and beyond, either way up or down river in search of boats. They found none or only a few light boats. (Some apparently went over 50 miles seeking boats. Non were found not even that far away.) Those boats not taken, had been deliberately scuppered scrapped and sunk.

Howe was determined to get to Philadelphia and finish this business once and for all. Washington would state later that only the Delaware saved Philadelphia that winter. *(Trevelyan American Revolution Vol III P22).* Howe decided in the meantime to issue a proclamation to the American public and what was left of the Continental Army. The British General offered the American public guarantees of safety to them and their property to all those who pledged allegiance to King George He also offered an amnesty to all those engaged in violent actions against British forces if they surrendered their weapons. Howe's earnest desire to quickly finish the job, was essentially torpedoed, for without boats, General Howe, s plans were duly scuppered. Just like the little boats the Irish had sunk to deny the British a dry crossing of the Delaware.

Trevelyan states that never had an army been in such a worse state as the American army and been able to hold itself together. The Americans had lost 90% of its army. Most of its baggage, stores, medical supplies, clothes, boots, food, and ammunition etc. had gone! The American army was now reduced down to sheer beggary. Captured American P.O.W.'s were in rags, more naked than clothed. Many, too many; would starve to death chained up in old British hulks in New York's estuaries. But before they starved to death, they all noticed their captures were all well fed and dressed. *(IBID*

P12 all American captured P.O.W.s, noticed that all the redcoats had great warm clothes and good shoes, were kept warm and had plenty of hot meals).

The Americans were the Viet Cong, and the British were the occupying well fed and funded modern professional army. What would happen next? Only time would tell.

CHAPTER 3

The American Via Dolorosa

The American army looked more like it would disintegrate upon its own volition, than rally to enemy action. Some young American militia would turn up later on, in their farm clothes! They had, not had, enough time to change into their militia uniforms, so desperate was the issue. The Americans joked that any more forced marches would ensure that the whole army would be nearly nude as their clothes and footwear disintegrated around them as they marched further south.

In Philadelphia, 70 deaths a day were now occurring, due to communicable army diseases and 3,000 citizens would die that winter. The loyalists of Philadelphia came out and congregated and started to dismantle the city's defences now that Congress had fled. Washington was forced to dispatch soldiers to restore proper order. The British knew victory was all but won, you could smell it in the air! They issued a proclamation to Washington's army that they would enjoy a full pardon, liberty, and property to all who pledged allegiance to King George in the next sixty days hence.

Hundreds of American civilians immediately flocked to the British to pledge their allegiance. Thousands more would follow suit over the coming weeks, to protect their homes and their families. These pardons and legal documents to safeguard their own property and person, were quickly and desperately being snapped up over the coming days, and had the British army administration, working long hours into the night to register everyone. These pieces of British paper became more valuable as word spread that the Hessians usually raided every house along their march and took whatever they wanted and that this carry on had been going on for months now. * The Hessians had acquired so much loot that it was beginning to slow them down. Each Hessian wanted a horse to carry his own personal stolen goods. From horses for each individual Hessian, they quickly moved on to wagons to carry their booty. Dozens and in some cases well over a hundred wagons were being used to transport this soldier's swag. These massed wagons would follow and desperately slow the Hessians down to a snail's pace as they advanced forwards. The worst freebooters were the Hessian women, they simply walked into Americans houses and showed the soldiers what they wished to pilth. Drawers were unceremoniously gone thru, clothes, curtains and bedding were all quickly purloined. Any resistance meant your house was trashed or possibly worse. From plunder to more wicked acts against American children, and females of any age, were now rife happenings in New Jersey. These vicious acts would result in the New Jersey militia coming out to kill both British and hessian soldiers, who were foolish enough to go about its roads in small groups. New Jersey descended into wanton lawlessness. To general Howe's credit he ordered that, British soldiers be hung for offences *see "Washington's Crossing" p/225-234 for a fuller description of these sad and wicked events.

———————————————

The British had promised the Hessians, land in America if they won. When the Hessians got to America they reneged on this agreement. On hearing this the Hessians all decided that American loot was theirs legally.

The Hessians and British soldiers also smashed up houses, burned libraries and churches of all denominations, and loyalists had their homes wrecked and ransacked too. The Germans made no distinction with loyalists or patriots, young or old or sex, all were open to be literally looted see *(IBID P31)*. They had looted New York and now the Hessians (about ⅓ of the British army) were now systematically looting New Jersey. The Hessians looted everyone; the American patriots only looted from Loyalists.

When the British arrived in Princeton, that academic institution was looted also, and all its scientific equipment smashed. The fine settlements of Maidenhead and Hopewell got a thorough looting, every house was looted one after the other, cattle and sheep were taken, what could not be removed was trashed and smashed.

This was the British bringing democracy to America – the "mother" country. No matter how hard the loyalists showed that they were pro King George and showed the Hessians and British soldiers their own issued documents, promising to respect property and people, it was all to no avail the British soldiers ransacked their houses anyway, and valuables were taken along with shoes, bed clothes – whatever they wanted they stole – soldiers' swag! (The British only seemed to have started looting too, after they saw the Hessians getting away with this behaviour for weeks)

Another new democratic device was housing the British soldiers in people's houses; they just came in and took them over. Well, whatever happened to their pledge or respecting personal property as General Howe had stated.

Every house in New York that had patriotic, republican sympathies, or ones the loyalists thought or just suspected had patriotic republican sympathies, had a large "R" painted on their doors. The loyalists all thought the day of judgement and reckoning was only days even hours away! New Yorkers seethed with anger and scores needed settling. But alas come December General Howe could only watch from the New Jersey side of the river, without boats his desire to finish of the game, was well and truly sunk! He decided to stay and make camp for the winter, this ragged, American, run-down fox could wait until spring to be chased down and torn to pieces. That is, even if it managed to stay together over the harsh winter! Which many thought was highly unlikely. The vast majority had left and only a tiny rump remained and their time was up in days. The American army was finished!

General Howe went home to New York to enjoy the high society life, good food, wine, warm quarters, and fancy New York balls. Howe expected a knighthood for his wonderful victory over these pesky American upstarts. Howe along with the rest of his high command thought the fight was well and truly over. And it must be said, so too did most Americans. Resistance among the New Englanders was practically over. Many had changed sides and allegiances, in order to survive or escape *retribution*. The American war of independence was a war amongst Americans themselves; unfortunately.

New England Brahmins now declared the revolution over too. And it must be said, that is what most estimated, with good common sense. British Commander General Howe thought nothing could be done now till spring, and that would be only a tidy up, thing at worst. If that!

"The vast majority of non-Irish American soldiers had deserted Washington's Army by the fall of 1776" So states Dr: Phillip Thomas Tucker, in his book; *"How the Irish won the American Revolution"*; p/124~445 pages. What Dr: Tucker rightfully states today; would prove to be a hard unpleasant fact, for the 19thCentury New England Anglo-Saxons historians to swallow; indeed, many possibly today, still find it too hard to face-up too. Dr: Tucker rightly points out that "the Resistance effort among the Anglo-Saxon populace across the colonies including the Continental army was all but over by the early winter of 1776". p/124~445 kindle.

Elkanah Watson of Plymouth, a proud New England patriot sums up most people's assessment of the situation as, by Winter 1776 most people had lost faith in the Revolution. Elkanah states by winter "we considered ourselves a vanquished people's" p/122 ibid. Dr. Tucker speaks well and rightly. It was all down to the Irish and 800 American/ Germans. The Irish were in no mood to chuck it in, yet. To the Irish this situation was the normal when coming up against the British "Sassenachs" (Ancient Gaelic for English) they were always outnumbered and had only rudimentary weapons.

Now for the first time they had guns *too*!

General Howe now Sir William Howe was ecstatic, dancing the night away at the New York Hot spots. He told General Cornwallis to return to England on the next available ship as all that could be accomplished had been done. The war was over till next spring, and probably finished already.

But not so fast, our British friends, as general Howe danced the night away, Washington was up to his old tricks of gathering intel on the British. He knew he had a much smaller army than the British. He also knew that good intelligence would be of vital importance, if his much smaller, diseased, and frozen army was ever to have a fighting chance. Washington had scouts everywhere. The Americans used young lads to saunter into towns, observe the set-up, count soldiers, cannons, reinforcements etc. and saunter out again.

German speaking patriots always got good intel from the Hessians. General Howe might be doing the right moves in New York, but Washington would soon have him dancing to a merry old tune of his own if he could. Washington was safe on the Pennsylvania side of the Delaware, but his junior Irish officers wanted action, and I believe the men did too. Nothing pleased the Irish soldiers more than getting one over on the Sassenachs. They had stolen their land, kicked them out of the country. Sold their families into slavery. Denounced their old Christianity as humbug if not the very seed of Mr. Beelzebub himself. They had resorted to sick public acts of extreme torture against Christians, just to name but a few of the delights of British Rule. The Irish soldiers were well known for being in good spirits no matter what. All European armies mentioned this fact, as did British commanders. With a few hot meals down them, supplied by the camp ladies who cooked in the woods nearby, their spirits would start to recover. Within days the rag tag Army was soon at work patrolling, entrenching, and keeping clean as best they could. New supplies had been dispatched from Philadelphia, clothes food ammunition blankets etc.

From the Irish perspective peace under British rule was no peace at all; they would get the full vengeance of the whole American affair. The Presbyterians had had too much of British rule too, more than they could stomach. The penal laws against both their religions were extreme. The Presbyterian ministers would chuck no compromise. So important were the Presbyterian ministers, that one sat in on a Washington battle plan briefing. *

WHY WE FOUGHT

At least one Presbyterian minister was at the inner circle meeting to decide for attack. What was he doing there? A second Presbyterian minister would be ritually stripped of all his clothes and butchered by the British.

Congress had even written to George Washington letting him know that if he so desired, he was to seek peace terms with the British and end all hostilities, if he so wished. Thing were so dire in Philadelphia that the congress had abandoned its home and relocated to Baltimore.

General Washington needed to address his troops and officers with these dire prospects but firstly he needed to address his small inner command, and then too his volunteers. Something very, very strange happened. We know the first to rally to the flag, when all else did not, were the Irish. George Washington's adopted son states this, quite frankly. Not only are they one of the first to rally, but they also made up the vast majority of those who were left. Which included a few English roundheads, fiery Scots, 800 Germans, plus officers, colonels, and generals; and the rest basically nearly 80% were Irish volunteers. Washington knew the Irish troops would not leave him alone to die. That is why he stated if all else fails I will retreat to Virginia and surrounded by the Irish make my last stand.

All would state, those that were *there* years later that ultimately, the American victory and Revolution was all down to the Irish, that is, all the Continental army's enemies… said that it was the Irish who made the best soldiers. They never shirked from the battle and drove bayonet to bayonet. Most American soldiers did not have a bayonet so when confronted by a redcoat phalanx of angry desperate men, with long bayonets and a driven conviction to kill them by thrusting this exceptionally long thin dagger into them at speed and strength, most fled. The British soon learned if they kept to this tactic, the American volunteers had no choice but to run.

Those left on the Pennsylvania side of the Delaware river would march into Hell, if need be, with Washington. The Irish were down to themselves and 800 Germans. All were recovering from being weak, diseased with typhus, tired and with bloody bleeding feet. All the soldiers were in a desperate need for shoes, stockings, and clothing. They were covered in lice, had camp fever, pneumonia, and dysentery to name just a few of the common ailments. They were cold and drained of all energy but recovering fast with hot food. Washington had sent the worst cases to a field hospital a few miles away (over 1000 were immediately sent to the field hospital). It is a wonder they were able to hang on in there most human beings could not have. **(to the Irish these sorts of conditions were, I am sad to say common, under British rule in Ireland) most native Irish in Ireland were poor with few clothes, no shoes, hungry all the time, and when they fought the British, in Ireland they were always outnumbered, and had few good weapons, much much spirit, but too few: guns, muskets, cannons, horses, and ancillary military equipment.

Most native Irish children were semi-nude many left totally nude. The Irish women had resorted down to grass skirts, Irish men had old raggy linen shirts, belts and hats made of straw, their horses reins and bridles were also made of straw. This is what the educators of European civilisation had been reduced down to! They were looked over by a tiny elite who in some cases looked down upon them in the same manner as the Nazi gauleiter's looked upon the Poles and Slavs. By 1740 all offending protestant sects had been successfully purged from this apartheid system, i.e., Irish Presbyterians and Irish Congregationists.

A little note here may add some light on the subject of Catholics in America, Pre-Revolution. Many Quakers imported Catholics to work and clear the land, a very arduous task indeed, so too Presbyterian's land owners. Land was plentiful but worthless unless cleared and worked into production.

Many imported Catholics, to work in Virginia plantations Irish child labour had been worked for centuries. Whether the Quakers, Presbyterians Virginia Planters or ship Captains declared them as Protestant, no one really cared. They had cheap labour and a good profit. No Catholic churches meant they became protestant by default. That is the real story of America. Irish Catholics were instructed by their Jesuits to declare themselves as protestant settlers on arrival and on-board ship. No one really cared as "Protestant" settlers they could carry arms .NO CATHOLICS WERE ALLOWED TO CARRY ARMS, WHAT SO EVER, UNDER ANY CIRCUMSTANCES, under British rule, another massive incentive to declare as protestant. Why should Irish People play ball with them, and be honest with them when they abused them, and had been totally dishonest in their dealings with them. The knife cuts both ways! What is good for the Goose is just as good for the Gander See page 8 Ireland, Irishmen and the American Revolution David Doyle.

For their part, the English officers were aghast at the number of Irish prisoners they had taken in the Long Island New York campaigns. British soldiers in the south would echo those comments later on, as the southern campaign got up and running, they too noticed the American Rebels were distinctly Irish. Many even just recently arrived Irish! The British regarded the Continental Army in good times as half Irish one quarter Americans one quarter English and Scotch. That was the good times, many stated its ranks were made up off Irish redemptorists i.e., recently arrived indentured servants, and Irish so-called Felons i.e., Irish freedom fighters, Irish people who would not bow down to British tyranny in Ireland. One English commander stated most of the rebel army was of this sort. And that this penal system should stop forthwith as it was only supplying Washington with new recruits.

To the Irish, 3,500 well-armed men with rifles were the best odds they had had against the British in 500 years. Normally they had poles with metal spikes on and a blade at the end, swords, and poles against British cannons and musket and guns… Yes, to these men, that had got kicked out of New York for sure; but with a few days rest and hot grub they would be ready to go again. Washington's would need to change his mind and forget all about peace feelers. This army may be down, but it was not yet out! Not by a long chalk!

At about this same time, of the American army's recovery, reconstitution, resuscitation and restoration, General Washington must have told his inner circle of his own command officers, that Congress had taken the woeful and dreadful step, of writing to him, giving him full legal authority, to consider the course of action, of opening peace negotiations with the British; if he felt that was an appropriate course of action to take. Maybe he confided in them that he himself thought the game was up. He must have told them that he thought the best two options available were either retreat to Virginia and make a last stand among the Irish Americans or alternatively move over the Allegheny Mountains into the western wilderness, both were options he openly wrote about at that time. A safe haven behind the Allegheny mountains in which to recuperate and raid British possessions from, must have looked like a sensible thing to do, too most. Certainly, Washington was thinking along these lines, when he wrote to his cousin saying all is pretty much lost. As it was to many American themselves. Retreat beyond the Alleghany mountains offered many good options.

It was the safest and most sensible option, as it secured the Revolution into next year and beyond. The response General Washington got from his inner command circle must have shocked him to his core! General Washington had many Irish senior officers. Two Irish officers recommended unbelievably an attack on Trenton! What!... had they seen the mess the American Army was in? If one could accurately still call it an Army? Nevertheless, Trenton was exposed, and for the first time they would outnumber the red coats. On paper both Irish officers pointed out the potential this ridiculous opportunity offered or presented. Far from retreating or making a last glorious stand, both Irish officers had been looking at ways to hit back hard. An Irishman colonel Reed, whose grandparents were Irish, Adjudicator and General Washington's adviser and another was also an Irishman colonel John Stark was all action and determined energy, he too recommended attack. American Historian Dr. Tucker p124/445 kindle. *"How the Irish won the American Revolution"* states "many in Washington inner command circle were totally against surrender under any terms". "Determined men like colonel John Fitzgerald born in county Wexford Ireland who greatly assisted Washington as a staff member were determined never to cease fighting against the invaders of America."

The Irish recruits both Catholic and Presbyterian would be amazed at such a proposal as accept peace terms; now we had guns! Now we have 3,000 troops! We can smash any British army which gets in our way. We have taken enough racial religious bile, vomit, persecution, hangings, digging up dead bodies and hanging our corpses, no! We will fight them into the ground, how dare they insult us or cower us; we have been their slaves long enough, we have sailed halfway around the world to get away from this religious trash, no more, no more, we attack, attack, attack! The Presbyterians suffered similar anti-religious totally unchristian laws as those specially selected against old Catholics. In Scotland Anglican protestants or miscreants would be a more honest word, had taken to, digging up recently buried Presbyterians, ritually hanging their dead bodies. After ritually hanging the deceased, the deceased head was chopped off, and their headless corpse thrown into the burial site away from the Anglican parishioners; in a part of the cemetery kept specifically for Felons, miscreants and other highly undesirables. This is what so called "Christians" were doing to presbyterian dead children, sisters, wife's old grannies and granddads. Whilst they were still alive, Presbyterians were hunted down like Catholics, to be murdered, with no consequences. They too just like Catholics, took to hiding in caves from murderous so-called Christian hunting gangs. Eventually they fled into the Scottish Highlands and islands which were Catholic enclaves themselves.

Suffering much discrimination, judicial murder, and other unsavoury acts by so called followers of Christ. The Catholics had their land, cattle, and farms confiscated. Eventually the Presbyterians fled to Ireland. The catholic Scottish highlanders fled to America for a new life. (President Trumps origins are in the dreadfully dirt poor Catholic Scottish Highlands on one side and Germanic on the other. As we have noticed Irish and Germans are an extremely, big element in this story.

President Obama's kin are from Ireland and Africa. Two very ancient civilisations and once again two very big elements in the American historical story. Pretty much most American Presidents have had Irish origins in them, as would most Americans citizens whose origins go back to the 16th, 17th,18th centuries of colonial and continental rule; even if they are totally unaware of it! As two American Continental officers observed wryly during the war *of* independence that many American *loyalist's* ancestors, came to America as *Irish Catholic rebels* in *chains*

Not to be out done, our brown African- American brothers and sisters too, generally have a good mix of Irish blood running thru their veins, many Irish men and women set up home, or made union with many African

Americans all over the Caribbean and thirteen colonies and in America's wilderness. Co-conspirators in the kick around gang, and they couldn't give two shoots for British peevishness, rude stares or righteous indignation. Both came in chains or were despised by Americas so called WASPs, *racial* Christians, a contradiction in terms and deeds. Indeed, a good element of old Afro-Americans have Presidential blood flowing thru them!

In the North of Ireland Presbyterians were subjected to the same anti Catholic laws. Catholics had no rights. Catholic people had their farms confiscated just for being Catholic, and loyal to their Christian old original faith. Hundreds of thousands of Catholic people were made homeless and beggars in their own country.

Once more, vile episodes of horrific public tortures were carried out by the New so-called *enlightened* "Christians". These consisted of, public hangings, public torture sessions for all to see including children. They were designed to cower the Catholics into submission. They included public hangings for petty offences. For more serious offences the Christian was tied to the back of a horse and dragged across the streets with their head and body bouncing along. This sometimes killed the Christian. So normally they were tied to a wicker frame so as to keep them alive, for more state torture. Once the horse had delivered the battered and bruised and broken body to its place of execution, the Christian was then hung until unconsciousness took over the bruised and battered body. Careful not to kill the Christian the hooded Government fiend then let him down, all the time the crowd were encouraged to laugh and jeer at the victim. Once down the government official then ripped open the torso of the dying traumatized man with a knife, pulled out his inners and placed them steaming in front of the government victim's eyes. Lastly the British government representative would chop off the male member. Hopefully by now he was dead. If not, this last obscenity would thankfully finish him off. The governments victims' body would

46

then be chopped up into four parts, arms legs, torso, and head. These parts would be disposed of, and the government victims bloody head would be placed upon a stake at a bridge usually.

This was not an uncommon experience in Ireland, or England. This is not barbaric ISIL, or Pol Pot. This was Tudor, Elizabethan, Stuart, Hanoverian England indeed two Irishmen were convicted of sticking up for, Ireland and Irish human rights and political representation and were condemned to this disgusting, vile and obscene sentence in the late *19th*Century. Thankfully, it was not carried out. But that is what the English enlightened judge sentenced them to! This state demonic violence went on for centuries in Ireland, in order, it was hoped to cower them. It totally failed in Ireland. Even though these practises went on into the 19th century. This state punishments for adhering to the auld faith was called "hanging Drawing and Quartering" many innocent people and Catholic rabbis were sentenced to this most demonic state ritual public torture show. And very popular they were to in England. It is no us denying its use, it was on English statute books and administered by its "Justice" system.

400 years of this degenerate and insipid apartheid laws were practised, and rabid sectarianism was introduced into Christian Ireland, and heavily enshrined in its laws even into the present era. With, it has to be said, mixed consequences. No matter how vile the laws, the Irish of the original faith and the Presbyterians refused to buckle under. The Irish Catholics and now Presbyterians refused point blank to accept the British head of state, or whichever latest familicide wore the crown, as the most supreme Christian in all private religious matters i.e., their English *Pope*, St Peters Representative, and the embodiment of all things Christian.

One must say after hunting them down, abusing their dead, murdering their rabbis, and chopping their Rabbis head off after a good hearty chase, thru the woods, one can only conclude that any devout sensible Christian would not blame them for refusing to kiss the king or queen's sweaty feet or baubles. Presbyterian and Catholic businesses in Ireland came in for special measures too. Catholics had no rights at all. If they went to trial the judge was an Anglican, the juries were usually all protestant, every lawyer was protestant. Every government job was exclusively for Protestants.

These usually were Anglican or Church of Ireland. Presbyterians and Congregationalists were in many cases excluded.

All government pensions were paid only to Anglicans. No catholic could buy land or teach their children Christianity. Not even in their own homes! This was banned by law by so called enlightened Christians. Presbyterians now came in for the very same Apartheid laws, laws of strictly enforced segregation and openly racial laws against Irish people. Presbyterian businesses were targeted and any business that competed with an English one, was barred, shutdown or had heavy taxes imposed upon it for daring to compete with British free enterprise. Lastly the British started arresting and imprisoning Presbyterians for co habiting with "strangers". The Strangers were the man's wife. The British refused to recognise Presbyterian ministers, their Marriages, Baptisms, or any other function they deemed worthy of religious ridicule. Husbands were legally arrested and placed in jails brought to court to answer for their lax morality of co habiting with strangers. These last measures meant that just like the Northern Catholics fleeing to America in their thousands upon thousands due to horrible persecutions, sectarian laws, racial and religious abuse, shutting down of all Catholic enterprises and businesses, they too were now joined by a flood of honest Presbyterians Fleeing with their Catholic practising Christians to America.

Ulster was the most Catholic part of Ireland in a short time it became the most protestant. Mainly Anglican or such other denominations, which stated that the high king or queen of England was their own appointed pope; anyone who disagreed with this new *fact* of Christianity could be tortured to death; but thankfully total exclusion in all matters; political, legal, social, or religious usually did the malicious trick. Stripped of any legal standing or redress before the law, and along with vigorous and energetic mass evictions in their hundreds of thousands, these measures rigorously applied not over years or decades, but centuries usually sufficed to kill them en masse or drive them out, again en masse.

In no short time, most Catholics lost all their land, and lively hoods they became street beggars hopefully left to die of starvation or forced emigration in their hundreds of thousands.

Too be honest the good protestants had their heads filled up with anti-Catholic bile and vicious propaganda, probably worser than anti-Semitic propaganda practised in 1930s Germany. This psychological religious voodoo, was practised and promoted by the British government over continuous centuries, and it deeply affected the good British population and sensible public. In some cases, an extreme anti-Catholic religious slant was embodied into their minds and souls. These anti Catholic measures legally embodied well into the 21st century. {British people could vote for a rabbi, a ranting vicar, or an Iman even an extreme one. But it was totally illegal to vote for any catholic priest. Prince Charles could marry anyone in the world except a Catholic, Catholics were banned legally! Prince Charles could legally marry an alien from out of space just as long as it wasn't a Catholic alien! This was the esteemed British law, as practised in England in to the 21stcentury. Some even derided Tony Blair although not a Catholic but having the affront to go with his wife and children to a catholic church no less and pray on his knees before God. Thankfully, times have changed for the better in most cases, but sly stuffy elitist Protestantism stills washes and swills about in empty English stuffy heads. Heads to stupid to know their own esteemed history.

As stated, the most Catholic part of Ireland i.e., the Northern bit, became Hey Presto! the most protestant, i.e., Anglican; due to the confiscated catholic farms now being handed out to British lackeys. Many, many Catholics fled to Europe much more to America. So, when General Washington discussed what Congress had implied, he received a mighty shock. The Irish officers and troops would not brook surrender or peace terms. Peace terms meant exactly what they had collectively suffered before in Ireland. Presbyterian ministers' great advocates for American Independence, would sooner march into hell than give in to this filthy lot. The Catholics who made up the large majority by far of Washington's Army, knew full well, all British vengeance would fall upon their shoulders or more accurately around their necks. Peace terms with the British always meant collective punishment. Peace terms in Ireland were always broken. Britain pretty much broke every treaty it had ever made with the Irish. Treaties were never binding on them. Only on the Irish. An historical fact not taught in British public schools. They were always broken later when it suited them. *(recently the American house speaker had to defend the American Brokered peace in Northern Ireland. Senior British Tory ministers & M.P.s openly stated that the Good Friday Agreement should be torn up as it was *no longer* needed! That's about typical for that lot).

So, when General Washington asked for advice, the Irish response would have shocked him to his marrow. This American Revolution to those left was an extremely religious endeavour. No presbyterian minister would brook any peace endeavour. To them and the Catholics it was liberty or death; and they meant that literally. That was not some catchy catch phrase conjured up for promotional reasons. This type of gusto must have shocked

Washington. His most trusted confident his Aide de Camp Irish American Colonel Reed was the main instigator of the bravado plan to go on the attack. Colonel Stark another Irish man was also pushing for this plan of action too. Most non-Irish officers must have been aghast at such reck-lessness. Had these two mavericks seen the Army recently? The Army was riddled with sickness, most had tattered rags on, the Army had been well and truly thrashed and trashed by these British regulars and their German hired guns. Time and time again.

This attitude must have shocked the Continental Congress too which had probably delivered their outline peace terms for General Washington's appraisal. What would he do? Washington's mind was slowly for chang-ing. He began to ruminate on this, about face. Attack! Had Washington gone mad. No! But he was surrounded by mad Micks many speaking an illegible language. "Sassenach" would be the only term anyone not an Irish speaker could make out. "Sassenach" was the Irish for the dreaded enemy "Sassenach" was the English Redcoats, their oppressors. Sassenach would be a word on the Irish and Irish Americans lips. And on the few hardy Scots sharpening their knifes, which they had every intention of driving right into any damned redcoat's inners.

To the assembled Irish this war had an extremely religious tint to it. Both catholic Irish and Presbyterian Irish wanted freedom from religious per-secution and British bigotry the type imported and heavily promoted by just William and his lot... To them, this was a most religious war indeed. A war in which they did not give two shoots about taxes, Tea or otherwise. All Catholics in America ever since just William and Mary had entered the British throne, were subjected to a veritable raft of ultra-protestant sectarian law, that had been introduced into America; Catholics, now had no rights to vote, automatically all rights were taken off them. Just for supporting Christ in a different way. They were made to feel totally unwelcome in their own country. Catholics just for being Catholics, had to pay double the land taxes, in America! Check it out. Fact check it! No catholic was allowed to carry any arms in America UNDER ANY, ANY CIRCUMSTANCES, or go beyond British demarcation lines of settlement. Some of these sectarians, segregationist, apartheid laws, also applied to Presbyterians in America. It cannot be ignored or denied that historically those parts of Ireland under British suzerainty always suffered sectarian divisions. Indeed, let us be honest with each other, the British elite bragged about how successfully they had sown division in Ireland to suit their own purposes and especially their own purses with loot and swag. And a jolly good job they made of it too.

Too both the Irish Catholics (by far the vast majority in the Army) and Irish Presbyterians; this sick nonsense must stop; they had not travelled halfway around the world to be once again kicked around by British Racists. Also, to our fellow American Catholics this tripe must be opposed in full. American Dissenters too opposed the religious tithe to the Church of England a Church many Americans did not even belong to, but were expected to pay in full for. German Americans indeed many Americans of the Catholic faith detested these twisted laws of Just William and Mary. The Americans had their own "glorious Revolution" and it contained liberty for all, religious freedom equality and the pursuit of happiness. Not like the British Glorious Revolution of 1688 which introduced apartheid, racism, religious intolerance, massive unfair taxes on Catholics. Enormous confiscation of land belonging to Catholics just because they happened to be Catholics. And mass enslavement programme of fellow human being in their millions upon millions, all to make a small British elite fabulously filthy rich.

This trite nonsense would all be sold to the gullible as "The glorious revolution". Glorious to what? Thievery robbery, sectarian laws, and special

Catholic taxes? This was not glorious it was state discrimination. State sectarianism. And this sick sectarianism would leave a nasty stain on intercommunal harmony, modernisation, equality, and good governance. Instead, it promoted, the vice of vile religious racism, segregation apartheid laws and social, political, and economic exclusion. Basic Christianity, and civic harmony was totally missing in Just Williams and Marys Sick sectarian religious bile. Anything but "Glorious Revolution" A sick sectarian revolution by people involved in murdering their own family members no less! This "Glorious revolution "was totally unchristian in nature and more akin to religious racism, and promoter of religious bile, filth, and jabberwocky.

Those few Scottish highlanders present would echo these thoughts too. They too had had their family's land taken off them by force, ridiculed and harassed, segregated and religious apartheid laws strictly enforced against them and all family members. Far worse than the jibes ever suffered by the Huguenots in France, by a long, long way. Religious racist laws abounded in Britain. Britain was totally a nation run on religious racist grounds at that time, and public exhibitions of extremely atrocious torture were practised by its elite, and the populous flocked to them for "entertainment"!

How any of this ruling class could claim to be Christian in any way, boggles the mind completely. Indeed, Mr. Beelzebub himself would gladly clap these unchristian sectarian laws; a card Britain would play to some effect on Americans. Benedict Arnold swallowed this religious bile and pronounced he deserted America because; Catholics were in its ranks. Benedict sold his soul to the enslavers. He wrote an address to the "true" Americans in the "Popes" Army, to follow him and desert too. They did not follow his patriotic or idiotic lead. Britain spread it muck far and wide. It even stated the American Revolution was run from the Vatican! No popery! was their next attempt to destroy the budding Revolution, when that did not work, they decided to become MORE Catholic to entice Catholic Americans into their ranks. Why every sane man knew Britain welcomed Catholics?

Next came the great Irish fiasco, the British Army was so pro-Irish sure they always had been. One of the largest St. Patricks day festivals was put on by the now purely pro- Irish British Army in New York. A massive festival and sumptuous feast were laid on for all true Irish men to partake in. When that jamboree failed, they resorted back to good auld no-popery, they turned up the No Popery voodoo to full volume Which had always worked well before, in Ireland. Many American loyalists actually swallowed this propaganda hook line and sinker, and them some more. No popery worked well in America, but not on the enlightened masons, Washington, Franklin or any of the founding fathers. They wanted what they publicly stated religious freedom and liberty, and they would not swallow British bile to poison and quench *their* revolution. Washington had been to long in the saddle to be fooled again.

To the Presbyterians and a growing number of Congregationalists this was all, old tripe, anti-Christian hogwash. The Devils "home Brew". And they wanted none of it! The smarter than most Masons both Washington and Benjamin Franklin had both seen the light on this sectarian issue, Washington had had his Damascus moment once the Revolution had got going. Without Catholic aid, muscle, and strength the American Revolution was a busted flush. Pretty much it was down to the Irish Catholics, and Presbyterians to overflow its ranks. And overflow they would. Popery and slavery went hand in hand, according to the Army of occupations propaganda unit. This was sweet music to the so-called loyalists. They gobbled up these religious hate messages as fast as the British propagandists could print them. A Mr. Southwick wrote an early Anti- revolutionary No Popery tract in 1774 called *"A master Key to Popery"* Mr. Southwick's own son continued in his father's footsteps, i.e., the print press. He was the editor of the

"National Observer" of New York. In 1826 he stated about his father's tract, that he too had seen the error and stupidity of his old ways, of religious intolerance and supremacist cleft footed Mr. Beelzebub clap trap for idiots. He stated a new light had burst upon them, and that they come to realise that actually, Catholics and the fighters of freedom went hand in hand and not the other way round. p/7&8 *Catholics and the American Revolution* volume 1 by Martin j Griffin.pub 1907. (Too true, Irish Catholics pretty much help free most South American countries)

When France joined in the fight for American Independence in 1778, many American *patriots* deserted, in disgust at Congress accepting help from a Catholic country. One must presume they wished therefore to remain subjects of the British crown, and under its rule. British no popery propaganda trumped their own wish for freedom (For the historical record and accuracy, the American Continental army was largely supplied with its guns and ammunition from Spain and France. See American Army's, "The war of the American Revolution, Robert W Coakley and Stetson Conn. Centre of Military History, United States Army Washington D.C. 2010)

Lastly the British Propagandists decided more psychops were needed to win and smash American resistance. If it wasn't No Popery! Then subterfuge might work better on stupid Americans. They started to distribute "honest letters" written by *discontented* American patriots, in an attempt to wear them down mentally. The "honest letters" written from the heart, went along these lines That their commanders had been lying to them, just look at us, we are in filthy rags, no shoes, badly led, badly fed, the misery of our situation is apparent to us all. The falsehoods of Congress are open for all to see, congress has abandoned us, we are all destitute, sick, and freezing to death, with cold hunger and nakedness. Our services are generally expired, this is the moment to fly from slavery and fraud. Other Letters would state, I can now relate to you that the affairs of England and Ireland are settled. And that Great Britain and Ireland are now firmly united with affection. I need not tell you; you have been cheated and abused.

The only people who were cheating and abusing, was His Most Highness Serene and Majestic and their adherents. Ireland had been turned into a veritable slaughterhouse, Century after century, decade upon glorious decade... And as for the Affairs of Britain and Ireland now being settled, they will be somewhat when you leave America and Americans alone; to find their own level without outside interference, which they are more than capable off without your advice given so magnanimously by the barrel of your guns.

These propaganda letters went on. In order to secure your liberty, you must quit your leaders and join your real friends. {what the people shooting at us!} Who will receive you with open arms? To any sane Irish man reading these tracts they knew full well they were wicked lies, told by Mr. Fork tongue himself. The British military see the Irish as their main protagonists in this venture. If they can smash the Irish, they can easily win.

This propaganda is very straight forward, as most of its complaints are too very true. They are freezing in rags, no shoes, little food, and most Americans have abandoned the issue by as early as the winter of 1776. As English Historian Trevelyan rightly states no other army could withstand such conditions and hold itself together.

The British propagandists would keep up a steady stream of propaganda all throughout the rebellion. On April 23rd, 1778, Washington had to person-ally warn his troops once again to be aware that the British are intensifying their efforts to get American soldiers to desert the American good cause. of liberty and freedom This was at the very same time as France rowed in behind America. And it has to be said British anti-popery propaganda worked very well towards Britain's goal of bringing America back under its heel; Thousands left the American army and its cause of individual freedom. Maybe it was just an excuse to get out of a most unpopular war, especially for American Anglicans. If the British could not win on the battlefields, then by George, they tried every way to win, off it!

Most New Englanders were fiercely *Pro*-British, And inherently more *anti*-Catholic than anti-British. They feared the Catholics more than their "cousins" the friendly Redcoats. For large elements of the American public, thru-out these difficult and treacherous times; they preferred to sit on the fence, they did not know which way the winds of war would favour. One way or the other. American liberty was a very hard-fought win. Much closer than most Americans like to admit or even think about. The Anglo-Saxon element in America were generally against liberty and freedom. They saw the "Mother country" as their great protector of their freedoms and selective Christian supremacy laws and irreligious liberties. So too did the vast majority of New Englanders.

New England had a hard core of revolutionaries like, Mercy Otis Warren, the first woman to write a history of the Revolution. "History of the Rise, Progress and Termination of the American Revolution interspersed with Biographical, Political, and Moral observation". 1805. Miss Warrens circle included; Samuel Adams, Abigail Adams, John Adams, Martha Washington, Hannah Winthrop, she advised: Samuel Adams, John Adams (2nd President) John Hancock, (Revolutionary president of Congress) Patrick Henry, (give me liberty or give me death) Thomas Jefferson (Writer of Declaration of Independence & 3rd president.) George Washington (Commander continental forces and 1st President)

New England was staunchly loyalist indeed the most loyalist area in the whole of North America by far. British generals stated it was ¾ loyalist other declared it 4/5 loyalist, under oath giving evidence to the British Houses of Parliament. It contained a small vociferous republican element who were just as staunchly for the continental congress, as the majority of New Englanders were for British subjugation, and religious supremacist apartheid laws and national enslavement.

Miss Mercy Otis Warren was in the latter group. After the Revolutionary war Britain would attempt to entice this loyalist stronghold out of the United States of America, during the war of 1812. When that did not work Britain turned its attentions to the Cotton south for undoing from the United States of America, on this enterprise it was extremely successful causing a war and arming the Confederate states to the teeth; to tear America apart. H.M.G.the British elite were always obsessed about splitting up the behemoth Continental America, its only really serious rival both militarily and economically; apart from later on another new emerging nation, Germany.

It was a British propaganda exercise to *re-write* the Revolutionary war, more to its own favour and religious and racial Prejudices. On this issue it found the New Englanders more than willing to write a slanted version up in the racist 19th century.

Half the names of the South Carolina Rangers were Irish. 43% of south Carolinas foot were Irish, 2nd Charleston company of foot were Irish, Maryland regiments were 60~70% Irish. (See p/173 "Irelands Important and Heroic part in Americas Independence and Development" by Reverend Frank Reynolds) p/175-chapter Irish in Army and Navy. States that the bare minimum of soldiers actually born in Ireland in the Revolutionary Army as 74,000. This minimum only counting those names that are distinctly and absolutely Irish. Many others are excluded which probably were Irish too; and these numbers does not take into account, the many solid and stoic Irish soldiers in the guerrilla war down south, in which we learn they are most prevalent. Needless to say, this figure does not consider in any way Irish Americans. Once again, who would appear in vast numbers too. Far, far, faraway the American Revolution was most certainly not an American Anglo-Saxon affair at all in any way shape or form as the New Englander brahmins have made out, over the centuries. This Anglo-Saxon American Revolution is a damn lie! Told by fools for fools to believe.

Just one Irish organisation, just one! In one place alone! Philadelphia the Friendly sons of St. Patrick, a Philadelphia based Organisation was openly out in public, vehemently pro revolution, from the start till its triumphant end. If you had sat down at one of its dinners just *after* the revolution. You would be sitting down with George Washington, postmasters, secretary of the American Treasury, secretary for war, secretary of the navy, attorney general, various diplomatic representatives of America, 27 generals, 1 Admiral, 3 Commodores, 5 Captains, Surgeons of the army, Director of the Mint, various Attorney Generals, State Governor's, 6 Majors, 20 Colonels, 5 lieutenant colonels, 5 Captains, I will stop there. That is some feat for just one Irish Association in Philadelphia alone. For example, General Henry Knox, the man who would drag the cannons all the way from Fort Ticonderoga all the way to Boston, the general who would oversee the river crossing on the night of attack upon Trenton, this man was a member of the Irish association in Boston an association founded by his father. General Knox was also a member of the extremely influential "Sons of St. Patrick Philadelphia" Thomas McKean an Irish signer of the Declaration of Independence, was a member of The Hibernian Society. Stephen Moylan Irish American patriot (born in Ireland) was an aide to General Washington, and commander in the field; he was the first person to use the term *United States of America in official correspondence.* Stephen was the President of The Friendly Sons of St. Patrick. General mad

Anthony Wayne, belonged to both the Hibernian Society and The Friendly Sons. Senior Capt. John Barry (born Wexford Ireland) is accepted as the founding father of the United States Navy. He was placed in charge of the first ever American warship the *USS Lexington*. He too belonged to *the Hibernian society and the Friendly Sons.*

GENERALS, -: Richard Butler, Edward Hand, William Irvine, Walter Stewart, William Thompson, to name but a few belonged to either the Hibernian Society or The Friendly Sons. Many other lower ranks Colonel and Majors also were members of one or the other or both.

These dinners they attended after the successful revolution, must have been jolly occasions. All could relax and exchange war stories. All played vital parts in bringing together the Americans Revolutions success. Many, many would be absent from the table. The host of the fallen, who died to create a country whose professed aim from the start was individual liberty and the glorious pursuit of happiness. What a tremendous feat. The Friendly sons of St. Patrick, had achieved their dedicated aim and pronounced goal. From then on, their pursuit would be to produce American engineers, scientists, chemists, construction workers financiers' farmers etc the eternal flame had been passed on to a younger generation. of fellow Americans.

American firms in the future, always before starting any big construction projects, firstly started, by advertising for good workers in Dublin and Belfast. Roads, Canals, Railways, Factories, Homes, Whole Cities, Wharfs, Harbours all needed to be constructed from scratch. Vast, enormous amounts of Land needed to be cleared always a tough job and brought into constructive production and cultivation These Americans were in the building trade alright, building a whole nation on a continental size from the foundations up.

The Friendly sons of St. Patrick and the American Congress had all this ahead of them. They had suffered much, but all those present had come thru a very arduous task, a veritable via dolorosa, the way of the cross. The American revolution was America's Passion play. Many times, America would stumble and fall, and it would have to pick itself up bleeding, to carry on this arduous struggle. Spat at and ridiculed by its detractors only a bloody thorny crown was its horrible embellishment. This thorny crown would one day be replaced with a seven spangled tiara a beacon of freedom and tabula ansata, inscribed with the date July 4th 1776. But for now, only Hells gates were open, and the fiery blast from its furnaces overflowed the land, burning hearts and homes together. Our cosy jovial, St. Patrick day dinner, seemed far off in the winter 1776.

What a lovely occasion to be at a warm dinner with friendly faces, at the very start of something big. At the very birth of a gigantic new nation, one that would grow up to conduct world affairs, and influence political direction and philosophy Surrounded by Americas Great and good the movers and shakers the fathers of the nation all sat down together to enjoy each other's company. But alas dear reader we must leave this warm lovely scene of the founding sons and fathers and return to more serious matters of revolutionary survival. Indeed, our joyous warm dinner by a cosy fire, a meal shared together amongst true and trusted friends, seems a long way off yet, if not, totally lost altogether for our brave sons of America. SONS of LIBERTY as one Irishman called them to the stuffy English elites faces in their very own parliament.

Whilst the American army was recovering on the banks of the Delaware, most Americans rightly assumed; all was but lost. Come late December 1776. No good tidings seemed to be on the horizon. No festive season of good will to all men seemed in the offing. Indeed, the revolution was fighting to keep its head above the water; in a pit of slippery vile quicksand, all seemed doomed to any detached onlooker. Washington and his Irish diehards were up a creek without a paddle. Things needed to change and change fast.

The Presbyterian ministers amongst its ranks, would never say die. Hell, or liberty was odds they had faced before. These ministers would sooner be burnt alive than give in to treachery. The fiery furnaces of hell scared them not one jot. They would far sooner die than kiss the king's ring, or any other part of his sacred body. (British sectarianism was rife all through-out its empire and the 16th 17th 18th and 19th centuries. The Presbyterians and Congregationalists had quite simply had more than a belly full of this nonsense to last a thousand life times, they left England and is sectarian discrimination, and travelled to the other side of the world, they were not pro-king. Also please remember this was the 16,17,18 and 19th centu-ries. British people today are extremely diverse and amongst some of the most hospitable people on this planet, and amongst its most tolerant by far. Every day tolerance by everyday people, the ordinary British folk are extremely and naturally fair minded and tolerant. Tolerance is very much a modern-day British society virtue. No other city or capital has seen such a large and dramatic dynamic change in its demographics as old London. A truly cosmopolitan capital of the world and its peoples. I digress we must march on with our dramatic story.

These guys were going nowhere fast, and they would gladly march with Washington into the very gates of hell. The game was most definitely on and to the Irish at least they must have felt that old scores needed set-tling. This was the most heavily armed Irish army ever fielded against the dreaded enemy, give up – hell no! we attack.

The idea of retreating was an anathema to these guys. To attack gave them a fighting chance to recover some much-needed pride., They had the best chance in centuries, they had guns and cannons too. The idea they were defeated was nonsensical to all of them. So, what, the New Englanders had left, so bloody what. This was the best chance Ireland had had in centuries; they did not intend to let this golden opportunity go. No bloody wonder George Washington loved the Irish, far from writing a letter outlining the Congresses peace terms – No! That was put into his back pocket. Washington would come across that letter later after the first battle.... *Oh, what sweet revenge!*

Washington would begin to consider Colonel Reeds daring attack. He must have ruminated on its execution. A three-pronged attack across the Delaware River and a sweeping attack on Trenton on Christmas night started to ruminate in his weary tired military mind. Washington was Rommel, Patton, or Napoleon in all but name. A letter is dispatched by Irish man, Colonel Reed to Washington, as late as December 22nd, Reed is inspecting the Continental Army. He has a razor-sharp military mind and is the closest confident to General Washington he writes Dec 22nd "we are all of the Opinion my dear general that something must be attempted" he urges Washington to attack he states, "even a failure cannot be more fatal than to remain in our present situation" Either we attack, or we might as well give up the cause. This is Reed's ultimatum and assessment, he has a good military head, one better than Washington's. And I think Washington knows Reeds military assessment usually are extremely good. Colonel Reed goes on "our affairs are hasting fast to ruin." To do nothing is to accept total defeat. Colonel Reed well knows Washington indecisiveness has proved fatal in tactics and battle performance over the New York campaign. Washington for his part, takes too much notice of the armchair patriots in the Congress. He is well aware that green militia cannot be trusted, up against experienced battle-hardened regulars of the British Army. On this one point he has been very badly let down by the Congress.

Congress was very reluctant to arm finance and sanction a regular army in the tens of thousands. Even though Washington had pleaded with them that a fully functioning, full time regular American Army could only beat the British hardened regulars. Washington knew the part time militia was not good enough for the job in question. He has repeatedly asked congress to act on this matter with much urgency. But to no avail yet. Colonel Reed needs to get Washington to act decisively. That is why he presses Washington to attack at all costs. (See Washington's Crossing p/257~260)

Washington does not think too long, he orders a council of war immediately. At this council, colonel Reed's plan to attack, exposed Trenton over the Delaware, is discussed, the council agree on the merits of Reeds plan. They quickly get down to the nuts and bolts of how to execute it. Things are now moving fast Washington reconvenes the council of war late Christmas eve, the fine details of this plan are gone over. Washington's plan is to attack Trenton with one blocking force to trap the Hessians from a retreat, and two independent lines of attack. Three separate river crossings across the Delaware are envisaged, all need to work in a synchronised action Plan. And this will be all done at night in the middle of winter. On Christmas night in bad weather across an ice bound river in full flow, with a storm fast approaching... What could possibly go wrong?

CHAPTER 4

"Resurrection" Into Your Hands Oh Lord We Commend Our Spirit

The ten most critical days in American history, the very turning point of the whole nation's destiny. Indeed, a turning point in world history, was about to unfold. This incomparable event for America. Was to be enacted by diseased, hungry, mentally tired men and boys. Would fortunes wheel turn in their favour? Would Washington's deliberators and doubters be silenced? Would hope and confidence be restored? This epic grandeur of a nations task, worthy of pen and paper, was about to open up. The fate of the whole nation and the story of the future of a free and fair world hung in the balance.

General George Washington needed this decidedly fantastic plan to work with the precision of a Swiss chronometer, to put a night-time amphibious three-pronged pincer attack onto the Hessians over the Delaware River? In the middle of winter, in a storm across an ice bound river; in three separate locations and hopefully all synchronized together, to meet up for the final assault on Trenton.

Washington for the past number of days had been having the American Army turn out for full parade in the late evenings along the banks of the Delaware river, for muster roll call, right in front of any British hidden eyes on the far bank. Washington was a crafty old codger for sure, he had many tricks in his quiver. So, on Christmas day evening, Americans soldiers gathering on mass in front of the Delaware had become a normal routine. Colonel Rahl in charge of the Hessians and British Dragoons at Trenton, pulled all his Aggressive patrolling out for Christmas day as the weather was too bad. Significantly he pulls patrolling along the Delaware river too. He kept his sentries outside Trenton on full alert. One American long-range patrol/probe deep in enemy territory south of Trenton would later on report the Hessians at this one outpost were all fast asleep Christmas night/ Boxing Day i.e., the night of December 25/26.

Washington's old original ideas about a possible breakout into small parties or retreat beyond the Allegheny Mountains or take his Irish diehards to Virginia those who wished to die with him and make a last bloody stand under American colours and surrounded by his choicest Irish troops. These ideas were now all yesterday's old cabbage. George Washington and the American Congress's thoughts; of peace feelers, now seemed so far away. Going on the attack was very much an about turn. Could the Revolution afford to take such a gamble?

The debacle of the New York campaign, when Washington's light began to fade must have wracked his brain with doubts. Washington had only achieved massive defeats, one quickly upon another. Many had begun to doubt his military acumen. Washington had only brought the American Army to the brink of a massive military disaster so far. Colonel Reed too began to ask questions about who should replace Washington. Washington was aware of these rumours and machinations and wise enough to know they were right; he had only brought the American people and its army, blood, sweat and tears.

The exposed outpost of Trenton offered the Continental Army a good chance of success as for the very first time the American Army would out-number the enemy. This was an extremely risky venture, was it much better to play safe? An all of nothing gamble on one last throw of the dice could augur a defeat and total ruination for the whole revolution. And that is one thing now the Revolution could well do without. Even the sniff of a defeat, would spell the end of the enterprise. Some of the Irish officers present knew full well what the Irish lads were still capable of. They knew what the troops had left, they knew they were not beaten, not by a long shot. The other Irish American officer of Washington's inner command pushing Washington down this extremely daring road was Colonel Stark* another brave no nonsense Irish soldier. He had been pressing Washington to attack the exposed Hessian fortified town on the far side of the Delaware; (Colonel Stark was Irish on his mothers' side, Derry Northern Ireland) for days now. Washington was well aware of the Irish community's zeal and commitment to the American Revolution. Its printers could be trusted and relied upon to print American propaganda for the revolution, no matter what Britain's enforcers threatened printers with, as regards legal conse-quences, fines or even confiscation of their printing presses. This was all old hat in Ireland, the British were always threatening them, with evic-tion, higher taxes, communal slaughter, hangings, the whole nine yards of organised government repression. The Irish people in America were extremely common in the Revolutionary public safety committees, enforc-ing republican ideals, principles, laws instructions etc. (The Irish played a big part in confiscating loyalists' arms pre the outbreak of hostilities; and once hostilities had commenced disarming them).

The Irish, American volunteers were all in… Presbyterians and Catholics, all knew the rope was awaiting any defeat or surrender for those born in Ireland. The British would hang them as traitors, especially the Catholics. The British hatred of Catholics was visceral and demonic in the extreme. Public torture shows of hanging a live Catholic to the point near death, cutting them down, disembowelling them and placing their torn-out innards in front of their eyes. Then whilst hopefully still alive (they always preferred to torture a live victim) then they would chop off the male member. That usually killed them. Hanging Drawing and Quartering and other vile government tortures hung deliberately over every practising Catholics head in the British Isles for centuries. Day in and night out.

Sir Walter Raleigh's H.Q. in Ireland was lined with the heads of Irish people stuck on poles, a bit like Colonel Kurtz Montagnard village, in *"Apocalypse Now"*. This type of pantomime military nonsense was played to the full in Ireland, especially against people of the auld faith. What faith Raleigh adhered to with his chopped off heads certainly was not Christianity in any of its forms. Montezuma and Aztec atrocities come to mind, more than Jesus and his twelve apostles when one considers this type of military activity. Whatever was guiding Sir Walter Raleigh s mind and thoughts it would not be found in the Bible. Certainly, this type of religious nonsense was practised by the British in Ireland as stated before; not over a few years or over a few miserable decades; No! this blatant perverted sectarianism was practised by civilising Britain over disgusting centuries. This was what the British called "civilisation", a most disgusting form of civilisation for sure. British soldiers were encouraged to hunt and chase down Catholic Rabbis i.e., Priests and if successfully captured, then the civilised ones would decapitate them in public for all to see, children too. This is not ISIL… this was just an opener on British civilised rule in Ireland. This sort of horrific nonsense had been going on for centuries in Ireland; and much, much more collective violence against the innocent Catholic population.

ONE OF THE " SCALPS," THE RESIDENCE OF THE CLARE AND CONNEMARA PEASANTRY DURING THE YEAR OF FAMINE.

Hundreds of thousands of Irish people and children were reduced down to this type of destitution and bare human survival for centuries. With each passing century more were added; to this miserable existence, in most cases just for being an original Christian

EJECTMENT OF IRISH TENANTRY.

THE EJECTMENT.

Hundreds of thousands of Irish homes were tumbled and wrecked, to get them off the landlord's land. Hundreds of thousands became abjectly homeless overnight, kid's, babies too. All cleared out even in winter to die on the roadsides in their own country. This cruel carry-on against fellow Christians went on for centuries and centuries against people whose only real crime was being Apostolic Catholics... For the last one thousand seven hundred years. i.e., following the teachings of Jesus as passed down to them from the Apostles time!

71

Far from retreating beyond the Alleghany mountains or making a glorious last stand in Virginia surrounded by his choicest Irish regiments, as any sensible man would have done. Washington was beginning to think the unthinkable, a mad gamble on a daring risky Attack with his hell fire and brimstone Die-hards. The bloody Irish. Scattered in amongst them were Scottish jocks, Highlanders no friends to the dreaded Red Coats the "Sassenachs." The highlanders had been kicked off their ancient lands too; they too had travelled halfway around the world to get away from these heathen swine. So too English Roundheads patriots to Republicanism, not royalty. Free French Catholics no friends to British red coats in America or Canada (British North America) plus German speaking American patriots. Some would be used by Washington to successfully spy on the Hessian mercenaries and the British Army. Both the British and the Hessians seemed to have trusted, the Germans Americans on face value as their trusted allies. A good supply of German American Patriots stayed on like the Irish.

Both sides ran spies into each other's camps. Washington used German speaking Patriots to socially infiltrate into the German Hessian mercenaries to gather vital information. George Washington seems to have got the better of the intelligence war. All throughout the American Revolution.

Enter an Irish man onto the scene. A man calling himself *Honeywell*. He claims to be a butcher and a bar tender in Trenton. A mystery man from Armagh Ireland originally. Now our mystery man is either captured by Washington Pickets which seems totally strange! What was he doing walking about the backroads of Trenton in the middle of the night and so far from town? He turned up in the wee small hours before dawn. And was "captured" Or he was met at a pre-arranged rendezvous? Either way he his brought to General Washington for a private interrogation. Washington ensures he is fed and placed in a Detention Area. Next there is a mysterious fire and Washington's "Prisoner escapes" Our mystery man goes back to Trenton to tell all the Germans in the bar, that the continental army is finished, mass desertions, fighting amongst themselves, badly fed, badly shod, a half-dressed broken-down rabble incapable of fighting anyone.

Our Irish man from county Armagh has done well. Undoubtedly, he has given Washington a bloody good rundown of the Hessians dispositions, gun emplacements and the like. Washington runs spies on his own, that only he is privy too. He keeps a large stash of money personally by his side at any H.Q. he resides in. Washington did well to subterfuge this meeting. His own camp had an active British spy amongst them. This generous bag of money was for these most secret endeavours. The spies are only known to him personally, and Washington pays them himself. As stated Ironically, the British have successfully infiltrated their own active spies in Washington's camp unbeknownst to him.

Our Irish spy, is later seen after the Battle of Trenton, fleeing with the rest of the town's loyalists back into the New Jersey Countryside. Undoubtedly to escape these Yankee swine, disloyal to king and country. He will settle into a loyalist stronghold and keep his ears and eyes open (On further research Mr. Honeywell by all accounts is a genuine historical man. Some American historians have cast doubt on his validity, but apparently, he lived and was quite a celebrity, he survived the war and had a good life after the Revolution) ... For now, the Hessians relax, with the good news that bartender Honeywell as brought back with his lucky "escape". As the noose it pulled tighter around their very necks, the Hessians were blissfully unaware of what the American Army was planning. Much later on in the Revolution, Washington would use an African American to infiltrate the British lines at Yorktown and achieve an American Victory, there too. The Black/brown African American would feed the British useless and false intelligence this required nerves of steel to pull of successfully. This brave black man delivered the victory at Yorktown on a plate to Washington. This very brave Afro American was originally used by Washington as a spy to infiltrate British lines and gather information. So, there must have been something about this African American that attracted American army intelligence officers to his ability to be a successful spy.

The British were so impressed with the cut of this black/brown man that they too, believe it or not, asked him to be a spy for them! And gather intelligence on Washington's army and its movements and dispositions. He duly reported back to his American intelligence officers this most generous offer of employment by the British. American intelligence got down to supplying this obviously honest black/brown gentleman with much tactical and strategic nonsense to fill up and please his British generals with. Washington's army at Yorktown knew a lot about the British; and the British at Yorktown knew an awful lot of bogus nonsense about the Americans. General Washington as stated earlier kept a personal money bag on his possession, whilst in camp. Washington let it be known he was willing to pay a handsomely for good intel.

Washington got to work to give the British a Christmas they would not forget, like the Battle of the Bulge during WWII. This would be a winter offensive, a daring night-time amphibious attack, and a three-pronged pincer attack. From three separate jumping off points across the mighty river Delaware.

Washington would have to attack at night and in a storm across an icy river, pushing and hauling cannons, up roads, onto a ferry, back off a ferry and down long roads by tired men with no shoes and little clothes with cannon wheels all wrapped up in cloth to hide the noise. Irish Americans neighbours would offer to guide the American army down the backway into Trenton. As Late as Christmas eve or early Christmas day Washington finally gives the green light... It's go! The American attack on Trenton is on! Soldiers assemble on the banks of the Delaware in the early evening now a usual daily routine, but this time with full rations for three days, and much needed ammunition. Once night falls, the cannons and horses are brought down to the river to begin embarkation in the dark. Washington's first troops over seal the embarkation area for miles around.

On Christmas night not a soul was stirring, snow was gently falling, and the wind was getting up. Soon an icy winter storm was brewing up and sweeping across the Delaware... Undetected and unnoticed, the American rebel army was on the move

This time they would not be defending, this time it was a night-time attack with triple river crossings. Washington knew he had the best of the American army left at his disposal with excellent riflemen from Virginia and excellent soldier material from Maryland. The British feared the Irish more than the rest.

Years Later, Confederate General Lee, the auld sly fox himself, during the American Civil War; whenever he heard that an Irish northern regiment was attacking a position, he instinctively ordered that that part of his position was to be immediately reinforced no matter what. He too feared the Irish, he knew like the British they would stick it out and stick it in and attack any position with guts and determination. It was the Confederate General Lee who nicknamed the Irish soldiers the "fighting Irish" After their repeated assaults at Fredericksburg, during the later American civil war. The Irish soldiers would come within feet of overrunning the confederate line. The Confederate line was well dug in, and defended Ironically by a lot of Irish, in Confederate grey. Apparently, the whole confederate army was cheering the Irish as they marched up over their own dead and those that had fallen early, then finally break into a fast run towards the

Confederate well dug in position. Most union soldiers only got to within 40 or 50 yards, but the Irish got nearer and nearer with each successive wave before they got mowed down., this falling wave was met each time with an "aaawwhh" when they all fell in good numbers just feet away from the confederate wall; each human wave crashing nearer, and nearer.

It sounds too good to be true but apparently it was the truth. Maybe the confederates liked to see so many of the enemy die? But most seem to think they were generally in awe of such reckless abandon and bravery. And genuinely felt sorry for each wave that was gunned down and knowing that each Irish wave got that little bit nearer and nearer each time. It was here on seeing the Irish repeatedly get nearer and nearer with each running effort that General Lee nicknamed them the "fighting Irish."

One Irish soldier who was there, described it as like advancing thru a hailstone storm so thick was the shot coming at them. The Commander of the Confederate Artillery boasted that if the Union sent their whole army against that Confederate line, he could obliterate the whole lot. He may well have been correct. He stated any chicken running around that field could not survive. And that was probably a true statement on this battlefield. The Fields of Fredericksburg were awash with dead and those in acute agony moaning, screaming and mutilated. Our younger generation of acutely politically correct interpreters should remember this next bit. General Lee was asked, should the Confederate Army chase down the defeated and retreating Union army, the Confederates could have wiped it off the map and militarily, should have jumped on them and trounced the whole lot. Lee declined; he informed his confederate officers enough Americans had died already today. General Lee ordered his men to leave the Union Army alone, let them tend to their sick and dying let them bury their brave honourable dead. The whole Confederate army turned about and without so much as a moan left the field of battle to fight another day.

That was the Confederate army and that was General Lee a fine American general, leading a good bunch of honourable soldiers. Not one Confederate soldier bemoaned that decision. Think on that next time you want to jump on his statue.

The Irish at these times were the choicest regulars in the British, French and Spanish Armies. They would go on to help as masses of individual volunteers, in the liberation of, most of the countries of South America believe it or not. They too were regarded as amongst the best sailors and soldiers there. A veritable Foreign Legion of Irish soldiers and sailors were regarded in all South American countries as the best toughest regiments in all of the southern American countries struggles of liberation against colonialism. Sounds fantastic I know but historically absolutely true. It probably has a lot to do with the living conditions back in Ireland, fighting and living half naked, fighting with rudimentary weapons, constantly hungry, living outside in all weathers. These types of conditions made the Irish soldier/sailor serving abroad in a foreign army or navy; a well fed, well-armed, very highly motivated soldier. Who was hard to crack, who never complained and could take and operate in conditions other regiments would collapse under.

The British army noted these qualities of the Irish soldiers, as did the French and Spanish Armies. All of whom fielded Solely Irish Regiments. Incidentally the Irish Regiments in the French Army pleaded with the French to send them to America, as did the Irish Regiments in the Spanish Army. The Famous Duke of Wellington commented at Waterloo about his Irish soldiers. I do not know what they will do the enemy but they sure as Hell scare me. He too noted that the Irish soldiers remained in good spirits when all his other regiments morale was rock bottom. As I stated previously no conditions the British Army operated under could come anywhere near close to the conditions the Irish soldier had left back in Ireland.

In Philadelphia, the good citizens only wanted the British army to turn up any day now, for to subjugate them; and for them to restore authority and their allegiance and custody. Most places in northern America felt exactly the same.

That stormy Christmas night the Hessians saw the storm come in and reckoned that no army could march through this and certainly not attempt a successful river crossing in this deteriorating stormy weather. The weather was just too bad these professional soldiers estimated.

Colonel Rahl called in all Delaware river patrolling but kept his pickets outside Trenton on full alert. This was the same mistake the Hessians descendants would make on June 5th, 1944. No Allied army would land a major amphibious operation in bad weather, upon the beaches of Normandy. Most high-ranking German generals saw the barometer plunge and shipped out to Paris for a bit of fun and relaxation June 4th and 5th 1944. They like the Hessians had miscalculated the prowess and determination of their deadly foe.

Washington's brain had gone into overdrive to carefully plan and execute this three-pronged, night-time amphibious attack on Trenton. He ordered fresh militia to go to the outskirts of Bordertown, create a mêlée but not to engage the enemy rather on contact they were to retreat quickly. Some modern American historians put this melee down to good luck and fortune, rather than Washington's directives. I'm more open to persuasion. Washington was a crafty old soldier he usually uses a ruse or false attack as a diversion to off foot the enemy. He did this at Yorktown to pull the British away from the genuine point of attack. So, it would come as a great surprise and not to running form for Washington to attack Trenton without some ruse to pull the British army away

Washington hoped to pull vital British troops away from any aid to Trenton. The British in Bordertown took the bait, and a large force was assembled by The British Commander Dunop. He marshalled together a force of 2,000 redcoats. The hounds had seen the Hare and gave chase.

For two solid days Colonel Dunop chased this elusive American regiment around the backwoods of New Jersey; so, when word of the night-time attack eventually arrived, they were over a good 12 miles away and could offer no support once Washington's attack had started. They had been truly fooled and led a merry old dance by the newly arrived green horn militia. Washington had used these fresh troops well. Not battle hardened enough to take part in a full-frontal assault but sure good enough as a large force to shoot and scoot and entice an enemy away.

One other American regiment of 600 men did actually get across and sweep the area below Trenton, they came back with the news that the Hessian forward posts were manned, all were sleeping! *(P234)*. American scouts got as far as Mount Holly. Other American volunteers secreted themselves in a doctor's residence in Burlington. Those who successfully crossed over the Delaware had to be withdrawn, when the rest of the regiments could not make it over on Christmas night, as the weather deteriorated, and ice made any further crossing impossible. Indeed, it took all night and the next morning with much trouble to get them back over from across the Delaware. 600 was not enough to sustain an attack or block the retreating Hessians from escaping if they decided to bug out. Meanwhile further up the river Washington was having his own troubles. Nothing was going to plan.

Washington's plan a daring three-pronged attack across the Delaware and a surprise pincer Night attack on the Germans was immediately coming apart; he was across the Delaware but most of his army was still waiting on the far side. Washington ordered those soldiers across to secure the perimeter and detain all leaving or entering this now secure military zone. Washington was gambling the whole Revolution, the whole shooting kaboodle, the full nine yards, the whole shebang on one last throw of the dice. He must have been deeply deadly worried. Nothing was going to plan he was three desperate hours behind schedule already, some were still on the far bank! His look may have been stoic, but underneath that thin veneer, every nervous tic must have been coming to the surface with its thousand and one worries, thousand and one unanswered desperate questions. What should he do? Should he call the whole operation off? Many, many military commanders had been in the same dilemma over time. Does he go on with a half plan or call it off?

The whole revolution rested upon this decision should he go for broke? or safely retreat over the mountains? All hindered on this point. He could definitely secure the Revolution by escaping; and that route was by far the most sensible one to take; or he could stare down the precipice and boldly go where no American Commander had gone before, straight down the jaws of hell, and face a risky battle outcome? Against the best regiment in the British Task force. Washington knew all now rested upon his solitary shoulders. As truthfully, it always had. Washington knew others around him were wondering about his military prowess and acumen. They described him as indecisive, unable to make the big decisions, lacking military experience. All this nonsense must have filled up his thoughts. What should he do? This was the million-dollar question. The fate of America rested in his trembling hands. He was the man on the spot. Like all generals before and after him, he alone had a date with destiny the fate of the country rested upon this decision and outcome He decided Straight down into the jaws of hell.... It was Go! Go! Go! America's freedom and date with destiny would be decided in a few wee hours' time. The wind was getting up, it was hard to see these brave men struggling in the drifting snow, horses excited, pushing, and pulling cannons, all tired, cold, and wondering what the day would bring. Washington must have thought; do these brave men know the spirit of destiny is in their hands. The whole universe of time was spinning around them, in a self-contained bubble of a snowstorm "There are more things in heaven and hell", "If you can hold the world in a grain of sand, hold infinity in the palm of your hand and eternity in an hour" The clock was ticking down... Time and tide wait for no man. Washington needed to concentrate; the die was cast. They had gone past the point of no return. Washington must have felt tremendous relief when the time of deliberation was over. This was the time for action. Carpe diem, seize the day, grasp the stinging nettle!

The American soldiers had their own date with destiny, every single one. All would soon be decided. Who would live, who would die? And that fate was not, in most cases in their own hands. These men had stout hearts, no shoes, full bellies for once, three days rations, and ammunition in full; Even so, much blood trickled onto the snow as this freezing, still half-dressed American Army quietly crossed over the Delaware, and began their final march on towards its final damnation.

Most could legally go after Christmas; their allotted service was up. Fear not; better to die fighting for freedom than live as a slave under the heavy British yoke of religious persecution. All the sensible men had left. As the bloody American Army quietly crossed the Delaware to the far side friendly Irish voices greeted them again, the man who ran the flat-bottomed Ferry was an Irish man, he and his Irish neighbours hauled the cannons and horses once again over the Delaware. More Irish neighbours who had previously scoured both banks for boats, helped cross the American Infantry over. Undoubtedly wishing them well. Washington placed the Marblehead sailors from New England with the precarious task of getting his whole army; cannons, horses, and all; successfully across the extremely dangerous ice bound river Delaware. These New Englanders did well, most arrive dry. Some had to get out to haul the big boats thru the ice bound shore; whilst others smashed the ice away. Eventually by this method the crossing was completed. But frighteningly three precious night hours behind Washington's synchronized tight schedule. Big Irish American general Knox is usually credited with his calm demeaner, booming voice and orders with seeing this military manoeuvre to successful completion. Many times, it looked a completely hopeless task, impossible to achieve. But General Knox never seemed to doubt its eventual success. He probably was putting on a good show.

The Yanks did well, against all the odds eventually all were over, cannons and horses too. General Knox was the man who came up with the mad plan to haul cannons all the way from Ticonderoga to Boston. To ensure victory there. He sure liked to punish himself. This would be the only successful crossing of the Delaware the other two crossing points failed to get to the far bank. * (as stated previously one other crossing did in fact get 600 soldiers successfully across; they immediately sent out a reconnaissance force to ascertain the Hessians disposition. One party bravely penetrated deep into enemy territory. The reconnaissance party returned. The Hessian advance guards were all at their sentry posts fast asleep!! The American army would literally in their attack later, catch them literally napping!) Washington now had everyone on the far bank. Worried sick, he could not make it now to Trenton in the dark. They would be approaching in daylight; the intricate scheme was unravelling in front of his eyes. Washington's other two units further down the river had failed to arrive, and it is now getting day light. Washington surprise three-pronged night attack is in tatters.

His army is Freezing, half clothed many only shod with bloody rags around their feet. A long way from their warm secure homes, family, and friends. Every volunteer contained within their own minds a thousand and one worries. What would happen to their families if they died?

If General Washington's was going to gamble all, on one last throw of the dice for freedom and liberty. Then by hell, he was going to do it all alone; with a much smaller detachment than he had bargained for; And without the added bonus of darkness to aid his surprise. As military men say the plan is usually only good for the first five minutes! Washington would need all the stamina, guts, resolution, brains steadfastness and determination to see the battle through to an American victory, on the continent of America. General Washington, one must assume, would have turned the flaps on his coat up and ordered the Continental army to march onto Trenton!... Very quietly!.. A strict silence was maintained. Washington's die-hards would slowly creep towards their foe. getting closer with every desperate hour. Every quiet step, into total silence they approached. Finally, finally, Washington's Army came across Trenton, they had made it. The future of America and the whole American Revolution rested on the next few minutes!

......Twas the night of Christmas, and thru Trenton not a soul was stirring. Not even the church mouse. When all of a sudden there was such a clatter and captain Rahl sprang from his bed to see what was the matter, away to the window he flew in a flash, tore open the shutters and threw up the sash, the moon on the breast of the new fallen snow, gave a lustre of midday to the objects below when what to his wondering eyes did appear but proud auld George Washington astride his white steer, soon cannons did roar with an awful fright, and many a Yankee put the Hessians to flight. Now cold and shivering the Hessians lined up, and walked into captivity, their festive. season so utterly, utterly, utterly mucked up *(Adapted from Twas the night before Christmas by Clement Clarke Moore).

Yes, the Hessians got a Christmas surprise alright. It had all gone well in the end; but Washington's three pincer entrapment never got off the launch pad. Very quietly while all else were fast asleep on Christmas night, the Americans appeared out of the dawn twilight and the foggy dew and advanced upon this sleepy Hessian outpost. They attacked with precision, vigour, and determination. Soon the finest troops in Europe, the best troops in the New York campaign so good the whole British army was in awe of them. Now they ran hither and thither, arose from their merry yuletide slumbers, to discover that the entire American army was outside, over running the whole town. The battle ensued, cannons did roar, muskets spitting smoke and lead. Some hit their targets for sure. Now it was the turn of the finest, toughest regiment in the entire British task force, to feel afraid, worried, scared. Now for the first time in the war the Americans would outnumber the enemy. Some ran straight away, straight away. Others fought back. Many died in an onslaught of lead, shot and cannons;.. within forty minutes it was over.

The hard nuts of the British task force gave up en masse! These fine fellows within 40 minutes had either run away or surrendered to Washington's army. Washington had pulled the rabbit out of the pot. An enormous amount of the best the enemy had, were now taken prisoner. A full nine hundred if not more, that's an extremely large force. If you lined 900 men up that would be the size of a large secondary school's full complement of first to fifth years. All rounded up and taken prisoner in a small American town.

American independence was back on. Washington and his army were sucking diesel. Merry Christmas everyone and an eventful New Year! The boys were back in town and all the Hessians could do was think of all that lost swag and loot, …. oh dear, oh dear.

The first Battle of Trenton on Boxing Day (St. Stephen's Day 26th December) was an unpleasant surprise for the Hessians. They were literally caught napping and within 40 minutes it was all over. 900 battle hardened Hessians immediately surrendered. Which amounted to 2/3 rd. of the entire deployment at Trenton. A couple of hundred escaped.

The American blocking force American Germans led by an Irishman * could not get into position quick enough and Germans and British dragoons just upped and left pretty quickly once the shooting started. *See Wikipedia article Battle of Trenton.

WHY WE FOUGHT

The defeated German Hessians like the defeated German Wehrmacht of WWII, who were paraded through the streets of Moscow 1942. So now too Washington had decided to parade the mighty Hessians through the streets of America's capital Philadelphia 1777. In both cases the citizens got a close look upon the German invincible enemy and in both cases the enemy did not seem so invincible or cocky now.

Washington knew every trick in the book, and he knew how to play it.

At the Battle of Trenton, a group of dejected, diseased, badly clothed and many non-shod, all hungry, all cold and most lacking sleep, American soldiers roused themselves from defeat, and gave a very bloody nose to the occupiers of their new nation. The patriots had smashed Europe's best, tout sweet whilst diseased, wet, half-shod, desperately cold, and tired foot sloggers. And, In the good old tradition of the conquered; the defeated Hessians the hardest most feared regiment, the hard men of the New York campaign were to be seen shuffling, all lined up en masse thru the streets of Philadelphia at American bayonet points! This scene or spectre, must have been an overly sweet moment for the patriots, after being so, so down and out. They came back from the dead like Lazarus, to rise up again. The American army had been lashed, whipped, scourged, nailed to the cross and crucified. And in good fable tradition they were resurrected...... The game was back on!

The American army got much needed equipment and stores at Trenton and rest for a while. America could be free for a little longer, just a wee small vital reprieve. The loyalists in New York would have to wait a few more days for their day of retribution on the patriots. The American army had won decisively its date with destiny. Howe called off any high society leisurely life in New York. Winter wonderland was put on ice for the moment and General Howe would have to resolve himself down to defeat these pesky American upstarts once and for all. Cornwallis was instructed not to depart for England but to return, with all haste.

Washington was not sitting on his laurels. He was sending young lads out into the towns and villages thru out New Jersey to garner information about the occupier's disposition. Regular army Scouts were being sent out to reconnoitre too. After the defeat at the Battle of Trenton, the mud-slinging soon started by the British Generals and high command. General Grant wrote from New Brunswick: -

> "I did not think that all the rebels in America would have taken that Brigade prisoner".

Howe knew that, that very German brigade had outmatched all other brigades with its bravery and tenacity during the New York campaign. All the rest of the British army were extremely envious of them as elite crack German Stormtroopers *(P225)*.

Lord George Germaine, colonial Secretary of State for King George III to General Van Heister, Hessian General i.e. (General of the mass looters);

> "Sir I have the honour to receive your letter January 5th. His Majesty has already heard of the misfortune which happened to the brigade of troops (i.e., looters) of his most serene highness...... It is hoped that the dangerous practice of underestimating the enemy may make a lasting impression on the rest of the army." *(P225 William Stryker battle of Trenton and Princeton)*.

The captured Hessians were eventually exchanged for American P.O.W.'s in 1778. Immediately upon being released back into the British army of occupation. Every Hessian soldier was detained and questioned about the debacle at Trenton. A special court was set up in occupied Philadelphia to look into how the magnificent Hessians got beaten by the diseased remnants of a rabble army. In sat in full investigation all of April, May, June, July, August, and September of 1778. But that would prove not enough time. It went on into the following year hearing hard evidence. And yet again into the following year. The year after that; and just to be sure to be sure for yet another year of investigation. The British must have heard from everyone including one presumes the church mouse! Heavy submission took place into this British disaster when victory was assured! These investigation of how Britain lost an early easy victory dragged on all through 1780 – 82.

The British army blamed the Hessians, but the British Dragoons stationed there were the first to desert the town. (See. p/223 Battle of Trenton and Princeton 1898 William S Stryker Boston & New York Houghton Mifflin Co. The Riverside press Cambridge.) When all the evidence upon this most British/German tragic tragedy was in; the special court martial made its official prestigious deliberations. April 1882 a full five years after the start of its enquiry. The battle for Trenton had taken about 40 minutes if that! To sort out and those 40 minutes had taken five long years to analyse in full.

Never in the field of human conflict had so many men inquired into so much over such a long time of an incident, so little in length to achieve so little, i.e., who was to blame? By the time the British got to the bottom of what happened the war was already virtually over! This victory by broken down patriots achieved so much.

> Never in the field of human history had so many received so much by so few, against so many odds.

The Americans would fight the occupier on the beaches, on the landing grounds, in the hills and valleys of North America. America would go on to the bitter end, and if necessary, alone. Washington could only offer the American patriots and people, blood sweat and tears.

WHY WE FOUGHT

The British knew they would have to quash this uprising, the spirit of independence and freedom from tyranny. The American people had nurtured their freedoms and liberty. British occupation was not the natural will of the collective American people, nor its 13 independent colonies. Their eyes had been opened to British occupation. Especially in New Jersey, very few eyes would shed a tear when the British left by the way they came; that is in fully loaded boats, back to their own harbours.

The Americans nurtured freedom and independence in their collective hearts, the British knew they would have to break their collective will upon this issue. Upon this rock the Americans would flounder and be smashed so they envisioned.

The Continental Congress could not know what lay ahead. They all knew America had a date with its destiny. Greater ordeals lay ahead, the enemy was far more numerous than the battered and beaten Continentals. All American hearts and homesteads began to see the true cost of British occupation, especially under the Germans. Washington was still pleading for a proper regular Army, not militia. Washington knew he must trade territory for victory and avoid set piece battles. Just as in Vietnam, the British could hold towns and cities; but the countryside was another matter. Washington would remain elusive, and only strike with precision when the opportunities came.

The Southern states which the British high command felt sure was loyalist territory, would turn out to be a hornet's nest of trouble. Indeed, more battles for freedom would take place in the south rather than in New England; where most people were content not to rock the boat. Vermont was a great northern exception not part of New England. For some reason Vermont supplied great tough soldiers for both the War of independence and the American civil war

In the civil war the only regiments with higher fatality rates than Irish regiments, were regiments from Vermont and the esteemed black hatted Iron-Brigade which would morph into the U.S.M.C. I think. During the civil war all states produced Die-Hard troops with extraordinary bravery, Wisconsin, Michigan Indiana Ohio, Minnesota, Pennsylvania all supplied troops to the Iron Brigade and New Yorkers and every other state would insist quite rightly that its own soldiers were the finest in the land, and we ain, t even gone down south yet were another tough hardy bunch, would produce one of the finest toughest armies comparable to the Red Army. As tough as old army boots, which few had.

The Americans must brace themselves for the challenges ahead. The Battle of Trenton was not the beginning of the end, but it was perhaps the end of the beginning. America would not lie down and be subdued or defeated; it would not prostrate itself and kiss the sweaty feet of King George or indeed any other King or Queen. So called treachery on the continent of America would have to be broken on the battlefield and in the hearts and minds of the American people.

The British court martial found Colonel Rahl and Major von Dechon were lacking in their leadership of the event. (The esteemed conclusion of the five-year court martial). On that deliberation, I am sure you waited with great excitement and anticipation.

The victory at Trenton electrified the American people. Out of the very jaws of defeat, the American army had snatched a sweet and vitally import-ant victory. The cause was no longer lost, and the American dream lived on in their hearts and minds.

Even the Congress was emboldened to strive on against all hazards and sacrifices involved in liberation. Just, as important as was the battle of

Stalingrad to the Russian people and its Red army. So too was Trenton important for the American people and its people's army. An American army of liberation......Uncle Ho Chi Minh was so engrossed with this example of stoic liberation and patriotic struggle by America; that he announced to the whole world at the start of their own Viet Minh struggle for liberation after World War two by citing the American declaration of Independence as his C.I.A. advisers looked on so proud. I bet they did not tell you that in Parris Island.

Galloway told the House of Commons *(P223 Ibid Stryker)* that after Trenton a new army of Pennsylvania was being formed and that before Trenton that could not have even been envisaged. Trenton was the pivotal battle of American independence.

The Governor of New York, William Tryon wrote that the rebels defeating that Hessian brigade, had given him more chagrin than any other aspect of the war (including the earlier defeat and departure from Boston by the British).

The British public too was shocked and stunned to the core. Trenton was a defeat of magnificent proportions. Trenton lit the light for freedom, and it would continue to burn brightly even as it does today.

British General Cornwallis *(P224)* knew the Hessians were one of the finest regiments in the task force, their sheer gallantry and bravery had been proved and awed by the rest of the army just weeks before at New York Cornwallis stated "That very brigade.... was the admiration of the whole British army. *

The author Stryker blames Cornwallis for the fiasco by leaving Trenton exposed from the British lines, it was too far forward and was thus unable to ask for help from anyone. Colonel Rahl, German professional commander, had repeatedly asked Cornwallis for permission to pull back to a safer less exposed position. Washington and his intelligence unit had noted this. Indeed, they liked the fact that each emplacement could not see what was happening elsewhere and Trenton was the worst case. Commander Rahl repeated requests were repeatedly dismissed. At these dismissals he seems to have become fatalistic in his attitude to the defence of Trenton. He refused the German military engineering officers requests to build fortified cannon emplacements, at strategic points around Trenton.

* At the first Battle of Trenton, Washington attacked the British exposed front. In the second Battle of Trenton, he attacked the British exposed rear.

Lord Germaine wrote: - (P224)

"All our hopes were blasted by that unhappy affair at Trenton."

The British Generals blamed each other and not themselves, for this debacle over the next four years and all through the court martial. The fact that the finest regiment in the army had been overrun by diseased, desperate, freezing cold, unshod, and dirty Yankees affected the whole war's situation. Slowly the British were concluding that this would be no quick easy victory or "a pushover". As was duly prophesied on the vast armada's departure. All they had to do was turn up and these rebels would surely flee. The roar of the British cannons and slices of cold British steel would put a stop to this rebel nonsense, and treachery. Slowly they began to understand this could be a long-drawn-out war and would later conclude it was an unwinnable war. But crafty intelligence led Washington to believe he was not finished with them yet. Washington saw more opportunities to be exploited. *(Irish Blood Story, www. Yankee Doodle with a Brogue).*

CHAPTER 5

Lazarus From The Grave

In an even more daring raid Washington was minded by his Generals to attack again as the British advanced towards Trenton. The British now knew the winter campaign was a real one. As British and German troops poured into Princeton, they immediately began to fortify the town into an impregnable fortress. The British and Germans would not be caught napping twice, both sent out deep patrols to see American dispositions.

Meanwhile the American vanguard entered the deserted town of Bordertown. All the Germans and British had left; taken every last piece of food and animals with them, they left it totally deserted save for their dead and wounded. ** *(P224 Stryker)*.

———————————————————

66% of all medals of honour have been won by Irish men in the American uniform. The medal of honour is the highest award America can bestow on a soldier. It is usually awarded by the President himself.

** By now, new news was reaching the Germans, and the large British pursuit force sent out to seek and destroy a large element of the American army on Christmas day, to attack the large militia force that Washington had sent out to entice them away. New news now reached them that they had been well and truly taken for fools, and placed on a fools errand, a chase about the woods and backroads whilst the real American army had captured Trenton, leaving them with egg on their faces.

The Americans got intel that a large German force was operating in the area but that they were much slowed down and encumbered by their bags of loot and swag. Wagon loads of soldier's swag accompanied them about New Jersey. Sometimes over a hundred wagons slowly accompanied the Hessians and slowed their columns down to a snail's pace.

Young American militia were now eager for some action (which is always a good point to be at). A large force of young inexperienced militia set out into the New Jersey countryside. They came back with a few German prisoners and a regimental standard of the Hessians which is still preserved.

Washington needed to turn the American army into a full-time army of professional soldiers, not sunshine ones or militia who stayed only for days, weeks or indeed months; he needed seasoned veterans.

After Trenton, Washington had used soldiers on good horses in fine civilian clothes to slowly ride ahead as if they were local gentry. They were instructed not to ride fast, just to gander about the place. Another small American scouting party came back with British dragoons and a commissary wagon stacked with supplies. Things were looking up for the yanks. Soon a new spirit would begin to mingle amongst the rank and file, a new much needed confidence of their own abilities and prowess was starting to show up. General Washington must have been much relieved and probably walked around as if an extremely heavy sagging weight had been lifted off his weary tired shoulders.

Some captured British dragoons told Washington that a large force was being assembled in Princeton to crush the American army once and for all. Washington on being led to believe a large British attack was imminent moved out of Trenton and occupied the high ground around it. He ordered fellow Irishman colonel Edward Hand to harass the oncoming British army and slow it down. * (I Just promoted Washington to honorary Irishman because he deserves it, in this battle for Americas Dream survival Washington was actually made an Honorary Irish man by the Friendly sons of St. Patrick. Apparently, he loved the little medal they presented him with) Hand put together an Irish flying column and deployed with good effect. This small flying column caused many British casualties, but more vitally important for Washington slowed their whole army up.

The second phase was about to begin, and Washington was about to give the British a lesson in tactics, tenacity, and skill. The old fox was about to pull another rabbit from the hat in front of the British eyes and noses and slip silently into the American wilderness for winter; whilst the British once again were out foxed, outwitted, and outplayed – yet again!

Washington was about to play his hand and give the mighty British a lesson in the art of warfare. As the British began to surround Trenton, Washington was trapped up against the Delaware, if he attempted to cross over the British army would destroy him whilst he manoeuvred his army to a very vulnerable and slow boat river crossing. He could not stand a long siege and a full-on attack would be costly for the British but even more costly for the Americans. A surprise attack on Brunswick which American intelligence had informed the General was well stocked with supplies and only lightly guarded with 250 troops. Cadwalader was ordered to straight away attack, but on his way an American patrol informed him the town had just been reinforced by 1,500 British troops and the surprise attack was called off. *(P21 Stryker).*

General Knox (an Irish General) was aware that a large part of the Continental Army's service was due to expire on 31st December 1776. General Knox was a fine Irish gentleman and tough as old boots soldier. It was he that had organised the Dragging of much needed cannons from Fort Ticonderoga and Crown Point, to cross over 300 miles of roads, mountains, rivers in the middle of winter, all the way to Boston, to aid in the siege of this American port now occupied by the British Army, in retribution for dumping tea into Boston harbour. A historic event known in America as the Boston tea party.

General Knox had achieved a momentous task when he delivered to the American army besieging Boston, these vital guns for bombardment of the British garrison. And thus, making their hold on Boston militarily untenable. The general had also achieved herculean heights of achievement when he successfully made the only military crossing of the Delaware, at night in a winter storm over an ice bound fast flowing river. Delivering over; Horses, Cannons, Wagons, Feed, and the main element of the American Army, in Secret and in enemy territory. General Knox knew most of the men's conscription time was up on 31 December. He therefore addressed these troops upon the dire situation in hand. A large British force of 8,000 or more was bearing down on Trenton to wipe the American army off the map. If they could just stay on a little longer then they could build on the Trenton success and achieve a greater good; if they departed on their due dates all the hard work and bravery would stand for nothing. Earlier in the campaign 500+ New Englanders had abruptly up and left the field, leaving the situation in a most dire position. Exactly one-year earlier December 1775.

Last December, the American generals had explained to them the dire consequences of their collective action would have upon the war and uprising; nevertheless, not one stayed behind to help out. They all upped and left on their due date. Leaving the revolution hanging on a thread, and the defeat that followed with a disastrous attempt to take Quebec City. The whole body of New Englanders apparently 500+, could not be persuaded to hang in there. And this my dear friends were only the start of the revolution.

Another American Commander Major General Thomas Mifflin addressed the ragtag army in a heavy coat made from a horse blanket and a large fur cap. His horse looked more regal than he did. He appealed to the Irishmen's patriotic zeal and duty. The Irishmen's own officers talked to the troops (lots of the Irish troops would only speak Gaelic) and finally General Washington addressed them: -

> "Yes, he acknowledged the troops had every right to leave they
> had already done enough, above and beyond the call of duty."

Washington stressed the virtue of their cause. The assembled regiments of the Continental army all listened. To many soldiers they could only speak ancient Irish so Washington's words would have to be translated to them. Washington asked the assembled troops; were they with him? then in one sharp snap drill, in Quick Army precision the whole American army Thousands upon thousands, poised their firelocks, like a well-oiled clock striking one. This the American officers assumed meant they agreed to their patriotic request.

Constant new recruits now became available to Washington although green and untried in combat, at least they "turned up." Washington's good regiments had been decimated. The Delaware regiment had 300 soldiers now only 100 were left. Maryland sent 1,000 soldiers and only 150 remained!

The Continental army had lost a hundred guns and hundreds of rifles and Washington had to strictly enforce that militia who came with no rifle could not take one issued to them, with them when they returned home as had been happening. (Washington was not aware of this habit. He immediately ordered it stopped forthwith) Washington's Generals were not sitting on their laurels, they sent out young green keen to fight militia to harass the Germans wherever they could. On the New Jersey roads, the Hessians were actually struggling upon these roads with all their swag and loot! Ambushes appeared out of nowhere by New Jersey irregular militia seeking revenge for German and British thuggery, theft, abuse, and other unsavoury matters. The British began to get twitchy. Orders were issued that soldiers were not to travel alone or in small groups around New Jersey. The New Jersey militia began to hit back down quite by-roads. Now the British began to feel unsafe once they left their fortified towns. Out in the New Jersey boonies,." in country" ... the British began to fear the unknown, every bend became a potential trap, every bridge a place of concealment for an elusive enemy.

When Washington was given good intel that a large British force was concentrating to attack him, as stated previously he immediately moved the army from Trenton to the high ground surrounding it. Washington immediately issued orders for the yanks to dig in and begin to erect strong fortifications. New Jersey militia were by now pouring into Washington's ranks around Trenton. The American militia were now pouring in as quickly as they had poured out after the debacle at New York.

Poising a firelock means to go from a rifle at rest on the left shoulder with the left hand underneath the rifle to bringing the rifle smartly towards the middle of the face, with the rifle shaft down the middle of the head and with the left and right hand holding the rifle in front of the face with its firelock facing upwards and visible.

Washington's orders were now to send out detachments of the Irish American Continental army to harass the advancing British and slow them down, as this large army advanced towards Trenton. As usual Irishmen were chosen for this job. Eventually the British advanced into the outskirts of Trenton late in the evening sun. They attempted to cross a narrow bridge into Trenton but were repulsed repeatedly. But one mad charge, a quick push and shove did actually get over the bridge. A little Irish drummer boy seeing the advancing British and seeing the patriots were close to losing the vital bridge, and close quarter battle, started to bang out an Irish tune with all his might over and over again, this rallied the patriots, and they repulsed the British back out of town and over the bridge which was again firmly back in American hands. Job well done. The British would not try a mad rush again. They had attempted about three very heavy and well supported mad rushes to seize this most vital bridge into Trenton. The last well supported mad rush actually did get across the bridge but were eventually repulsed back over it. they settled down for the night sure to despatch the trapped Patriot Army in the morning.

A Presbyterian minister died in a nearby skirmish, he was stripped naked and had his watch stolen and was bayonetted seventeen times, and his skull had many sabre marks upon it. These were not ordinary battle wounds; the presbyterian minister would be seen as a root cause of the whole trouble. He was unbelievably having something to eat in a tavern in Trenton when the Hessians advanced in. The minister attended Washington's senior military meetings with his Generals. His input to rally the troops on, would be seen as vital. The presbyterian ministers would be as good as 10 men or even a full 100 and they would keep the troops buoyed up to achieve a victory in every battle. Many British officers laid the whole insurrection down to their fiery sermons. Thus, this pastor was stripped, repeatedly bayonetted, and his face was repeatedly slashed with sabres i.e., an officer sword or one swung by the mounted soldiers.

With the American army locked up in Trenton. The morrow would bring their total annihilation; guaranteed! There was no escaping now. Washington was trapped. This time for sure.! So, the British high command thought.

Not so fast my British friends, two of Washington's senior officers knew Trenton like the back of their hands. Colonel Joseph Reed went to Princeton College and was born in Trenton and General Dickinson who lived in Trenton. Their plan was to use a minor road out of Trenton that circulated it at a distance.

As the bad storm aided their attack on Trenton as the hardened Germans estimated; no army could cross or march in such atrocious weather over the Delaware. Now a fierce cold snap made apparently the transport of cannons much easier on an icy back road. During the wee small hours Washington now did the unthinkable. The whole American army silently slipped out right under the redcoat noses. Washington maintained a strong working party making as much building noise as they could; fires were kept lit and new ones started; all sentries remained visible to the British army. As like a collapsing box the sides and tops of the army folded in and all that was left was an outer edge a mere gossamer a thin show of sentries and much digging noises, and building shouts, metal tools striking metal. Eventually the digging slowly subsided in the late night. And slowly ever so slowly the sentries crept away. Leaving strong fires still burning.

When the morning arrived like the morning dew the entire American army had disappeared. As the Continental army left Trenton behind and neared Princeton, miles to the rear of British lines Its front column unfortunately came upon a British column rushing to Trenton to join the expected battle there.

Unfortunately, this British force of about 300 men with bayonets and cannons smashed into the advance party of the Continentals who at this point were militia soldiers. The next paragraph

gives the reader just a little idea of how things could change so fast, on a beautiful morning in quiet sleepy New Jersey backwater in the middle of nowhere.

General Mercer was down, bludgeoned, and bayonetted; Colonel Haslet was down too, shot through the head; Captain Shippin of the Continental marines had fallen as had Captain Fleming of Virginia; Captain Neil of New Jersey's militia artillery was also down, his two-gun batteries were overrun and turned against us.

Quickly Washington turned up with reinforcements and led the British fleeing with much encouragement. This little article says much more than I ever could about close quarter combat, it could all happen so quickly and be so deadly. The American militia would have been mightily scared, but they held their nerves to get two shots off. Into the oncoming screaming British hard cases. They did well for raw first-time militia.

But inevitably the strong determined British troops began to over run them. Soon Washington Turned up with reinforcements; the fight flew in the patriot's favour, and it quickly turned into a rout... But the whereabouts of the slippery American army was now known. Soon other British units would be alerted to the whereabouts of the elusive American army. Soon they would get organised and attempt to run the patriots down; bring them to battle and annihilate them once and for all. If the British could catch up with them the Americans knew it would all be over. Now the hare would be hunted down by a pack of wolves. Everything depended upon the patriot Army keeping a good distance between them and the rapidly advancing British. Meanwhile General Cornwallis had aroused from his slumber to finish off these dastardly Americans. But when he got there, he could only see the smoke rising from the fires of the American armies deserted camp. The camp smoke was rising in unison with his indignation and stupidity and mounting and rising anger. He had been royally duped.

He quickly aroused the redcoats to about face and chase after Washington but no matter how hard they chased, Washington was always one or two steps ahead.

The rear guard of the American army tore down bridges to make any pursuit much slower. The Americans were getting much keener, 400 British redcoats had died in action, in the Quick smash and grab blitzkrieg American attack to take back Princeton.

The Americans got two brass six pounders and much food and clothes from taking Princeton. They burned what they could not take, to deny these stores to the redcoats. They quickly moved out of Princeton with its damaged university and headed to their secure winter quarters at Morristown. Washington pushed his men hard, all the way at a relentless pace. He forced marched the army all day and night. If the green militia could not keep the pace, then they would be left behind. Washington pushed them all on, militia too. They became straggled out, but all eventually made if safe and secure to Morristown. Washington as usual got the exhausted men to reinforce their winter quarters right away. This would have been a baptism of fire and fitness for the militia, if they could not keep up, then they would be left behind. On the punishing forced march over a night and day, they must have wondered what they had got themselves involved in. The winter campaign was over for the Americans after thoroughly ruining Howe's Christmas and his New Year celebrations. Washington's, stoic leadership, and general ship as a leader of men had won through. With a small attachment of determined loyal Revolutionary die-hards, whose time was up; together they ensured the American revolution would see into another year. With whatever that beheld! All alone whilst others fled these brave few saved Americas bacon, and the Revolution.

The Destitution and suffering the soldiers endured, can hardly be imagined never mind described. Physically and mentally, they had been thru the wringer, not all had come out the other side. It is to these weary men that America owes its hard-earned everyday freedoms to. This weary bunch are the genuine and real founding fathers of the country, that goes by the name of the United States. What a raggy start. "Only a tiny part of the population performed truly extended military service" (P/21 *A people Numerous & Armed*). Remember that on St. Patricks day when you next witness the parade. Just a few hard and hearty fellas stood between you and state enslavement. The Story of the Revolution is essentially about the Irish, and not the New Englanders, who stole its legacy.

Washington force-marches meant they reached safety, ahead of the British. Men were falling asleep by the roadside whenever he stopped. This was typical Washington, he was a hard taskmaster, but one who cherished his men and especially the hard-line full timers, but the militia was beginning to learn what was expected of them. They had to keep up (as Washington was not going to wait or slow down too much for them).

A small American cavalry scouting party on the forced march, came across an outlying British convoy of supply wagons alone with an escort of 200 redcoats. Captain Stryker decided to attack at night. The silence was suddenly broken by musket fire hitting the British from all sides. The Americans yelled out instructions in such a manner that the redcoats feared they were under attack by a substantial American force, they decamped tout sweet. Now it was the American's turn to get some swag of their own. Merry Christmas one and all and on the last day of Christmas, January 6th (the same day the three wise men turned up to congratulate Mary an un married very young teenage mother, with gifts of gold, Frankincense and myrrh for her new baby) Washington made it to Morristown safe and sound, carrying the gift of an American Army intact and the promise of freedom and liberty, for the new born country. Ahead for both lay scourging and crucifixion. A veritable _via dolorosa for both._

Washington would have to endure his thorny crown a little longer in his ministry.

"Not to that city on the plain,

Where pilgrims flock from many a clime,

I watch tonight that shadowy train

Pass down the solemn aisle of time;

Onward they march with banners red

WHY WE FOUGHT

With blood from Calvary's crimson tide

The followers of the thorn-crowned head,

The warriors of the Crucified

..And o;er the burning desert plain

And thru the trackless forest wide

With dying breath, he tells again

The story of the Crucified. *Taken from The Followers of the Cross by Ellen Clementine Howarth The Trenton poetess*

This winter campaign was most successful to the American dream because they risked their lives and gambled on a victory. America would emerge into an independent country with the pursuit of happiness high on the agenda. The American Revolution was on a razor's edge. The rag tag diseased army had pulled it off. They had taken on a crack regiment in warm quarters and beat them in battle. Two American soldiers died on the road to Trenton from the cold, not battle wounds!

The American soldiers had shown themselves to be doggedly determined and mentally extremely tough to carry on, against all the odds by any definition most professional armies would have collapsed under these conditions. Before Trenton, the bold Declaration of Independence was all but dead. After Trenton, the Americans could build on a successful winter. 1777 came in with a much better prospect. Washington had been lucky at times and unlucky in others. He needed a full-time regular army for sure. For now, the men would have to build sheds to sleep in and set up emplacements to fortify their winter quarters. Life in Morristown would be tough. Very tough and basic. The situation was still militarily precarious. Patrols would have to be organised and conducted. Washington light began to glow a little brighter, with Congress.

Washington had answered his critics, deliberators and doubters. Americas revolutionary hope was restored. The eagle might not be soaring high, but its wings were neither clipped either. The one great object, an independent country had survived a massive onslaught. Trenton truly was a turning point in the Nation's history an incomparable event, against all the odds, and the Gods of ice, snow, wind, and water, hunger, pain and dejection. The American Army defied the greatest odds when it had no sensible right to exist at all. Washington had confounded the odds and frustrated and beaten the British and the dreaded Huns.

> They faltered not, though worn and spent
> that sad and weary band
> upon their holy mission bent
> to free their native land.
> they faltered not though snow and sleet
> was crimsoned with their bleeding feet
> not ladened they with food and tent
> but rifles old and banners rent
> was all their store as forth they went
> those men of 76 poem Ms. Ellen clementine Howarth
> Trenton Poetess

Oh, wherefore soldiers would you fight
The bayonets of a winter storm in truth it were a better night
For blazing fire and blankets warm. We seek to trap a foreign
Foe. Who fill themselves with stolen fare, we carry freedom
as we go. Across the storm swept Delaware.

David Ramsey; the very early Revolutionary historian, and
one of its leading politicians wrote
"THE VICTORIES OF TRENTON & PRINCETON
SEEMED LIKE A RESSURECTION FROM THE DEAD.
Amen to that brother

CHAPTER 6

The Eagle Has Landed

Joseph Galloway 1731 – 1803, was an American politician, a soldier, a loyalist, member of the first continental congress, a close ally of Benjamin Franklin. He was part of Americas political elite. He was a Loyalist to the British crown. He joined with British General Howe and accompanied him during the continental war. So Mr. Galloway had a bird's eye view of the situation. He also personally interrogated American P.O Ws, so he knew what he was talking about and stated before the House of Commons enquiry into why the war was going so badly for Britain in America. Galloway informed the House of Commons enquiry into the American War of Independence that half of the Washington army was Irish, *27th October 1779.*

The British were totally surprised at how many Irish made up the ranks of this American Army. Officers had noticed the vast amount of Irish P.O.W.s they processed. The Battle for Long Island had shocked them, with the Amount of Irish Prisoner's that they had Captured! These cries of Irish soldiers making up most of the American Army would echo down thru the war years and down thru the battle sites, wherever they may be, whether up north or down south.

Lord Mountjoy himself testified on the 2nd of April 1784 that the ancient Irish language was just as well-spoken in the American ranks just as much as English. Mountjoy stated America was lost due to the Irish. "I am assured from the best authority that a major part of the American army was composed of Irish it was the Irish valour and determination that lost us America and sealed our fate" …

All the British officials and Generals all testified to that same fact. As did the French, who were America's ally. The French stated, without the Irish we would have lost. The birth of the American nation; would like all births. A bloody and painful experience for the masonic midwifes, to successfully deliver the birth of a new independent country called America. Then this new country, could only be born with much labour pains, pushing, shoving, forcing and much blood, sweat and tears, would inevitably flow before it could be successfully delivered.

Mr. Cobbet a well-known British historian {keeper of the official parliamentary records} a man of abject truthfulness no matter what, and a great recorder of events and accurate observation.

"Hansard" the official record of British parliamentary proceeding in the House of Commons, was established as a direct result of Mr. Cobbett's own desire to have a written record of daily events, which nobody could argue with. His honesty is apparent in all his writings and dealings with authority. He had brought charges against four of his fellow senior British officers; for stealing pay from the enlisted men whilst fighting in the American War for liberty.

Even though he was threatened by senior officers with flogging to death, he still insisted. His charges were true and accurate. Later the British Secretary for war would have to admit to the House of Commons that unauthorised deductions were customarily made from soldiers pay book. Cobbett a Sergeant Major in the British army fighting the American revolutionaries also stated, that half of Washington's army was made of Irish volunteers.

He was later on, imprisoned after the American War of Independence and Liberty for criticising the (brutal flogging of British enlisted men by their officers in 1810 – 1812 American war). He was also accused ridiculously of being behind and organising the NOVA Mutiny (Spit Head Mutiny) in the Royal Navy in 1797 (which was more to do with Irish Republicanism than any English farmer). In these "rebellions" in the Royal Navy, the Irish rebels took control of 31 Royal Navy ships in Plymouth and Portsmouth (the Channel fleet) whilst Britain was still at war with Napoleon. Soon many other ships joined in, in the River Thames.

Other rebellions happened in Royal Navy ships at sea, in the West Indies, off Ireland, the British fleet off Spain and the Cape of Good Hope. The Royal Navy was very heavily manned mainly by Irish sailors, mostly non-officers, just ship crew; and the crews were in a rebellious mood for sure. It was Irish republicans in the British Royal Navy that organised these rebellions throughout the Royal Navy. They took over ships in the River Thames, the large navy port of Portsmouth. You will not find this history written up into British history books as it shows up the Royal Navy in bad light. Indeed, throughout The War of Independence Irish captains under American flags were sinking hundreds if not over a thousand British merchant ships sailing around Britain and Ireland.

Others echoed Cobbett's, observations of as to who were really decisive in kicking Britain out of America.

In July 1775, Lieutenant William Fielding wrote "how above half (of the American army consisted of) Irish and Scotch (Northern Irish). The largest line in Washington's army was known as the Irish line (Pennsylvania) line. All testimonies into the British parliamentary investigation into how Britain lost the American war, all, everyone stated their victory (The Americans) was down to the Irish in its Army, down to its support in recruits and supplying it with its needs both commercial and financial.

The Irish community was 100% for independence and self-rule. Not so the American population most British Generals and politicians in America state over half the American population wanted the status quo? Testimonies by: - Lord Cornwallis, Joseph Galloway, Sir Henry Clinton, Major General Grey, major General Anderson, Sir Guy Carlton, Major General Robertson, Lord Dartmouth, Sir Joshua Pell, Ambrose Serle (secretary to Lord Howe) All stated America was lost due to the extremely large amounts of Irish in their ranks. Plus, one testimonial quoted American General Lee whilst a P.O.W. In conversation with a British General, Lee openly admitted to the British General that half the Continental Army was Irish. Plus, testimony of British General Robertson who testified that a full $4/5^{th}$ of all those with English ancestry remained loyal to England during the Revolution. Most British generals regarded New England as the most loyal part of America towards the British crown as regards its general population. Some estimated it was $2/3^{rd}$ loyalist other estimated its loyalism as high as $4/5^{th}$. American Historian, Lorenzo Sabine in his voluminous and meticulous study of American loyalism would also claim most New Englanders were loyalists. This historical fact has been misplaced. When the New Englanders began writing their version up of the Revolution, they always came out on top smelling of roses and patriotic zeal. What humbug! The British generals testified under oath 4/5ths of New England was loyalist. Indeed, it was the most loyalist part of the whole thirteen colonies! New England was awash with loyalists.

Yes, a hard core of New Englanders was very patriotic and vociferous, among them was Mercy Otis Warren the Countess Markiewicz, of the American Revolution. She was the first female to write up a history of the Revolution, the three volume "History of the Rise, Progress, and Termination of the American Revolution.pub.1805. She was a personal acquittance of Samuel Adams, Abigail Adams, John Adams, Martha Washington, Hannah Winthrop. She advised; Samuel Adams, John Adams (2nd President U.S.A.) John Hancock (Revolutionary President of Congress) Patrick Henry (Give me liberty or give me Death!) Thomas Jefferson (3rd President U.S.A. and principal author of the Declaration of Independence. A document with many Irish, forebears in Colonial America) George Washington (Commander of the Continental Army, during the Revolution, and the United States first President, and real founding father of the U.S.A.) Ms Warren was a propogandist, playwright, poet, and pamphleteer for the Revolution. She was involved in all its intrigues and machinations from the start to the bitter end. There were many patriots swimming in a sea of British loyalism in New England. The Patriots were the few. The brave few.

One famous case of reconstituted loyalism parading as a devout Patriotism, involves the American historian Mr. M. J. O, Brien an American historian who devoted his entire academic life to study of the genuine Irish effort in the American Revolution. He wrote hundreds of peer revied articles and numerous books on the matter. When confronted by a famous New England Brahmin family, the Lodges the very epitome of American protestant Anglo-Saxony, more American than the star and stripes, themselves, and certainly far more American and patriotic than the lowly and thoroughly detested Irish. With Numerous 19th century American Historians, rediscovering that it was the Irish that actually won the war for freedom and liberty. The complete opposite of what the New Englander historians were peddling and had been peddling and falsely fabricating a falsehood

on the American mid-19th century public. Mind. Mr Lodge the very epitome of New Englander elite; took Umbridge at Mr. O Brien's, outrageous
and dastardly conclusion that American freedom was won by the lowly
filthy Irish; and not by the Anglo-Saxons Teutons.

Well, let us go back to the outrageous 19th century, just to see where this bias
came from. All thru the racist 19th century the subhuman Irish effort was
belittled, and the spurious New England element lifted up to the supreme
all conquering, never wavering, total effort, and this assessment generally
pervaded into the American sub-conscious and into a false narrative disseminated thru totally biased and historically totally in accurate educa-
tional material. Thus, Brahmin Lodge the true blue American challenged
Mr, O'Brien's facts, sure its common knowledge we freed America, and the
Irish only turned up after the famine everybody knows that!

Well, let us just say that Mr. O Brien wiped the floor with this stupid untrue
but widely disseminated common American clap trap. He produced the
muster rolls of the continental Army awash and overflowing with distinctly Irish names and the hundreds of times these common Irish names
appeared on the rolls. It was openly Irish blood running thru the American
soldiers, and definitely not English blood as the New Englander American
historians peddled all the 19th century, pure codswallop.

Mr O, Brien produces an Appendix 48 pages long of Irish American officers or officers of Irish descent. And that is just for the page after page
after page of officers never mind the ordinary enlisted men. Next the true
Historian then produces 83 pages of just a few of the most common Irish
names he introduces just 12 common Irish names of just these 12 Irish
names they fill a mini telephone directory a full 83 pages full of just 12
common Irish names, and that is on the official lists. So, God only knows
what the real figure is just for these 12 Irish names! I can assure the New

Englander Brahmins of perverted history that Irish people have a lot more than 12 common Irish surnames.

Lots of Irish soldiers did not even have enlistment papers they had joined up in droves and large crowds' whole townlands. The Irish joined up in large groups usually, and not as individuals as the New Englanders had, those that actually turned up or had sent their slave to represent them on the Battlefront.

One American General rightly stated at the very start of the Revolution. The Americans will enlist in ones and twos; the Irish I am assured will enlist in crowds. And so right he was too; Most Irish soldiers were never even individually processed their recruiting crowds were just too big. So, put that in yer pipe and smoke it. Apparently, the vast number of Irish names on the Continental Army's muster rolls is amazing. American true patriots with a true and accurate understanding of the American Revolution should also keep in mind the vast support the Irish Parliament was openly supporting the rebels and not the King plus Irish MPs in London were openly pro-American. Any way to finish the point after Mr. O, Brien the Historian produced these mini telephone directories of just a few Irish names. Remember that point these telephone directories are just for 12 common Irish names; only 12. The true historian then confronted Mr; Lodge the famous New England Brahmin patriot with the coup de Grace; he informed him not one "Lodge" Appeared on any American Army muster roll. Not one! So much for that man's patriotic credentials.

President Kennedy went up against a very well-respected Lodge in New England, who was a seasoned politician of long standing, nobody gave Kennedy much hope... he won. And dislodged a lodge from his high perch.

WHY WE FOUGHT

The American Revolution was predominately Irish in Character historical fact! The Irish, the Revolution, Washington D.C....The White House... Irish merchants supplying the rebels... Irish merchants helping, to establish a bank, just to finance the Revolution and keep it going... Irish townlands acting as reservoirs of recruits, to quickly fill up depleted ranks in the Army in emergencies. Everyone knew during the Revolution you could trust the Irish to be all in for the Revolution. Everybody else was treated with extreme caution and suspicion, including all Americans without an Irish accent. Strange but true. Truth really is stranger than fiction. The rebels acted on this assumption. You could not trust Americans nor Germans on face value. Were they loyalists? Or for the American Republic? All new recruits(non-Irish) were never trusted on face value alone, in the Continental Army not until everyone was satisfied that they were not a spy from the British. Extreme caution was the order of the day. Both the British and the Americans ran spies claiming to be recruits into each other army. Disenchanted soldiers could become a deserter ready to tell all, for some money. Washington kept a full money bag on his personal possession and dealt with many spies on his own only known to him in some cases.

American intel seems to have gotten the better of the British effort. This was a most unusual intelligence war. Both sides on the American side loyalists and patriots might know each other very well neighbours almost.

The British tried every technique to gather good intel about the American Army. Sympathetic settlers would help them and possibly inform on their neighbours. Other settlers would gladly help them with provisions. The continental army could trust Irish townlands 100%. The British regarded these townlands as very hot areas to operate in or around. Many Irish townlands became no-go areas for the British Army unless they were well equipped and prepared for trouble. The Irish people were all in and would face vicious retribution if they lost. All American Generals knew Irish townlands would give them full support no matter what. The Irish and the American Revolution are inter twined like a twisted metal cord, they go together one hundred percent, hand in hand, and I am sorry to say, that is the very opposite for New Englanders as a whole. Ask George Washington or indeed any American General. What was it that Washington said when he first saw the New Englanders in action! "I never would have accepted this commission to lead the Continental Army if I had first seen them first. (See p/80-81 *Hidden Phase of American History*) For General Washington's written appraisal of the New England soldiers how useless they were, lacked motivation and how much they blowed about themselves, their efforts and had deceived Congress and himself into the bargain. Or his other comment about how the New Englanders were leading everyone to believe they were true patriots and what a brave bunch they were, winning every single battle on their own. What utter humbug. Washington knew they were blowers, deceiving him and the Congress up the garden path with their Battlefield Buffoonery. And biased battlefield reports. And blowing up their own chests with puffed up patriotism. Most New Englanders were loyalists, they would blow with the wind whatever way fortune was blowing. Britain looked on New Englanders as their cousins; and the feeling was reciprocated. After the war, New England was so pro-British that the British wished to entice it out of the Union.

To the British, New England was the most fertile ground for this secessionist policy The British would later claim ¾ of New England was loyalist, others stated it much higher. (4/5ths) The New England History of the American Revolution would have had George Washington Spitting and foaming in his grave. It is a total fabrication and fraud played upon the American mind. And written by a pro English elite mid-19th century when Irish people were being openly and repeatedly, depicted by Britain as sub-human. New Englanders could not accept the thought that America was freed by sub-humans, so they rewrote the history for a more discerning audience. A racially new fable was concocted, a racially more hygienic one was found more pleasing. Out went the main fighters of freedom all agreed it was them. Out went the Massive Irish effort the main one. Out went the blacks/browns; they made up 1 in 4 soldiers at Yorktown. And in came in believe it or not, the people who ran away, the people who supported the crown. The people every American general thought little of, the very same people George Washington stated and wrote if he had seen them before he never would have taken the commission to lead the American Army and what's more, he stated no amount of persuading or back slapping could ever have, made him change his mind. For your consumption, Ireland and the Irish were not only 100% all in, in the America Revolution in America; but back home in Ireland they were attacking wagons with goods for the British Army of occupation in America, burning down Irish factories that sent them supplies. Also, Irish privateers were sweeping the British fleet out of its home waters with tremendous effect. The Irish on their own were rapidly destroying the British merchant fleet.

Young Dublin Irish men, probably with a fishing background, began to attack and confiscate British merchant ships. From the proceeds of their cargo, they then moved onto bigger British merchant ships. More profit meant the Dublin Lads could afford to buy large heavily armed French warships Which they renamed and flew the stars and stripes from. Soon the Dubliners were attacking the Royal Navy, and Britain's merchant fleet, and doing considerable damage to both. The Irish people also, openly supplied American warships with food water and whatever else it needed fast and surreptitiously

The Irish lads had nabbed Royal Navy ships and placed American flags on them and got about sinking the entire British commercial fleet and many Royal Navy Vessels in British home waters no less! No New Englanders did this. Ireland was under British occupation, yet it still managed to service American Continental warships. Young Irish lads in armed vessels sailed into British ports and harbours and used subterfuge or open threats to start bombarding the port if their warships were not fixed up quickly! What utter bravado and guts.

The one escapade under subterfuge, was when the Irish Warship on station around England's home waters flying the stars n stripes suffered damage. It needed repairing in a harbour. The Irish Captain simply renamed his ship and sailed in, in his American Armed privateer.ie a pirate operating under the American stars and stripes. He simply sailed into a British harbour and demanded the locals fix up and provision his "Royal Navy" warship. Which is what they duly did; and the Irish privateer was soon back in action flying the stars and stripes all around the British isle leaving sunken vessels in its wake, fact! English schoolbooks revel in the antics of Sir Walter Raleigh, or Francis Drake, English school history books celebrate their brave exploits and bravado. For example, Drake's attack on the Spanish ships in Cadiz Harbour Spain in 1587 is jollyingly called "Singeing the Kings of Spain Beard". But its complete hypocrisy when a couple of Dublin latchico, s singe their own king's beard. Then when it's done to them, they are not Heroic acts, but criminal fiends. It's very much do as I say not as do, principle. The other occasion the Irish Captain just sailed in trained his cannons on the ports warehouses and buildings and informed them that they were to fix up his American ship quickly or he would begin to destroy the ports facilities. His ship was duly fixed up and returned to duties sinking more British ships in their home waters.

These Irish Privateers flying the Stars and stripes would be replenished in France or secretly in Ireland. Nobody asked them to join the fight for American Freedoms. There was no recruiting station to go to. These Irish lads just up and captured small British vessels, then captured large British vessels. These Irish Patriots were so good they ended up buying modern French battle ships manned by hundreds of sailors. And they quickly got down to the business of destroying the large British mercantile fleet, and many royal navy warships, to boot. Benjamin Franklin over saw these Irish Activities, he instructed them to get him British Prisoners of War, which the Americans were in dire need of; with which they needed to make trades for American Prisoners of war detained and starving to death aboard British hulk ships in American Harbours. These Irish boyos, s pretty much swept the British merchant fleet from their home waters.

Irish and Scotch Irish, (Presbyterians) guerrillas worked well for American independence and liberty in the swamps of South Carolina. "Humping the boonies", "in country" in the swamps and woods of the south, ambushing British patrols a la the Viet-Cong. Even when the Continental army was driven out of the south and things looked low for the American side, the Irish and South Carolina patriots still kept the flame of independence burning in an irregular asymmetrical guerrilla war against the British. The New Englanders never did this! And yet they like to tell Americans how they, yes, they won the war. What utter nonsense and 19thcentury racial tomfoolery

www.Irishcentral.com, How the heroic Irish won the American Revolution.

To some extent the Irish were the very backbone and sinew of America's hard struggle for freedom, liberty, and independence, from its beginning to its end. Others came and went, and some worked well in their own localities, but the Irish were in it for the long haul. Their colours were stuck fast to the stars and stripes 110%.

The American victory of The War of Independence was very much an Irish win on American soil. The figures and statistics all back up this premise as do the generals from all sides. Who were actually there those who actually fought, all of them, all of them blamed the Irish for the defeat at the time and years later to the House of Commons, the British house of commons that is… Not one! Not one! ever mentioned the New Englanders in any way shape or form, not even in passing as being important towards the American final victory on the Battlefield! Not one. They only mentioned it as regards its steadfast loyalty to the Crown. Fact! On the historical record for all to see and read.

The Marquis de Chastellux, a French officer American ally stated: -

"Congress owed its existence and America possibly her preservation to the firmness and fidelity of the Irish."

Washington stated: -

"Ireland thou friend of my country in my country's most friendless day."

Cobbett a proud British man and one described as one of the greatest British men of all time by some. Up there with Winston Churchill apparently, I read somewhere recently … (William Cobbett…the greatest Englishman ever? Book review Richard Ingrams "The life and Adventures of William Cobbett" wwwbuddawalksintoawinebar. blog. blog Book review William Cobbett…the greatest Englishman ever).

Cobbett would say in Ireland on 10th November 1834 *Cobbett in Ireland P194*: -

"In carrying on that war that part of the army which never flinched for General Washington, as other parts of it did – the permanent and useful part of that army was the Pennsylvania line, they were the regular troops. Now, I assert upon my word; and there are many persons here who know

I would not state it if it were not true, the greater if not more than one half of that Pennsylvania line in number 20,000 were Irishmen."

Cobbett would allude to the Irish in the American Continental navy during the War for Independence and Liberty. On 10th November 1834, *Cobbett in Ireland P22.*

Mr. Cobbett, the proud English gentleman farmer, British army Sergeant Major, recorder of House of Commons events, historian and social commentator alludes to the people who manned this new navy. With regards to The American Continental Navy, English historians of the American War of Independence do not tell the truth he states.

Mr Cobbett, the historian acknowledges that whenever we were beaten (and we often did get a good thumping) the British historians always says it was by the British sailors we were beaten. They do not say Irish sailors! "Here we have sent from Ireland men to beat us at sea. And beat us they did to some tune." The obvious fact that the Irish kicked the British out of America was apparently well known in the United States post Revolution. It seems that the British and the WASP elite and New Englander historical brahmins, wanted to paint a picture that they were the hard-working patriots who worked night and day to deliver freedom to Americans. Nothing could be further from the true history of the Revolution. The clean pressed New Englanders with their fancy uniforms, deserted! The obvious fact that the Irish community did most not all, but most of the fighting, the obvious fact that the Irish volunteered en masse, the obvious fact that Irish townlands were used to refill the ranks. The obvious fact that wherever the Irish community resided, that was where the area's most hostile to British occupation were to consistently be found. The very fact that Irish traders openly accepted American currency even I.O.U.s. Irish traders saw it as their patriotic duty to supply and support "their" Army. The protestants did not. Snooty New Englanders looked down their well-polished noses at the pathetically dressed Irish "mob", the Patriotic Volunteer Continental Army; who were doing the actual battlefield fighting, in well-worn fatigues, and not at all dressed for the occasion; in snappy colonial uniforms. The New Englanders much preferred the lie and the fairy story that stout hearted Anglo-Saxon types liberated America from British sectarianism, religious animosity, and political, hegemony. Nothing could be further from the truth. Hogwash history for lunatics!

The Irish could not give two shoots for the stamp tax, tea tax or any other tax. They collectively wanted rid of British rule, full stop. And they had every intention to fight for it. Support it militarily and provision wise; and by hell even financially it need be. It was the bloody Irish in Philadelphia, the Friendly Sons of St. Patrick who significantly helped set up the Philadelphia Bank to emergency bank roll the bloody revolution, its arms, army, munitions, debts, wages, and. Provisions. Three of the biggest businessmen to bankroll the whole Revolution were Irishmen. Blair McClenachen an Irish man was the biggest contributor to set up the Revolutionary bank in Philadelphia. The real cockpit of the Revolution and not loyalist New England. Mr. McClenachen was followed by fellow Irish man Robert Morris Who actually at one time was personally paying the wages of the entire American army out of his own pocket. No New Englander ever did that. Lastly Irishman Robert Pollock was also bank rolling the whole revolution. Two went bankrupt saving the American dream. (Morris & McClenachen) No New Englanders come near to their collective financial support. These three Irish men all based in Philadelphia, supplied the whole continental army with food, clothing, arms, ammunition, to supply the whole full assemble of a revolutionary army in the field. Oliver Pollock lent 1 billion dollars in today's money (2019) of his own money. It is these three Irishmen who paid financially for the freedoms all Americans enjoy today.

Not just satisfied with that massive effort to free America, Robert Personally re-arranged the whole American economy onto a sound footing to pay for the bloody revolution. He personally controlled and managed the whole illegal pre-1776 and after that date the proper importation of all Arms, ammunition, cannons, muskets, medicine, cloth, gunpowder and every last item to keep an Army in the field, fighting a world No;1 power. He organised and oversaw the whole operation from France into American East coast ports Fact!

Oliver Pollock yet another Irish American Patriot, Oliver oversaw and ran personally the whole operation, of Arms and army equipment from Spain & Cuba into the Gulf of Mexico. All vast amounts of war material were landed in New Orleans, and transported up the Mississippi into the theatre of operations. Oliver ran this whole show. Fact! again. This Mississippi route was the equivalent of the Ho Chi Minh trail during the Vietnam war. Oliver also oversaw the vast amounts of Spanish dollars which Spain pumped into the financial system to keep the Continental dollar afloat. Fact check it with a good American Historian if you like. and not one New Englander in sight. Not one! So let us be clear of the hard facts. The Irish set up a bank to bank roll the whole revolution, one of the main contributors, even ends up paying the wages of the Continental soldiers himself! The Irish mainly man the whole American Revolution, they supply it with goods, unlike most others, they are willing to take Continental funny money and I.O.U, s. They essentially supply it with ships, man and pay to arm those ships and go thru unbelievable hardship as a community to achieve American liberation. Not on their own Germans, black/brown Americans and southern Hillbillys and backwoods men and frontiersmen all chip in, but very few Anglo-Saxons New Englanders, appear at all. Indeed, they are noticeable by their absence! South Carolina had it much tougher than anyone else or indeed anywhere else. And indeed, most American Professors of Revolutionary history know this to be true.

It was the bloody Irish soldiers and merchants and their far-flung homesteads, towns and villages that supported the whole revolution. And not the bloody New Englanders. Most by far refused point blank to aid in any way the rebels sell them food or clothes, blankets, or provisions of any sort. They refused American revolutionary money. Only British crown money would they accept under any circumstances. Aid the enemy they would with a whole plethora of produce. So much for their American Patriotism.

Come the war of 1812, many New Englanders wished to secede from the bloody United States and back into a union with Britain? God help us and save us! Britain was forever attempting to split up the United States. The war of 1812 was one such occasion to try their hand again. And they targeted New England as prime real estate to entice back into the Anglo fold. They failed and moved onto the Cotton South where they were more successful, in their desires and machinations.

But alas true friends back to the main menu of the real revolution, and those who were actually engaged in it at that time. And not those who say they were years later. It was the Irish parliament right under the Britishers' own noses, who voted for support and liberation in America. It was the Irish in Ireland that were burning down factories and warehouses that supplied the British army in America. It was the Irish in Ireland whilst still under British occupation who were ambushing wagons bound with goods for the British army in America. It was Irish merchants that were supplying the American patriots with arms ammunition from Ireland. This trade carried on illegally was so profound British warships had to patrol Irish waters to intercept this openly illegal trade to Britain's enemy. Ireland was "America mad", one British commentator observed.

Whenever an American victory was announced bonfires would light up the Irish night sky, to show to the British just who they supported. Just in case they had any doubts. It was the Irish who insisted on feeding in many cases chained up American P.O.W.s, captive in Royal Navy ships holds, many half-starved to death, whenever a British naval ship pulled into an Irish harbour. Irish members of Parliament in both London and Dublin spoke in defence of the American patriots and their open support for them. Indeed, as the endearing term "Sons of Liberty" was a phrase used by an Irish member of the British Parliament. actually, in the British Houses of parliament! ("Manifest Destiny" was another Irish ism) This type of open support by the Irish even in the king's own parliament got right up the royal noses of Britain's establishment.

The Irish in Britain and Dublin did not view England as a mother country, or indeed one with cherished liberties. The only liberties dished out with any quantity towards the Irish were ones from the hooded hangman, head chopper, shackles the noose, transportation to the other side of the world. Stripping Irish people of any Human Rights. Floggings Pitch capping's, slavery and other generous libations of British civility, control and management, thru threats of violence, Segregation, Apartheid, Religious ridicule, Racial animosity, racial laws, discrimination, policies of mass starvation, mass slaughter. To name just a few of Britain's enlightened rules and laws.

These British practices lasted not years or even decades, but over centuries. Indeed, their racial denigration reached its peak mid-19th Century. Just one single week of this nonsense would embarrass the Huguenots; and give them some yard stick to judge their harassment under French rule. It was these centuries of misrule, debauchment, tyranny, and Asiatic despotism;

that would make the Irish flock in excessively large numbers to drive the British Army out of America. And tarnish all of them with a patriotic zeal hard for ordinary colonists to understand or emulate.

The American War of Independence and Liberty was won by a population of two and a half million, in which half a million were Irish. Minimum! Washington loved his Irish volunteers as would President Lincoln. "God bless the Irish" both would say, repeatedly! The staggering facts are that those who were there clearly state; "that it was the bloody Irish who made us lose America.

As I began studying for this book I was struck by these facts and would quickly conclude that according to the enemies of America, the people who fought against independence; the British, all say, it was the bloody Irish that lost us America, plain and simple. So, one can only come to the conclusion that what we have had so far is a" know nothing" interpretation of the American War for Independence and Liberty; and that many of the foot soldiers, the sloggers, and the die hards of the Continental army were Irish and not New Englanders in fancy uniforms. I am not putting the New Englanders down. They fought bravely in the civil war and all wars since to proudly represent their country. But the part they played in the American Revolution has been vastly overstated by them by some measure indeed, and to totally downplay the Irish and Black/ Brown element for 19th century racial ideas, was and is treacherous in nature. Totally un honest history.

An Irish and Scottish contingent and southern Hillbillys kept up a guerrilla campaign against the British in South Carolina for two years. All on their own and with their own resources. Also, the population of South Carolina contained a good many British loyalists. More battles were fought in South Carolina than in any other State to achieve American independence and liberty. Not only South Carolina was doing its Heroic bit, all southern states and beyond in the illegal wilderness [The British had drawn a line down America, in which no settlers were to pass. Many Irish ignored this British line and populated the Wilderness any way. Why should they show respect to British laws when British laws paid no respect to them, nor ever had done?] Wherever the Irish turned up the rebellion was still on. The British Generals and it, s officers in the field noticed this.

George Washington's own adopted son stated: -

"When our friendless standard was first unfurled for resistance, who were strangers that *first* mustered round its staff when it reeled in flight? Who more bravely sustained it than Erin's generous sons? Who led the assault on Quebec and shed early lustre on our arms in the dawn of our revolution? Who led the right wing of liberty's forlorn hope at the passage of Delaware? Who felt the privations of the camp, the fate of the battle or the horrors of the prison ships more keenly than the Irish?

Washington loved them for they "were the companions of his toils, his perils, his glories in the deliverance of his country" *President George Washington's son;* and yet the films and books would make one think that the wasps did it all. Without the Irish there would be no American nation, all said it was the bloody Irish! Ask the British who fought them. p/102 *(Hidden phase)* One British General states. it is the Irish Catholics and Irish Presbyterians; it is those two elements that hold the whole southern sector together. Washington himself knew the Irish were his most fervent supporters. P/157 *Hidden Phase of American History* Quote of an English traveller about the American Revolution "for whilst the Irish immigrant was fighting the battles for America, by sea and land. The Irish merchants particularly in Charlestown, Baltimore and Philadelphia laboured with indefatigable zeal and at all hazards to promote the spirit of enterprise to increase the wealth and maintain the credit of the country. Their purses were always open (just as the New Englanders were usually shut; uncomfortable fact I know, but one borne out by the historical commercial ledger) and their persons, devoted to the common cause. *"On more than one imminent occasion, Congress owed its existence and America possibly her preservation to the fidelity and firmness of the Irish"*. "These observations were noted by an accomplice of Major General Marquis de Chastellux another noted that the moment that an Irishman steps a foot on American soil he becomes American i.e., a Rebel (taken from *A Hidden Phase of American History* p/157.)

In studying for this book, one gets a sense of the golden thread of History, the historical continuum, how it all fits together, and one leads and inserts into the other nicely. The whole historical jigsaw of the unabridged, unimpaired, unexpurgated picture, comes into view and finally Americans can see the majestic painting of the American Revolution, No longer is it a puzzle as to how a country with *no standing army,* could defeat the well-armed, well fed, well clothed well shod, well supplied British expeditionary force with its hard case Hessians, hired gun slingers, and sustain that national struggle thru hard, and desperate times to ultimate victory on the continent of America.

Later on, a full century later in American history, one cannot lead into the biggest battles ever, in all of Irelands ancient 6000-year history i.e., *The American Civil war!* A war in which once again extremely large elements of the Irish population took part in, *on both sides.* It is estimated that nearly 200,000 Irish born took part, never mind the enormous pool of Irish- American soldiers born in America to recently arrived Irish refugees. Then one could easily argue the American Civil War would have sucked in possible *½ a million men and Irish boys, many just recently born in America, and just as many recently arrived.* It is well known the massive

WHY WE FOUGHT

Irish Participation in the American Civil War, but ½ a million is an enormous, figure. and definitely the biggest battle in Irelands history of over 6000 years.

Just as the massive famine effected the massed ranks of the Union and Confederate armies, and squares historically into the muster rolls and ranks of both the Union and confederate armies So, to Irelands oppression under England fed the whole congregation to fight, die and support the American Revolution come what may, even bloody hangings en masse! Ireland involvement in the American revolution, has been deliberately obfuscated and belittled if not totally written out.

Irishmen's valiant involvement in the fights for individual, political, and societal basic human freedoms and rights, is colossal, on both North and South American Continents. Unbelievably, nearly all south American countries also owe a large debt to Irish soldiers and Irish sailors in getting independence from their colonial masters. This massive involvement in liberation both in North America and South America is a phenomena no other country, or peoples, in world history, ever come near to replicating. The fierce determination of Irish people to stick up for the little man and woman, has to be almost by now a genetic trait, inbuilt after 800 years of English domination. Amazingly this historical phenomenon is little known in Ireland. Its only when they travel abroad, that they come across statues to men with Irish names as a liberator of this or that country. True! Statues to Irish men; in piazzas plazas, boulevards, squares, parks, and streets. No other race on earth has acted in such a staunch fashion for individual freedom and liberty, wherever Irishmen and Irish women turn up.

Nearly every South American country owes it freedom in part and many a large part to Irish Patriots sticking up for the little man and sticking it to their colonial oppressors. Fact! Fact check it if you like. It will totally amaze you, how nearly every South American country owes in a large part its freedom and independence to Irish soldiers and sailors serving amongst their ranks.

Let us all refresh our memories and continue with our true history of the American revolution and of what contribution the Irish had already made to free America from the British empire's tyranny, misrule, and taxation without representation. For it is only in understanding Irish history that one can get any idea of the Irish community's fierce resistance to British rule in America. A pathological intensity to see it thru to the bitter end no matter what end that may be. To pay any price, to bear any burden, meet any hardship, support any friend, oppose any foe, in order to assure the survival and success of American liberty.

As stated no other country in the whole world can come close to the Irish struggle for the oppressed everywhere. There is probably a statue to an Irish Patriot in the capital of most South American countries! Most people in the world recognise this Irish trait, or phenomena. Especially when it has affected their own countries destiny and freedom struggle. The only topic of issue, is most Irish people are totally unaware that their ancestors were involved in multitudinous liberations movements from hegemonic autocracy or plain foreign occupation, and towards individual free-doms and national independence all over the globe in the 19th century... "Government of the people, by the people, for the people *who ever those people may be*, The people may be, black, white, mullato, rich or poor, it made no difference to the Irish, all peoples should be in charge of their own destinies and not have it ruled over them by a clique or political racial elite. On these issues the Irish were found to be steadfast, globally wherever and when ever they turned up. The Irish under British rule were born rebels to the poor and wretched of the earth. With them they made common cause repeatedly, and globally.

Indeed, even today Ireland has a very strong commitment to work with and for the United Nations for social justice and human rights and dignity. If you join the Irish Army more than likely you will be deployed overseas to serve for the United Nations. For its relatively small size the Irish Army dedicates a lot of its training and resources for United Nations deployment. Possibly to a far greater extent and proportion than most other countries.

After our little interlude into South America, we must now return our gaze back upon north America.

As previously stated, Philadelphia as the capital and location of congress was abandoned in December 1776. So precarious was the American situation, that they even informed Washington that, if need be, he could open up peace negotiations with the British. This was by far the lowest point in the whole Revolution. Pennsylvania and Virginia with their vast pool of patriots willing, to engage would have pulled his thoughts south. Washington had already stated if all else fails he would retreat down to Virginia and surrounded by his loyal Irish troopers make a last glorious stand. If New England really was the Cockpit of the Revolution? Then it must be over. As the cockpit was over run and totally subdued. One must also ask why did not the New England patriots take up an asymmetrical guerrilla war against the British like the Patriots did for year upon year in the south? All on their own. {sure, some good units did emerge from New England. Vermont Especially, always produced hard hitting loyal soldiers for America Vermont is not a new England state.}

New England's population was never the cockpit of the American Revolution, that was Pennsylvania. New England's population many state was pro-British, indeed the most pro-British element by far. They looked upon England as their cousins, the great benefactor of their religion, liberties, and institutions. If New England was the actual cockpit of these events, then it was all over by December 1776. It was because it was not the cockpit, that the Revolution lived on. Pennsylvania, Virginia North& South Carolina all kept going whilst the population in New England did bugger all to attack or harass the Army of occupation.

Pretty much all the Guerrilla and Partisan Activity was done in the south by fellow Americans not willing to sit by whilst their country was being occupied, by a foreign power. They did not sit back and leave it all to the Continental Army. Irish People in Ireland not even living in America were doing more to fight for American freedoms and independence, than the whole New England population in general. And they too were living under occupation. Make no mistake about it whenever the Continental army won Ireland was ablaze from cork to Donegal with Bonfires. Irish ordinary people not soldiers provisioned American warships in Ireland. They demanded the right to feed American chained up P.O.W, s on board any British naval vessels that pulled into its ports. They set fire to factories and warehouses with goods for British troops occupying American soil. And they did all these things and much, much more, even if it meant hanging from a bridge a common experience in Ireland. Or the British coupe de grace of Torture i.e... Dragging a tied man behind a horse with his head down over the road to his place of execution It was customary to ensure this first part of the public festival of torture ensured that he was still alive to enjoy the second course. And we all by now know what that second course entailed His bloodied body and head was placed inside a noose hopefully kicking and screaming and gasping for air. Hung until near death He would be carefully cut down and on into the third course of British legal justice. Every Christian effort would be strenuously exerted to keep the poor Christian alive for more gruesome laws on this Christian country's statute books of legal, demonic nonsense.

This was legal law, and practised quite well upon Britain's uppity individuals, subjects, who dared to think for themselves or question the status quo. These evil practices were on the crown's statute books well into the 19th century. Indeed, in the middle of the 19th century three Irish men were condemned by a British court for this very wicked public practise of what can only be called demonic legal spectacle. This behaviour is the work of thoroughly sick perverse minds. Irish people would face this penalty 24 hours per day 7 days a week 365 days of the year for centuries. But come the American Revolution they were all in, no matter what the bloody consequences. I rest my case.

The American officers knew full well, Pennsylvania was home territory for them. There a good percentage of the rural population was Irish and to a man all knew that meant and spelled rebellion and full support to its Army which was mostly Irish in good times and was now pretty much all Irish in this most dire of times. Who were these Irish? let us be certain on one thing, many non-Irish colonies fielded a large number of Irish volunteers. For example (P/43 in James Haltigans excellent book; *"The Irish in the American Revolution"* 1907 Washington D.C. free download internet) Mr. Haltigan notes that the predominately Dutch colony of Albany fielded an absolute plethora of Irish names in its officer corps. This number was totally out of all proportion to its alleged Dutch population. The Irish would turn up in large numbers in many supposedly non-Irish counties.

American General Lee, told British General Robertson, half his Army was Irish. (P/46) Most American Historians recognise this number as historically factual.

From 1718 a very steady flow of Irish constantly continues to pour into America. Both disposed Catholics and Presbyterians. Indeed, even in the 17th century American colonies were used as a dumping ground for Irish rebels their families and their children. America was used as a penal colony right up to the 1770s. Between 1718-1775 52,000 prisoners were shipped off to America. (www.American penal history *"Bound with Iron Chains"* by Anthony Vaver) This just for those years. Many thousands of dispossessed Catholics and their children were shipped off and sold at markets in the American colonies in the middle of the 17th century, by sectarian Cromwell in his religious racist wars. Later on, another sectarian tyrant, robber king William had his fair share of even more Catholic deportations and once again these dispossessed Irish and children were sold to American colonies. To be worked to death. The New England puritans and rabid anti catholic Virginians cared not one jot for these people. Indeed, during the Revolution, the New Englanders feared the Catholics more than the Red Coats. Papists was a word on all the puritan's lips. These so-called Christians pilgrims' fathers and their offspring fleeing persecution sure knew full well how to dish persecution out, their hypocritical selves. Most American British colonies were awash with religious intolerance laws against each other's Protestant sects. They could hardly live together in the same states, never mind break bread together, as they had been instructed to do by the great preacher himself! Anglicans against Presbyterians, Presbyterians against Quakers. All protestants Christian sects enacted laws of intolerance against each other!

This type of racial/ religious sectarian chatter was meat and two veg. during the 17th, 18th, and 19th centuries. Both the Catholic Irish and Presbyterian Irish had both been on the receiving end of this racial and religious abuse and tyrannical despotic rule dished out to them by the shovelful under enlightened British rule in Ireland. It was to these Irish Presbyterians and Catholics that made up the hard core of the American Revolutionary Army. Make no mistake about it buddy. It was to this stubborn hardcore that America owes its freedoms and liberties to.

To these two congregations, things had never looked so bright. Now they had arms to hit back with; and at Trenton they would outnumber the Sassenachs. And they had every intention to drive these hounds into the sea and off their soil. They had not been kicked out of Ireland to be kicked around again. No! they had arms and had every intention to follow Washington into the gates of hell and back out again.

Those, the British under Cromwell detested to the core were shipped off to the Colonies by religious racist Cromwell. Extraordinarily little is written about this aspect of American history and the history of colonial development. Irish people and their children were sold into the American labour market. Sold as slaves! Since the middle of the 17th century, British policy was to force the Catholics out of Ireland and repopulate Ireland with English protestants. William Petty British government Advisor advised H.M.G. to depopulate Ireland to 300,000 Catholics only. ¾ of the Irish population were to be transported to England. His Majesty's government envisaged Ireland as its massive private ranch. Ireland would breed livestock.

H.M.G. thankfully rejected Petty's proposal. For now! In many ways the very same attitude prevailed towards America, it was to become a place for raw produce not manufactured goods. British colonial policy was to turn America into its larder, ranch, farm, forest and general supplier of raw goods. This is exactly what the masons presumed and feared. They had absolutely no intention of letting America become the second fiddle or a British commercial appendage, or dancing to a British commercial tune or drum, whenever it banged or played its tune for America industry and enterprise to dance to.

The British would increase the screw on the Presbyterians in Ireland by putting tariffs upon all their enterprises, any that infringed on British merchants. The Presbyterians rightly took, Umbridge on these commercial penal laws and they too began a steady stream to the New World and away from this elitists commercial and religious cabal. Lastly the pro-British authorities in Ireland began to arrest Presbyterians upon the charge of co-habiting with Strangers! The strangers were their Presbyterians wives! The British establishment refused to recognise Presbyterian Ministers nor their Marriages baptisms or whatever their pious and holy royalty deemed fit to sanction.

American historians especially need to remember Ulster was the most Catholic part of Ireland. Many ships from Ulster's ports were dislodging thousands upon thousands of Catholics as well as Presbyterians into American ports. British policy was to take over Catholic farms, force them to emigrate and give those farms to loyal English Christian Anglicans. Most of the people being disposed from Ulster were by far Catholics not Presbyterians. Lastly many, many ships from the other three provinces. Leinster, Munster, Connaught all thru out the ,17th & 18th centuries were discharging passengers into all the American ports. Indeed, *Ireland was by far the main commercial supplier to the American colonies. It was only Ireland that sent aid to New England when its towns were over-run and burnt to the ground, during kings Phillips's war. It was Ireland that supplied the colonies with farm animals, labourers and farm implements and tools.*

This historical American nonsense by New Englander historical brahmins that only Protestants stepped off Irish boats bound for America from Ulster is historical racist tomfoolery, which ignores what the ships captains reported, the papers at the time commentated upon, and the plethora of Irish place names in America, and Irish recruits in its army. (see comments about the ridiculously enormous amounts of Irish names in the *official* roll calls for the Continental army)

To ashamed to tell the truth; that Americas army was heavily manned by Catholics, that George Washington's personal body guard was mainly Irish Catholics, that Irish Catholic townlands existed in pre- revolution America and it was to these numerous townlands that the Continental army got most of its recruits from and that recruitment from Catholic and Presbyterian Irish townlands was massive and that recruitment did not dry up, as it would most elsewhere in America. And that this massive Irish; Catholic, Presbyterian, Congregationalist effort was endured over a long and hard fought bitter martial struggle, of years of torment, defeats, hunger, and chronic shortage of money, pay and even rudimentary clothing and footwear. The New Englander 19th century interpretation of the American Revolution made up to suit British racial sensitivities needs to be exposed for its lies and misleading historical jabberwocky. Hoity-toity Hogwash history, for sure. Fancy uniforms included

Once again, it was the *Catholic* population that was targeted in Ulster for forced Transportation out of Ireland. Where in God's name do these historical deceivers think the forced Catholic population ended up.? Are we honestly meant to believe that every ship out of this most Catholic province when Catholics were being forced out of their houses and farms, and totally depopulated, that every ship leaving Ulster transported Presbyterians only? What utter, utter, humbug, historical nonsense, history for Chimps by Chimps. See J. Stor "*The Derry Watershed Religious and Political Demography* 1622-1911. This academic article states in 1659 Catholics are in the majority in Ulster. In three Ulster counties Catholics have large to very large majorities. In the 17th century 50,000 to 100,000 emigrants from Ireland of which 75% were Catholics. See also J. Stor, Demographic factor in Irelands movement towards partition 1607-1921.

In 1600 Catholics owned 99% of the land in Ireland. In 1641 that was reduced down to 59%of the land finally by 1688 it was down to only 22% of the land. Where did all these Irish Catholics go to? From shipping records, we know a vast amount were constantly pouring into America whether officially or unofficially, all thru the 17th century indeed the Catholics were in the majority in America all thru that Century. Land records in Ireland clearly show who was getting shoved of their land and who was expelled, exported, or driven into slavery. If we take the proper historical view 500,000 bare minimum, Irish were in America Pre-Revolution of this ½ million 100,000 – 250,000 were Presbyterians. Figures are varied so if we accept a minimum 500,000 Irish at the start of the revolution then the Catholic population is either 400,000 or 250,000. Most serious American purveyors of shipping records, births, marriages, county records agree on this minimum figure. Then the Irish Catholics are either 250,000 or 400,000, and not 10,000 as Wikipedia states. Incidentally in 1800 the Presbyterian church had only 15,000 church members which seems dreadfully low. Each member could have a wife and children but it still seems very low to me. See page 59/60 Ireland Irishmen and Revolutionary America. The presbyterian population in Ulster declined a little to very little over the 16th and 17th century. Most are right to state they emigrated to America. For example, between 1733-1776 the Presbyterian population in county Tyrone fell from 71% to 62% a significant drop for sure. Derry/ Londonderry a major shipping town saw very little drop in its town's population of Presbyterians over the exact same period. Most probably went to America. But by far the main drop in population i.e., those leaving were expelled, disenfranchised, kicked off the land Catholic small-time farmers, nearly all the Catholics lost their land during 1640-1740 in Ulster, they were by far the biggest losers in this land confiscation process. See (J. Stor *The Derry Watershed Religious and Political Demography* 1622-1911 also J. Stor *Demographic Factor in Ireland's Movement Towards Partition* 1607-1921)

WHY WE FOUGHT

The Idea that pre-revolution America only had a small population of Irish Catholics flies in the face of historical facts. New Englander historians have just automatically counted ships from Ulster discharging passengers all of whom they state are Presbyterians or Scotch Irish. This is a blatantly racist lie told by people who could not accept the historical fact that Irish Catholics freed America, fought for its rights and liberties, and won over the Tarzan Aryan types they so love and aspire to emulate. History for chimpanzees. Quite large landed estates in America were owned by Catholics, we know this because protestants complain about this travesty i.e., rich Catholic landowners with influence. My God whatever next. A Catholic President, dread the thought. Catholics owned land and businesses; Indeed Washington D. C was built on Catholic land designed by an Irish Architect. The original Whitehouse is the same building as Leinster house the Irish Parliament.

Who were these American Die-Hard Patriots? And why did they fight! Presbyterians were penalised like the Irish. Their marriages were not recognised by the Church of England. Presbyterians like the Irish lost all religious liberties. Things had become so bad in Scotland, the "established" kingly recognised so-called followers of Christ. Christians in name only had taken to digging up recently buried Presbyterians, hanging them, then chopping the corpses heads off, then throwing the abused corpses into the area for burial in the cemetery that was kept aside for miscreants and criminals. This was life for Presbyterians under royal British rule.

In Scotland, many Presbyterians were hunted down like wild animals and they resorted to living and hiding in caves. All the vast wet wilderness of the Scottish Highlands and islands became a refuge of the Presbyterian population. Fed up with being hunted like wild animals the Presbyterians emigrated to Northern Ireland. The Scottish Puritans had resorted to digging up recently buried Presbyterians hanging their dead bodies, chopping their heads off and then dumping them on a patch of land on the cemetery grounds reserved for miscreants and criminals. Once in Northern Ireland the Anglican establishment did not recognise Presbyterian marriages or births, they excluded all Presbyterians from government jobs, government pensions and if they set up a business that competed with a British business, large tariffs were imposed upon them. The last straw was when the Presbyterian men had been arrested for co-habiting with strangers. The strangers were their wives!

Indeed, in Scotland many Presbyterians were hunted down like wild animals they had to hide together in caves and disappear into the vast wet wilderness of the Scottish Highlands and their many islands. The Presbyterians fled to Northern Ireland en masse to escape this totally depraved behaviour. Slowly but surely the exiled Presbyterians began to be systematically abused once again by the British State in Ireland. They were excluded from any government job, office, or government pension.

Between 1720-1730 large amounts of people from Northern Ireland began to enter American colonies. (p/29 Haltigans "the Irish in the American Revolution). Large amounts of Irish Catholics had been pouring into America and as usual these would be written out of the official history of America. Cromwell had sold Thousands of Irish as prisoners to the American colonies; many to be worked to death by Protestants high on English Anti-Catholic Bigotry and religious voodoo. White Anglo-Saxon History by white Anglo-Saxons for white Anglo-Saxons was to be the official tooth fairy story of how America was formed and how America won its Freedom.

50,000-100,000 Catholics were expelled from the Great Dictator Cromwell's one-party state. (p/71 The Irish in the American Revolution) Cromwell would set up in England a dictatorial puritanical tyranny. More akin to Pol Pot than Jesus or his disciples, not Christian in any way shape or form. A sort of proto fascism was concocted by the great dictator and yet, he stands outside the British parliament as a representative of egalitarianism. Richard the Lion Heart was more egalitarian than the Great Dictator. To the penal Colony of Virginia, in 1625 went 1800 prisoners six years later only 800 were still alive. The Irish were heavily prevalent in all 13 colonies prior to Revolution p/8 (*Ireland's Important and Heroic Part in American Independence*).

Both Cromwell and just William and Mary, dumped Irish citizens into the thirteen colonies. The Irish were sold and infants too as indentured slaves. Did these dumped Irish indentured slaves and some under Cromwell sold as slaves for life. Did all these captured people die of disease or were they pushed over the edge? The vast majority were worked to death as the slave population needed replenishment every few years. Since the inception of the development of the 13 colonies; Ireland was the prime commercial supplier to these developing enterprises. Ireland was the first and only government to come to New England's aid during King Philips war when New England was devastated. New York and the Government in England refused to send any aid

Working Irish prisoners to death was stock in trade in the British Caribbean islands. In 1652 under Cromwell, Irish women and probably Irish children were. sold to Virginia merchants, by Cromwell's Commissioners. Immense numbers of Irish were trafficked, men, women, kids, babies, under this penal religious scheme. Sir William Petty mentions 6000 women and boys bound as penal prisoners to the Caribbean. This was the same man that was pushing and advising for total depopulation of Ireland. And its repopulation by English. It really is a pity to see such wasted talent; envisage such a vista before its time had come. If only he had been born centuries later in the Third Reich where Mr. Petty's advice would surely have got a warmer reception, and possibly have been put into action, so one could see the fruits of this sensible man's racial hygienically clean idea.

In the Caribbean, the Irish mix and marry Africans, especially in Montserrat.

The Irish organised slave rebellions one of many down through the ages in the New World and in the Caribbean. The Irish would combine well with the African slaves to overthrow their British masters. Black slave rebellions are more common than officially written about in America colonies.

Famed British historian, Dr Lingard makes it 60,000 Irish sold as slaves. Broadin a contempory of Dr. Lingard's estimates 100,000 Irish prisoners were sold. These two are well respected British historians, with a vast wealth of knowledge and time into British history. Dr. Lingard was probably one of the great historians of England. He revolutionised Historical analysis and would only use primary sources. What he therefore states, is in the historical primary record. Dr Lingard revolutionised British historicism into its modern emphasis upon primary sources. This type of Irish Rebel child slavery or child slavery for Catholic children was never hereditary i.e., penal children were born free only their parents were Penal prisoners. Horrific whippings were common especially to anyone who escaped and was captured. This episode in no way takes into account the massive industrial size trafficking of young Africans in their millions and millions into permanent chattel slavery, where their innocent children would be born *into* hereditary slavery,

That was never practised upon the Irish, but it was still a bloody harsh life, and an extremely brutal one if you got caught escaping. Thus, the Irish and blacks always when mixed spread sedition, freedom, and rebellion. The British slave holders in the Caribbean soon learnt that Irish indentured slaves and black chattel slavery was a mixture for sure trouble. English slave holders soon learned not to mix the two as a rebellion was always on the Irish indentured slaves minds.

The Irish could never be trusted and always stoked rebellion in the ranks. Possibly because the Irish were white the black/brown African slaves maybe used to taking orders of white masters, thus when white people started talking of a slave rebellion that might have helped them cross the psychological Rubicon of rebellion. I'm only conjecturing but maybe just maybe it might have, more successfully stoked resentment or acted into some sort of organised action. The two mixing always breed rebellions. For some black/brown slaves, also being brought up as a slave to another human since inception, if they had never experienced any psychological freedom. To act against the slave master would need some new catalyst. But to be sure, black/brown slave rebellions were a lot more common than history lets on. A lot more common!

King Williams glorious Revolution was a disaster for Catholic Americans they lost all their rights! Thus, the glorious Revolution imported into America religious intolerance, British sectarianism, and overt racism. There was to be no religious or liberty of conscience in H.M.G. run America. Freedom of conscience was a Catholic virtue allowed in Maryland a Catholic Run colony but when the puritans turned up, they, made it into a one-party intolerant Stalin-esq religious state.

Freedom of conscience was brought to north America via Catholics not Protestant sects; read your history books. Slave based indentured servitude was used to build up another colony Jamestown in 1619. Alliances between Irish Catholics and Black slaves united by their bond of servitude lead to many slave rebellions and stricter racial laws had to be introduced to stop the black/brown slaves from mixing with the Irish indentured semi-slaves. (Virginia slave code 1705) A new colour bar was now to be strictly enforced In North America, as it was never enforced in South America, Blacks/ Browns mixed freely with native South Americans and southern European slave holder's merchants and freemen of any persuasion, under the Spanish and Portuguese tutelage, in South America. All slaves under Spanish and Portuguese tutelage were baptised and treated as human beings and not as cattle or a person's property. Creole or mixed marriages were quite common in South America; indeed, it was the norm. Under the British system in North America a draconian colour bar was strictly enforced and had to be tightened up Negroes were never to mix with whites. Never a real issue in South America.

America was a British penal colony just like Australia. Well over 100,000 Irish convicts were sent to America from the 17th century thru to the 18th century, and that does not include the vast number who went as indentured servants/ slaves. How the Irish won the Revolution, P97, P472. For people who harped on about religious persecution and fleeing from religious persecution they sure as hell practised it a lot in America themselves i.e., Presbyterians were kicked out by Anglicans from certain states. Presbyterians forced the Catholics out of Maryland. It was the Catholics who brought religious tolerance to America and the only ones to practice it. The Great State of Maryland was the only one with religious tolerance written into its constitution. All protestant' Sects ironically practiced religious discrimination upon each other.

As per normal it was divide and rule, the Irish rebels must not mix with the African American slaves. Black slaves were to be very heavily segregated communities. Once again never a real problem of heavy distinct colour bar in South America. Britain promoted an extremely rigorous colour bar in North America; with its tragic consequences still felt today by young black Americans, as somehow being a lesser American because of the pigment of their skin or not truly accepted as real Americans as white New Englanders are. Thankfully at last, that last vestige of human ridicule and stupidity is running out of America. The death knell of imported white racial superiority has been rung across the land, and that residue of generational bigotry is fast dying out in multicultural America.

Today young Americans are sickened to the core with this racial filth, and see it for what it is and always was the work of childish spoilt decayed minds denying their common humanity. A common fact the racists seek to deny and fight against. Essentially, it's a psychological form of neurosis which can lead to psychosis and erratic destructive spoilt behaviours Racism is the work of a diseased mind. For people with chronic psychological insecurities, or societal insecurities, for childish people who have not grown up.

Religious puritan fanatics burnt down Catholic churches in tolerant Maryland and devolved this tolerant religious state down into a one party statelet. This is not your schoolbook American History this is real history, red in tooth and claw.1740 Georgia not to be out done in unchristian bigotry it too now banned Christians of the old original faith, from living amongst them in their Klan of white supremacy Volksland.

American protestants constantly fretted about the blacks and the Irish amongst them. They became anxious, neurotic and in certain cases psychotic a well-known ailment in Victorian Britain. A psychosis of No Popery was transplanted from the Old World to the New. This unchristian poison would cause problems for American civil life right up to the present day. British no popery was disseminated down into American colonial society *on purpose* as an ideological construct, to make them more obedient to British rule. Enslavers do not believe in freedom of thought, they believe in enshackling it

The American Masons, the racist ignorant ones were heavily prevalent in disseminating this unchristian poison amongst its own people. Being an old faith priest in liberal New York in 1741 was a crime punishable by death. Masonic regalia and pointy hatted brigade of slave owners and pagan worshippers went hand in hand and imaginary slave rebellions sprang into their fevered heads full to the brim with religious mumbo-jumbo

Most Presbyterians would be of Irish stock, so they knew each other pretty well. Whatever their differences, they were laid at the altar of American freedom and liberty and that was the way it was without exception. Not only did the Catholic Irish dominate on the battlefield; they pretty much came to dominate its new Navy. The first naval engagement of the war of independence was a wholly Irish affair Jeremiah O Brien and his brother both old faith; captured two British ships. This would all be written out by the white Anglo-Saxon New Englanders masonic types. Out went the fact that it was mainly the Irish who kicked the British out of America. Out too went the massive black brothers on show in the ranks. In their stead came the patriotic slave masters in nice, neat carefully pressed crisp uniforms straight from the props department. Out went the Catholics and in went the square jawed Anglo-Saxon types of New England. Out went Irish P.O.W.s prisoners and the whole penal history of American colonies for 200 years prior to the revolution and in came the true-blue protestants, the religious puritans who planted themselves onto America, s virgin soil and built up a puritan paradise; not be sullied by Catholics, rough Irish, or the fact that America was for 200 years a penal colony. Oh no that just would not do for our Pilgrim fathers, fable story of heroic religious planters. Who let us not forget would not have lasted two years without native Americans helping them?

In the annals of the war of Independence, America first Congress complaints abound that the Catholic Irishmen's Massive and courageous involvement to win American freedom was being written out and that the History of the American Revolution was being heavily modified. A full quarter of all men who lined up at Yorktown were black! What happened to that story? Where did these black patriots go? Down the proverbial sink hole of W.A.S.P. history we know this because the Hessians on the British side wrote about it. Where have all these black people come from.? Let us have it right. The first non-Americans to live in America successfully were free or escaped Africans from the Spanish colony in Florida a full 100years before the founding fathers even set their delicate feet on to American soil.

The very first successful European colony on American soil was St. Augustine and not wasp Jamestown. The founding fathers were predated by the French and the Spanish in their thousands if not tens of thousands, decades before any founding father steps his delicate foot onto American soil. Black African slaves were sent by their masters to fight in their stead in the War of Independence, the Black slaves were fighting for their masters' political rights. These African slaves were not even fighting for their own freedom, they were fighting to free their slave holder from political servitude. Their white masters got their pay. These black Africans were going nowhere. They must have felt awful funny seeing the white part time New England patriots come and go. 1773 two years before hostilities breakout, 4 African American slaves, petitioned a member of the Assembly......Sir the efforts made by the legislator to free themselves from British slavery. This made the four slaves highly satisfied that good men with good intentions to fight slavery and the noble intentions to fight those who enslave them. They expected many good things, to flow from this development. Well, our dear black/brown sisters and brothers I have to tell you now very few good things flowed at all. Black/ brown Christians were and would be still chained up by armchair Christians.

As the prospect for victory seemed more secure and certain; the white masters would have felt more confident to lend their slaves for the patriotic endeavour. In the desperate days of the Revolution in 1776, states had to resort to buying black slaves at markets to fill their quotas, once again that went down the proverbial plug hole of History. As the war came near to its end white slave masters to show how patriotic they all were, were now more than willing to send slaves to represent them and eh, they got their Army pay too. This would always curry favour after the victory to show how patriotic the new Englanders really were. And also, to receive, some well-earned army pay for the slave master, safely miles from the front. But we must remember supporting it wholeheartedly from his armchair in front of his nice warm fire, whilst a good hearty dinner was prepared for the patriot himself. As General Washington would call these lackeys, snugged up, all nice and warm in their "chimney corner".

Thus, I believe this may account for ¼ of those at York Town being black/ brown, and then being duly written out of the official white New Englander masonic version of Independence. American history of the wasps by the wasps for the wasps. An historical myth. You see the History of the Esteemed American revolution was to be written by the armchair patriots. The Chimney corner gang.

Remove the Irish and Blacks and whitewash that 90% of Washington's New Englanders deserted the cause. Many changed sides. I mean after all, they were English, good King George, jolly ho. It was the New Englanders those that saw Britain as a caring mother Parliament, a mother country. It was the New Englanders who wrote the American fairy story of freedom to suit their own purposes. They decided what the myth should say and how that myth was spun the Bloody New Englanders became the True patriots. And the real die-hards were written out, to soothe English sensibilities, and tastes.

The New England Brahmins morphed over time into true patriots by the time the 19th century came around with much British cajoling and encouragement New Englanders as British lackeys were more than willing to re-write the Revolution to suit themselves, belittle the Irish and their efforts, to free America and its people from British sectarian slavery. Whitewash the blacks/browns who appeared in good numbers and sometimes quite large numbers, especially on muster rolls. Wipe out all this truth. American history was to be hygienically cleaned, racially pure. Out went the coloureds, the Irish, ridiculed or just plain, had their massive contribution ignored, belittled, and replaced with New England Teutons, patriotic Anglo -Saxons, who did it all. New Englander historians would produce and promote a sugared coated hygienically clean pro New Englander interpretation of the American Revolution. The Irish struggle, to strike a blow for common humanity, religious freedom, and individual rights, free of Monarchy and its special privileges, was unfortunately watered down after the revolution. Many of its aims and beautiful ideas were deemed unworkable unachievable. America was broke and needed rebuilding.

The real Die-hards who made up the vast majority were written out. Black, brown soldiers have been erased completely, with such propaganda zeal that Stalin, Goebbels, or Orwell would be proud off such a feat. Most American historians are not even aware of Americas 200years as a penal colony, or that 1 in 4 soldiers at Yorktown was black/brown; that coloured soldiers turned out in some cases in dominant numbers on muster roll.

That the Hessians stated that hardly any American outfit was fielded without a good contingent of black/brown patriots both as slaves and freemen. What happened to that history?

The history of the American Revolution has been twisted to fit a New England agenda and that all stems from the heavily racist 19th century.

We should all be aware that the New Englanders were blowing their own trumpet at the start of the revolution. Washington and other American Generals commented on this trend plus their heavily biased battlefield reports held little integrity. Let us listen to a man who was there, a man who oversaw it all and was in charge of the whole revolutionary effort on the battlefield. Let us listen to what General George Washington has to say about the New England brahmins. General Richard Montgomery writing to General George Washington october5th 1775 during the Canadian campaign. Montgomery states" the new Englanders are the worst stuff imaginable" Montgomery states they lack any zeal for the cause. Washington writes January 31, 1776.... These thoughts I can say exactly fit my own observations of these soldiers. Washington goes on; "shoot they will from behind a fence but dare not ask them to move over open ground to attack the enemy". Washington in a letter to General Joseph Reed November 28th 1775 states…as regards the New Englanders "that I should not at all be surprised at any disaster that may happen… later. Could I have foreseen {the new Englanders in military action} ... no consideration upon earth should have induced me to accept this command." Washington in another letter at another time writes…...August 20th, 1775, in this letter Washington is referring to how the New Englanders have led the American Congress up the garden path with regards to New Englander patriotism "The people of this government have obtained a character which by no means they deserved" (i.e. the N.E. are blowing their own trumpet and battle field facts do not back them up!) He continues "In short they are by no means such troops in any respect as you are led to believe of them from the accounts which are published."

That's pretty damning evidence from the private letters of the commander in chief of the American Revolution. He states these things not in a temper but coolly over a full year of hearing and witnessing himself their actions. Now let me state quite categorically I am not running them down I merely wish to show that the American Revolution was a mainly Irish affair. I am aware that may surprise some, but the historical record needs to be put straight it was not the patriotic New Englanders who freed America it was Irish Catholic and protestants in the main plus hardy frontiers men southern patriots a vast effort by German Americans. A vast effort by black, brown Americans with the New Englanders bringing up the rear if that! If that! And that's being mighty generous. See *A hidden phase of American history* p/178-182 Even though all enemies agreed if it were not for the bloody Irish, America, would most definitely be still under the British yoke. Look it up ask yer mates. The Irish, the Catholics, the black, brown people were not good enough for them. Only pilgrims and their descendants were true patriots. Let us just refresh ourselves again as to what George Washington stated about the true patriots, he stated if he had seen them before the revolution then no amount of persuading could ever have convinced him to accept the job of leading the continental army. Washington's observations of them were echoed by his other generals too.

Washington stated if all else collapses he would go home to Virginia and go down fighting with his Irish soldiers! Washington too spoke about the New Englanders habit to blow out of all proportion their small efforts and belittle everyone else's. What appears to have happened is that after the Revolution, everybody knew the full part the Irish had played in freeing America from British religious discrimination, and demonic rule. As the 18th century turned into the heavily racist 19th century with the Catholic faith being demonised by Britain and the Irish being depicted as subhuman, simians, with tails growing out of their backsides. Children too had tails apparently. I am not too sure how this fit into Darwin's Protestant *"Origin of the Species by means of Natural Selection or the Preservation of the Favoured Races in the Struggle for Life"*. But I think we can all guess who those favoured races would be.

As the 19th century progressed. The New England history brahmins could not bear to have America freed by Simians so thru out the 19th century the Catholics were dropped and a racially purer protestant foundation story was slowly concocted a foundation fairy story which all New Englanders can and should be proud of. As it makes them out to be the storm troopers. Britain was heavily promoting this game of rewriting the American War. It detested the fact that now that the Irish had turned into subhuman species the History books needed to be written with a New England slant. And boy what a slant it was.

France sent Troops and its massive navy to liberate America. Both Spain and France declared war on Britain. Both sent massive amounts of troops to liberate American soil and its peoples from British domination. On hearing the news that France had joined the war with America, many "patriots", Thousands, left in disgust, or left stating their disgust. Whether this was the truth or because they could not take the hardships anymore, we may never know. Washington had personally warned the army that Britain would stoke up the no- popery to high heaven, in order to defeat the cause. As far as the battlefield was concerned, and the fight and struggle for American independence if they could not win on it they by hell they intended to win off it, by any means necessary, fair or foul.

By 1778 the war was becoming unpopular with the American citizenry, and would steadily become more unpopular with each coming year. The hardships involved were immense and the non-Irish American citizenry were unaccustomed to the physical nature of war, farm burnings, cattle stealing or requisitioning, husbands and brothers away for long periods, the intense insecurity in an internecine partisan war. All these horrors were new to American civilians who just wanted a quiet life {This paragraph excludes the southern states}. But to the Irish this Partisan guerrilla war was more a way of life, for them and their descendants. The Irish were well used to the deprivations of war both conventional and guerrilla. And the horrors both entailed. Too the Irish they were more than willing to keep the fight for America burning for decades or centuries if need be. To them, both Catholic, Presbyterian and to a lesser extent Congregationalists this was their fight, and they intended to partake a full part in it no matter what!

Spain liberated West Florida, Florida, and parts of todays, Louisiana, Mississippi, and Alabama, apparently a southern heartland of British loyalists. Parts of the deep south would maintain both French and Spanish influence, well into the 19th Century. Irish soldiers were heavily embedded within both the French army, and the Spanish armies in liberating America. An Irish man: born in Ireland was the Governor of Spanish Florida from 1793-1811. The Liberation of America, was it has to be said, for the most part, a masonic led Catholic run enterprise! Ironic I now but historically very true The Irish Catholics and Irish Presbyterians were at the broken bottle end of things slogging it out with the slaves representing the new America free from Britain and its debouched sectarian rule and gross religious Anti-Catholic diatribes, and the tyranny of kings white Trash no more Christian than Haitian voodoo. The detractors of the American Revolutionary army, labelled it at the time as a Catholic Army, The Popes army. The Vatican was behind the scenes controlling it. Sure. The very discovery of America was a purely Catholic venture. Every evening just before sun set, Christopher Columbus, s argonauts boldly going where no man had gone before, would sing the Salve Regina. From Chesapeake to Massachusetts these brave Europeans planted crosses in American islets, bays, and estuaries. A full 100years before the Puritans "founded" America.

Jacques Cartier discovered the St. Lawrence, not the puritans. Robert Cavalier la Salle was the first European to navigate down the Mississippi, first to travel in Ontario, Texas, Erie, Michigan, the French were all over America and its interior the mid-west, they were the original pioneers of the American west not New Englanders or Puritans who hugged the coast Read your good history books.

As one historian wit wrote as regards American exploration the first shall become last and the last shall become the first. The Spanish were all over the southern states and southern border and California for a full century if not more before the puritans finally turned up 150 years later! The Spanish had discovered America and settled in St. Augustine and spread out all over the southern United States at its earliest, even before the Pilgrim fathers were born. English did not come to America with the Pilgrim fathers it was being spoken all over what would turn into the southern states by Irish men and women. Free black Spanish slaves were living successfully in Florida with native Americans a full century before the famous pilgrims ever turned up! When the American government banished the Native Americans; off their own property in Florida; they also stipulated all native Indians and free black people are to vacate Florida by a set date. Black and brown African Americans had been openly living in Florida with Native American people since the 16thcentury. The very first non-native people to celebrate thanksgiving were Spanish, French, and Free African settlers in the 16thcentury. A long, long time before the Pilgrim fathers. Historical Fact!

The Catholic settlers came long, long before the Dutch or English. Catholic missions were established and operating in America in a full century before the Pilgrim fathers. Catholics not New Englander puritans were the first to navigate the mighty Mississippi and Missouri river systems. All the while the pilgrim fathers hugged the coast and would have perished without Native American vital assistance. The southern European adventurers pushed on into Lake Huron, Lake Superior, the Fox river Wisconsin, The Ohio river system, Arkansas the Illinois river system, and Lake Michigan, among many other smaller back waters of the American Continent. Southern Europeans, Spanish and French adventurers were all over the mid-west long long before the pilgrim fathers were born. France and Spain were deep into American territory long, long before the pilgrim fathers were out of nappies.

The first English speakers in America were all Irish a full 100 years before the pilgrim fathers stepped on to a rock in Massachusetts. An Irish man was with Christopher Columbus. And Irish soldiers were very heavily embedded with the French army and even more so in the Spanish Army and Navy. Irish men were all over America a full century before the Plymouth Pilgrims. The Irish too were fleeing religious persecution. The Spanish and French were building settlements in the Southern states in the middle of the 16thcentury a previous century, never mind decade to the so-called start of colonialization. Dr. Baird states in *"Irelands important and heroic..."*. P/99 from 1729-1750 12,000 arrive annually from Ulster alone never mind the other three Irish provinces. That well over 252,000+ Irish in just 30 years! Never mind the massive influx of Catholic P.O.W.s and children in 1640s (Cromwell) and the 1690s (Williams religious intolerance laws i.e., sectarianism) One Protestant Irish Bishop of Derry, states that about a massive 300,000 Irish have left Ireland and it is to these Irish that all the trouble in America was down to. At one stage even the American Red Indians began to complain about so many Irish in America! Honest! And yet Wikipedia would have one believe no Irish Catholics existed in America before the famine save for 10-40,000 over the entire period of 1492-1845. What utter, utter, utter, ridiculous claptrap. History for chumps and chimpanzees. How in god's name does Wikipedia account for the massive Irish involvement and enormous amounts of Irish on the roles of the Continental army? The prodigious number of Irish Settlements in America? Oh, I get it all these people suddenly turned into Protestants to suit a New Englander Approach to the Birth of the Nation. The birth of a lie would be more accurate, with regards to this perverse writing out whole segments of Americas real past, when she was still young .

In *Famine Fenians and Freedom* by an English man Richard Brown P/40 he states that there was a massive import of Irish as early as 1650s into the colonies in America, he gets it to 10,000. The Catholic community of Ireland was being disposed of millions of acres of their own farmland all thru-out the 17th & 18th centuries in many cases they fled to America. From Ireland too went cattle, pigs' hens and sheep to help colonise its plantations. Irish Children too were rounded up and sent to work in tobacco plantations in Virginia.

In 1754. 28% of Washington's troops were actually born in Ireland! Irish Catholics were working in good numbers in Virginia prior to the so called "Pilgrim Fathers" ever having placed their feet on any rock, sand, sea or mud on American soil Virginia county records, land and probate records old parish records allude to this fact according to Reynolds in his "*Irelands important and Heroic part in Americas Independence and Development*" see p/113 Jamestown in Virginia had been founded 13 years earlier and according to Mr. Reynolds the Irish were already established before them.

A good exchange went from Cork to America as Sir Walter Raleigh had much land in Southern Ireland. Apparently, this is where the potato connection comes in. Mr. Reynolds estimates that 100,000 Irish were transported to either the Caribbean or the Colonies. This he calculates as a true and accurate number according to contemporary sources.

Irish place names litter the early colonial period of the America story. Yet Wiki states it was only 10,000 in total over the whole 180 years. That would not even come anywhere near what the contemporary sources state for just Irish children. The history of very Early American pioneers expanding into the west is awash with Irish settlers. Many Americans who can trace their descendants down to the 18th century are descendants of these very early Irish incursions into the American wilderness with or without British approval to enter the virgin territory. And, yet the New Englanders would have one believe only square jawed Anglo-Saxon of the better class populated America! In many cases the patriotic New Englanders detested the Irish Catholics and German Catholics more than they did their brothers in arms the Red Coats!

So, let us be clear the New Englanders wrote the Fairy story of how they discovered America and how these part time patriots freed it. America's enemies all play a different, consistent, and more accurate tune, and it goes something like this. America would still be ours if it were not for the bloody Irish, they all every one of them sing that same hymn and tune.

An Irish man from Maghera County Derry wrote out the American Declaration of Independence from Jefferson's draught. It was an Irishman who read the Declaration of Independence to an American Crowd from Congress Hall. The very first facsimiles of the declaration were produced and printed by an Irish man in Philadelphia. Many Irish signed the

Declaration of Independence. Irish printers were turning out propaganda leaflets, and not scared to print them too.

The federal city of Washington was founded on An Irishman's Farm, a free gift from a founding Catholic to his new country. The original White House was built on catholic land, was designed by an Irishman on the plans of Leinster House, the Irish Parliament building in Dublin. So, the United States White house its seat of government was built upon the plans and design of the Irish seat of government. Somehow that's seems just about right historically speaking. Much of Washington D.C. was catholic land. At The very first congress a General Reed remarked that the Congress was attempting to deny the massive Catholic Involvement in the fight for freedom. This at the very time Irish catholic officers were most meritoriously filling the higher ranks of the bloody continental Army. Never mind the masses in the ordinary ranks of the continental army. This is the same old story we will hear more of this native New Englander historical nonsense from the no-nothings in the civil war And aptly named they are too!

It's as if they discovered America and how they freed it from their Armchairs. {many ,many Protestant Americans are not even aware that they have Irish blood in them Catholics made up the majority in 17th century America, as indentured slaves and P.O.W.s Thousands upon thousands of real old time protestant true blue Americans are not even aware they came to America as Catholics, sometimes in chains!} The totally fabricated version of American Independence would gain more ground as the 19th Century progressed and in line with British demonisation of the Irish race as sub human and dirty simian ape like creatures; just one small step above the negroes,in their heavily promoted racist rag mags and education for idiots, fools and those inflammatory types, easily lead astray with racist voodoo, or prophesies of racial superiority; playing to their foolish smug arrogance, silly minds or just plain infantile jabberwocky.

This was pure 19th century racism. Very, very prevalent in Britain and its lackeys and New Englander acolytes. The chosen race or as Darwin would espouse it "the preservation of favoured races in the struggle for life". And yes, no one would struggle more harder than the armchair patriots of the favoured races of New England. Yes, to the bugle they would rally and hang fast to the star and stripes, never let it be said they ran away, or gave up or dallied with their British cousins in trade or sustenance. And if they were not there then by Jove their very own slave would have the proud honour to represent his heartless master to the full complement. And many a full complement they did make too. But as they are black their white master gets all the credit down thru the annals of New Englander history. History for chimps! Which comes with a full 19th century guarantee of historical racial hygiene.

During the American army annual St. Patrick's Day celebrations whilst in the field Washington would cancel all normal duties and fatigue work. The day would be spent in camp. All officers had to stay in camp, provide the food which was traditionally a hogshead and supply the drink. All volunteers had to stay within their own designated regimental areas. Washington informed the officers that discipline had to be maintained at all times. Washington usually had dinner with the French and toasts to American independence and Irish liberty were common. One St. Patrick's Day the Irish soldiers saw the American Germans volunteers make an effigy of St. Patrick which they then began to ridicule. The Irish soldiers took umbrage at this and American officers had to quickly quell any violence. They were unsuccessful. George Washington himself arrived to see what was going on. He informed the Irish that he would personally discipline any German soldiers that the Irish picked out as being personally responsible. The Irish volunteers could not pick out any individual German soldiers as there was a gang of them. Washington took control of the situation and ordered more drink and told the Germans that they would have to celebrate St. Patrick's Day along with everybody else. He told the Irish "and you are not to get drunk." Washington was very afraid of the Irish volunteers getting out of hand with drink. Every St. Patrick's Day he would inform his officers "one drink only." Like the Duke of Wellington later in the 19th century who stated about his Irish troops "I don't know what they'll do to the enemy but they sure as hell scared me." On another St. Patrick's Day Washington had American papers distributed amongst the ranks, for some unusual reason! Quickly Great excitement ensued, and a loud cheering was heard all throughout the American army. The American papers declared that the Irish government in Dublin had come out in favour of American independence and were fully supporting it against British wishes I told you Washington never misses a trick

The new Americans wanted a puritan history of how they won America. The British themselves were heavily pushing for this false narrative of the American revolution to be taught in American schools whether this was an anti-Catholic bias, or an anti-Irish bias or a pro-British interpretation a mere squabble amongst friend's cousins in fact or a mixture of all three; its effects were profound and totally false

The New Englander brahmins were more than welcoming and needed little persuading to write this false narrative of the American Revolutionary tooth fairy story.

December 1774 two raids on fort William & Mary confiscate for the rebels, gunpowder, and cannons One raid is led by Irish man, John Sullivan. New England Patriots make a good show. New Englander involvement was large and good at the start but come November 1776 it deserted and never rose again. That is not until the mid- nineteenth century, when American school books were printed with them to the fore.

During the actual revolution, wealthy Irish ship builders, who had relocated all along the Eastern Atlantic seaboard, of America; had vast fleets involved in fishing and commerce across the Atlantic and in between Colonies. The Irish ship building industry was run out by the British who insisted all boats must be made in Britain. Also, Irish fishermen had to apply to England for a permit to fish off Ireland, Plus Irish Fishermen were not allowed to fish off the Grand Banks that was for the exclusive use of English fisher men only. One wealthy Irish ship builder and sailor Capt.; Daniel Malcom had business premises in Boston; it was in his premises that the first Colonial President of Congress President to be Hancock, Adams, Otis and Ward met to discuss America's future and the coming revolution. (See p/135 Irelands Important & Heroic Part in American Independence) So here we have the very instigators of the coming American revolution bringing it all to fruition and planning it in an Irish business, man's office. A very safe place indeed to discuss rebellion against the British Crown. This book along with *"The Hidden Phase in American History"*, carefully lays out the massive importation and constant flow of Irish into America 17th century and 18th century. The Irish from all over Ireland were coming over in 10s; 100s & 1000s and tens of thousands, Year on year. Boat load on boat load in Irish ships.

The Irish settlers were pushing into the frontier and were the first to settle in that vast wilderness (p/124 Irelands Imp & Heroic) Many American Protestant families stem from these immigrants, many of whom were originally Catholics. Both Georgia and South Carolina paid for the passage from Ireland for small farmers. Large tracts of idle American land were non-productive, the wealthy Irish landowners needed to import settlers from Ireland to clear the idle land, farm it, and pay rent to the large landowner. Plots of 100 acres plus 50 acres more for each woman and child was the normal contract. Large tracts of land were set aside in many southern states for the exclusive use of Irish settlers. The large landowners had much land but few to farm it or even clear it. To the poor Irish this seems an attractive offer. Many came and settled, it was the Irish settlers that broke into the wilderness and left many a mark or place name of their early presence. The Irish seems to have been the main recipients of these schemes; even though they were offered to the Dutch, and German settlers. (p/122 Ire Imp Heroic. for a good overview see *Hidden Phase's/* 241-373 & see chap; 1 &3 *Irish Heroic*) p/1229(*heroic*) "But of all the countries none have furnished the province with so many inhabitants as Ireland" Both Rich Catholic merchants and very large landowners and Jesuits all helped the Catholic Irish to Emigrate and settle in America. Americans were glad the land was being cleared and brought into cultivation. The thousands of Irish place names speak for themselves. The richest man in America was a Catholic, Mr Carroll, George Calvert, (lord Baltimore of Baltimore Ireland) William Penn, James Oglethorpe amongst other imported many Irish Catholics, many would become protestant by default. No Catholic churches were allowed, no priests; so, if you wanted a wedding or baptism or funeral the only choice was a protestant one. Many official complaints abound about the surge in papists both from Germany and Ireland the Irish papists are now freely mixing with the savages i.e., native American Indians Gosh! "Scarce a ship sailed from any of its ports {Ireland} for Charleston that was not crowded by men, women and children" p/123(Heroic). Complaints about Irish papists being dropped off on the Delaware river, or general complaints about the number of papists increasing. Whether these people are lodged officially or not they are all over each colony. In passenger lists, paper reports etc. South Carolina was inundated with Irish place names. The colonial records office of North Carolina remarks: "The immigrants from Ireland in companies sufficient to form settlements, sought the wilds of America by two avenues the one by Delaware river at Philadelphia or through Charleston" The unofficial Irish begin to overflow into Tennessee. Many of today's American families stem from these Irish settlers and are probably unaware of this genetic fact.

Well educated North American officers During the American Revolution talked amongst themselves of this hidden genetic and religious fact, that a lot of protestants are not even aware that they came to America as Catholics from Ireland and that the revolutionaries were awash with Irish blood. But the two continental army officers knew all about America's early settlers and got a good laugh out of this farcical comedy American states had handbills printed and distributed in Ireland inviting the Irish over to settle in their states all thru the17th and 18th centuries Many, many southern states are literally swamped with Irish place names. In 1770 an Irish Community wish to emigrate to America they complain of very high rents in Ireland. They petition the provincial council of Georgia and ask them would it be possible to settle in Queensborough where their neighbours already are. No sooner asked than done, the provincial council of Georgia allot them 25,000 acres for their sole purpose. Savanah was another place in the south that the Irish were pouring into in good numbers.

New England itself had a large Irish population. Surprisingly, in the early part of the 17th century ships from various ports in Ireland are dropping off Irish settlers. Most of these early settlers are not from Ulster but the three other Irish provinces! Just because a ship comes from Ulster does not automatically mean that its passengers are automatically of the presbyterian persuasion. Or indeed vice versa just because immigrants come from Munster, Leinster, or Connaught does not mean their automatically Catholics. What we can say for sure it that the figure of only 10,000 Catholics in colonial America is a racist lie of mammoth proportions;

deliberately concocted for vile racist and religious dogmas. To wipe them out of "The Birth of the Nation"

Ulster was predominately a Catholic Province it was the Catholics that were being forced out, it was the Catholics that had vast tracts of farming land confiscated off them. So many rich Catholics were leaving Ulster in very large numbers because of this sick sectarianism heavily promoted by Britain for its own selfish ends and desires. It was the Catholic landed population that was being targeted for forced removal. Many of these Catholics must be among those early catholic settlers in America because ships from Ireland are continuously pouring settlers into all the colonies. These early settlers were recusants, Catholics who refused to automatically accept the spiritual supremacy of who ever happened to be sat on the English throne at any one time.(p/134 *Heroic*)

Shakespeare was an unreformed recusant; Shakespeare was a papist! The only work he really cared for at the end of his writing career were his two early blood curdling mesmerising, "The Rape of Lucrece"& "Venus and Adonis "Both are very bloody and probably both contain cryptic clues to the real aim of the poem Both describe to the initiated the intimate process of Hang, Drawing & Quartering Shakespeare's teachers became Jesuits when Jesuits were rare and hunted down like wild vermin. Shakespeare apparently knew intimately one Jesuit who was Hung Drawn & Quartered. Shakespeare final Will & Testament left money to buy a residence which was the centre of Catholic resistance to state debauchery. Like his father Shakespeare was fined for being a recusant, and fled Stratford upon Avon when he was caught at a Catholic safe house! The local Sheriff an Ultra Protestant had it in for him, he did not leave because he was caught hunting Deer! Romeo and Juliet is not about feuding Italian Families, it is much ado about the rival Gangs in the House of Commons. If they refused to believe that whoever sat on English throne was spiritually supreme in all matters then their ancient farmlands which they had farmed for over a thousand years were confiscated and given to an English lackey. This policy was rampant in Ulster. So, American historians automatically assuming ships from Ulster only carried protestants is extremely naive. As I stated it was the Ulster Catholic community, which was subjected to land confiscation and forced eviction, off their own land. It was the Catholics, who were specifically targeted for this type of selective religious treatment from Ulster. In many respects disenfranchised Presbyterians and those fed up with sectarianism, were an added bonus, to this British expulsion business.

As early as 1639 Catholics all over Ireland were losing vast tracts of land, to English royalty and their sycophants, and lackeys enriching themselves thru these means. And in the process gaining fancy titles such as Dukes, Lords, Viscounts, Earls to name just a few of the titles these land robbers allotted to themselves. Remember In the 17thcentury more Catholics came to American colonies than protestants

The Irish were unceremoniously written out. Even though all British Generals, American Generals, French generals, all, and everybody in Britain's own parliamentary findings of their own courts of enquiry all concluded the American Victory was down to the perfidious Irish. All witnesses testified it was the Irish that kicked us out of America. It was the Irish merchants that sustained it. It was the Irish townlands that supported it with men material succour and 100% support no matter what. It was the Irish but not wholly them who came to the revolutions rescue; when they along with fellow patriots put their money where their mouths were; and started a fully funded Bank to financially keep the American Revolution afloat and not let in flounder due to lack of financial support. An Irishman at one time was actually paying the whole continental army's soldiers with his own money! The Pennsylvania bank scheme was established by three Irish men, and other Philadelphia merchants. It was Philadelphia that was the real driving cockpit of the revolution and not pro-British new England, by far. It was they and the Irish merchants that put their heads on the block and came to the Revolutions rescue in the nick of time. Irishman Robert Morris put his own money in to start this bank, backed up by Irish merchants in Philadelphia. It was Philadelphian Irishman, Robert Morris that paid the American soldiers their wages out of his own pocket when congress had no money to pay them! It was the bloody Irish all down the line Paying, supporting, feeding arming, volunteering and yes fighting and dying over eight hard years of hard slog, with frontiersmen, southern guerrillas and northern patriots especially from Vermont, Marblehead Massachusetts, and German Americans, and finally our brown brothers whether free or slaves representing their white cowardly masters in their stead.

One in four American soldiers at Yorktown was black/brown. Where did they end up? On the mid-19th century cutting room floor of white Anglo-Saxon, hygienically clean, New Englander myth-making hogwash history of their American neatly pressed, fully outfitted uniform, white only revolution. It was Irish merchants that supplied the continental army when nobody else dared or would. It was Irish merchants who accepted American congress money when every other American business would not. It was Irish townlands backing up the whole revolution with men money, merchandise, food. It was not the New Englanders for sure. Not one not one in all the courts of inquiry not one witness ever said it was down to the New Englander Patriots not... one.... Yet today what narrative of the American revolution is taught in schools? Are American children taught that one in four American soldiers at Yorktown was Black/brown? If not, why not? Because it is true, maybe an uncomfortable one for some but it still remains the historical truth no matter what. Are American children taught that many black slaves went and enrolled in their master's stead? This was not an uncommon Practise. Are American children taught that many, many black/brown soldiers appear on the continental army muster rolls? Many free black/brown men of their own volition joined up. Are they taught that American Generals preferred the slaves to the New Englanders? If not, why not? Because it is true. Washington and his officers knew the black slaves were in it for the long haul. Their duration was not for a few weeks or one or two months the black slaves representing their masters were in the fight for years; just like the Irish. These black soldiers were not minute men they were full timers for a long time. If Washington could have 500 slaves for two years or 500 militia which came and went but was always an enlistment of 500. From the written records the American officers much preferred the long-time slave soldiers' p/21 "*A People Numerous and Armed*" by Prof; John Shy. "Only a tiny part of the population performed truly extended military service." If your opinion of the American Revolution is one of square jawed Anglo-Saxon types in nice, neat uniforms then you are as far away from the historical Revolution that one can sanely get to. Yes, neat uniforms and square jawed picturesque Hollywood types make a nice mini-series. But in reality, the American officers looked good, but the foot sloggers had a variety of poor mish mash linen hunting shirts, unusual footwear, and many looked raggy round the edges. The real hard cases of the American Army probably looked pretty ropey and ragged. Unshaven and hungry, with hunting knifes and tomahawks inside their belts. Which I can assure you were not for show. The real hard cases looked like they had been in the field for years. Which was probably the case.

One of the only days these die-hard American Patriots got off was to celebrate St Patricks day. Washington would issue the Army's orders for the day Usually the night before. All the Army will observe no fatigues or working parties. He would stipulate a little drink only, soldiers were to stay in their own regimental areas, no one was allowed to leave camp, but officers could go out of their own regimental areas. Officers supplied food and a little drink for around the campfires. Food was traditionally a hog's head. Officers were expected to maintain discipline. That was in many cases the only thing this army in the field for years had to look forward to. One day each year to sing, eat drink and be merry. They missed their homes, children, and their wives, and probably dead comrades. People do die in wars. The heroes don't always make it out, to see another winter {if you google the Vietnam memorial wall and you look up the young American soldier's facts about their service you will see very few made it past 4 months, most died within the first 3 months of arriving in Vietnam} They would constantly worry how they were coping without them. How their little farms were doing. The Irish would traditionally help each other to run the farms. All children and neighbours would help work each other's fields, cattle, cows, hens, pigs etc the men did the fighting, and the community kept the farms going.

This was how battles had been fought in Ireland against Britain for centuries. This was what their fathers did, their grandfathers did, and their great grandfathers did... and on down the line.

The Irish Army against the Red Coats could and would stay in the field for years. Fighting away from home was the normal course of events in Ireland. The New Englanders its militia at least detested being away from their homes. Washington put them guarding bridges or some other static tactical point of importance. To the Irish who could not give a highland fling about American taxes. This was all about freedom from oppression against the old enemy. They had no fond memories of the "mother country". Or for its much-vaulted institutions. All the British sassenachs and its red coats had done for Ireland was to debase it and its peoples. Things were going to be different in America. This time they had guns too. And they had every intention in using them.... too the full measure.

171

The fact that New Englanders have the Irish Catholics down to 10,000 in total from the Famous pilgrim Fathers-1776 goes to show how deep this quackery has sunk into the History of America just disappear half a Million Irish. If the Irish Catholics did not exist prior to 1776 then how does one account for 100,000 Catholics in its ranks and roll calls and rosters. If the Catholics townlands did not exist, then why was the American Army and its Generals instructed to go into them in an emergency to get recruits urgently. And what happened to all those birth certs marriages etc? The New Englanders have pushed their tripe history long enough. One British General states as regards the Southern sector it is the Irish Catholics and the Presbyterians it is these two elements that hold the whole continental Army and partisan, and guerrilla war together. p/102 of 445…

"How the Irish Won the American Revolution" General Washington himself regarded the Irish has his most fervent supporters. The whole history of the American Revolution seems to have been re written in the 19th Century to get rid totally of the Irish, Blacks and Catholics. The bedrock of the Pennsylvania line was Irish Catholics many spoke only Gaelic. This once again most Historians accept as historical fact. The Pennsylvania line was predominately Irish this was the bedrock upon which all else was built upon and around. When all others had fled the Irish both Catholic and Presbyterian were going nowhere, they had every intention of returning British coinage in kind with added interest accrued over years. While all else fled en masse, they sharpened their knives and cleaned their weapons. Now too, the Irish for the very first time, they too had guns and the mighty American long rifle could and would kill and take out British officers at 300 yards no problem. Possibly even 400 yards! Considering all action was normally at 50 yards, these American snipers began dropping many British officers tucked up safely in the rear; or so they thought! Now, the Irish Catholics had guns; no longer pikes, sticks with a piece of metal on the end. They had guns and they had every intention of using them against their

oppressor so too did our Presbyterian brothers in arms they too had scores to settle with this lot!

They had both come to the other side of the world to escape religious bigotry oppression, political disenfranchisement, and dreaded penal laws. They were going nowhere, even if 90% had fled! When I began to read for this little chapter i started to read about the American War for Independence, I was stuck solid to the ground after Washington got his pants kicked by the British again and again around New York; I was dumbfounded to read 90% of his Army had absconded and what does he do next? he attacks! He attacks! What was Washington playing at? did he think he was Rommel? I put the book down. Something was very, very wrong with this narrative. I Was not happy with just accepting this version of events; my historical heart and head knew, something was amiss; what was bloody driving General Washington on? In his own mind he knew the game was up! All was lost. He wrote privately upon this too a relative. Indeed, congress had probably already written out its outline surrender terms and set them on to general Washington for his perusal. What caused Washington to attack? What changed his mind? What indeed! I was not happy I knew some hidden force was obviously at work but what? I read on knowing full well the accepted historical narrative was missing a trick. Bingo! A few weeks later I hit the jackpot. In an account to the British Parliament an American loyalist (loyal to the British crown) in the British army stated that America was lost due to the Irish, it was the Bloody Irish who worked against us to achieve American Liberty and Freedom, well nothing new there, that is what they all stated Its what he stated next that lite the fuse and delivered George Washington's thinking onto our historical platter. This American loyalist in the British Army stated from Maine to Georgia the Presbyterian Chapels were preaching American Independence and Rebellion non-stop. these chapels were hotbeds of rebellion, so too the Congregationalists had started this too. Viola! All now fitted into place. Washington's rebel Army consisted of Irish Catholic with Every intention of Sticking it to the British, alongside them were, hotter than hell Irish Presbyterians hopefully with a few of their fiery blood and thunder preachers preaching nonstop, sedition, rebellion, and Independence from the dreaded Sassenach. The filthy heathen Red Coats. If Washington did not know this fight was personal, he bloody well knew now alright! These men and their hot head preachers were going nowhere who cares if all the rest ran away, these men meant business; and knew exactly what that entailed in full measure.

One could argue the American southern states were more patriotic than the New Englanders even though the continental army was driven out of the south, the southern patriots kept a war going for years in the southern states. Even without the continental army or its supplies or pay. These southern guerrillas kept it hotter than hell for the British army of occupation to operate freely in. This war was long and hard on the southern community. Men would be gone with their sons for long periods. Most would know the persuasions of their foe. House burnings and farm burnings were common. The British intended to lord it over these people. The loyalists would egg them on. The southern sector of operations the British soon learnt was no walkover. But still these hardy bucks fought on into the night. Ambushes and small skirmishes were common, so to the odd large battle was conducted if a good opportunity showed itself. The porous western border up against the wilderness might have looked empty, but in this vast wilderness were men with long guns. Men used to hunting, Shooting good and straight. Probably better snipers than the best Britain could field. These bands of frontier men with their sons could work in small fast mobile groups or sometimes coalesce into a sizeable force and smash an exposed British stronghold. The Southerners intended to make this partisan area of operations extremely hostile to its army of occupation.

Nothing like this hot guerrilla war was ever conducted in New England. If not, why not? They had the arms to conduct similar operations if they wished to do so. The New Englanders got down to a quiet life with their distant favourite cousins. And were more than happy to trade with them, just as long as they did not pay with dirty Yankee funny money, only good solid English money was good enough for the so-called New England patriots. A name and moniker they probably named themselves because the American Generals sure did not give it to them.

Some of the Irish in America, were direct descendants of dumped P.O.W. s from Cromwell's timeline. mid 1650s sold in America to English colonists. Indeed, as stated earlier many of America's early protestant families are routed in this penal history, unbeknownst to them

These early American settlers, were worked to death in many cases. Forcibly removed from Ireland and in most cases, they had to leave their wife's and children behind, who were sold separately in the American colonies or to English colonists in the Caribbean islands. These abuses against the Irish people and its race would drive the Irish Americans on too never give in and once and for all smash British hegemony into pieces in America, their new home. This visceral determination of the Irish and the Irish Americans cannot be underestimated. Washington knew it and so did most of his generals They certainly were not afraid of the English or their hired gun slingers. They only wished to close up on them; then annihilate them on the battlefield. America was flooded with Irish Catholics and Presbyterians fleeing British, religious in toleration, supposedly supremacy, religious ridicule, sectarian laws, enforced irreligious segregation, political disenfranchisement, loss of civic rights, all political rights. Indeed, Catholics had absolutely no rights in their own country under enlightened British rule!

WHY WE FOUGHT

Many Irish Catholics and Presbyterians had had enough, of this nonsense they were determined to rid America of this abject nonsense, and religious buffoonery. Too the Irish it was plain and simple Cromwell had thrown them off their land abused them and their children "To Hell or Connaught" was his battle cry; well now the Irish Presbyterians and Catholics had one of their own" Death or Liberty" and they wrote that on their battle jackets too. To all the Irish it was simply Get out of our country and stay out; with your stupid sick sectarianism and take your hired thugs with ya. And they had the fierce determination to back it up 100%

In their tens of thousands and hundreds of thousands, the Irish fleeing political persecution, Torture and Religious persecution of a most wicked kind had poured into America all 17th Century apparently more Catholics than Protestants (thousands upon thousands of Irish P.O.W.s and indentured slaves arrived escaped or were sold. Many thousands came from all the ports in Ireland. During the 16th & 17[th]18th centuries the Irish Catholics were forced out en masse from Ulster, Leinster, Connaught & Munster.

Ulster during the 17th and early part of the 18th Century experienced massive confiscation of land belonging to Catholic farmers and Forced emigration of the Catholic population. This policy went on under Cromwell and during the so called "Glorious Revolution" of unchristianity, and land robbery. This confiscation of land of Catholics went on well into the 18th century. Not everyone who came to America from Ulster was a Presbyterian. Nor should they historically automatically be assumed to be one. Ulster was after all the most Catholic part of Ireland. It was the British that wanted them removed off the land and out of Ireland.

Thus, when America sounded the battle bugle hordes of fired up Irish men and their sons rallied to the cause. Both Presbyterian and Catholic. American Freedom and Liberty was sheer music to their ears. Both

176

encapsulated a desire to rid America of British misrule - full stop! That was their aim, design and with fierce determination they had every intention to carry that thru, to a bitter end if need be. Come what may!

In Virginia, a large number of dissenters were pushing for religious freedom i.e., from the pro-British Anglican Church in the build up to 1776. Irish Presbyterians and Irish Catholics and American dissenters made a phalanx of opinion that wanted a disestablished church i.e., a separation of church and state in Virginia. Plus, a tithe tax had to be paid by all, to the Anglican Church. Thus, in Virginia and other dissenting states or colonies a large amount of citizens had a liability towards republicanism ideals. Why should they be made to pay for a church they did not belong to, or recognised?

Plus, just like Ireland a large amount of exceptionally large, landed estates were established in Virginia; and these exceptionally large, landed estates rented out smaller plots of land to small homestead farmers, at a particularly good return for them. The Virginia landlords were forever increasing the rents to these homesteaders or small farmers. All these forces led to many loyalist politicians being voted out of office. Republicanism was heavily lent to small farmers and dissenters. Thus, a large population of Irish, far larger than officially claimed later made very good cause with these elements in the southern states. The southern states were by and large more patriotic than New England. The British themselves claimed after the war and during it that 4/5ths of New Englanders were pro crown.

The southern states even, without any American army presence still made it hotter than hell for the British army once they ventured out from the big cities of Savannah or Charleston or indeed got away from the coastal strip. If the British could not win on the battlefield, then by Jove, they wished it off the battlefield. There are many ways to skin a cat! They played the No popery card to entice the Presbyterians away from their pact of steel with their fellow Irish Sufferers the Catholics. They had every intention to drive a sectarian wedge straight thru the very heart of the American Revolution. They failed! Presbyterians would not be fooled by such childish incantations, snappy slogans or rhetorical pamphlets arousing no popery voodoo to jingle jangle in front of their eyes and bamboozle them, like easily led fools on a fool's errand. Away with such child's play of Christian tom foolery. Away and bedazzle others with your jiggery pokery, no popery nonsense. Religious prejudices dressed up as virtues, and sold to the masses like…, life's essence. Which emits a very peculiar unchristian odour. A foul-smelling concoction which hangs around the British Empire and lives in its wake of religious supremacy and snobbery.

The fact that the first American Congress wanted more Irish in America shows their deep concern for Ireland, Irish people, and the fact that Ireland as a country was very pro-American under the British heel of oppression. Ireland was the first country to recognise the thirteen colonies as a united country. The Irish parliament backed them up, as did the Irish nation. Did the New Englanders ever act with such patriotic zeal? Did the New Englanders ever light bonfires at night whenever a continental victory was announced? Ireland was occupied by the British too. So too were the southern states, yet they still carried on a guerrilla war for years on their own. One should remember this was being done in Ireland Occupied by the British when the Irish did not even have guns or horses. They operated in a heavy militarised countryside. If caught they would be hung. Yet they too kept the spirit of American freedom in their hearts. A win for the little man always warmed their cockles. Hope sprung eternal. The American patriots were on everyone's lips in Ireland.

The first Congress was willing to give Irish people the right to live, reside and come to America even into the future. Large elements of Irish settlers remained written out of the official record and this was why supposedly the Dutch, English and German townlands and counties were all producing militia with Irish names common amongst them in large numbers. Plus, it needs to be written, many, many rosters contained a lot of Afro-Americans, black/brown patriots sometimes well over 50% of those in that actual muster roll that day. What happened to all these black/brown soldiers turning up for muster roles all over America were they too whitewashed out of the official New England Pro British cousins' version of American History?

The British put a lot of the rabble rousing in the north and Southern colonies down to the Irish agitators. Benjamin Franklin wrote wherever the Irish people congregate they are always for American freedom whether in France, Spain, Italy, or Portugal. *(P37 Hidden Phase of American History).* Ireland went mad with excitement when America declared its independence. Irish regiments in the French and Spanish armies Begged to be deployed to America The British public was mad with seething rage, the British population wished to destroy America and turn it into a ransacked, ravaged countryside; destroyed like ancient Carthage, *(P36 Hidden Phase Cry of Delenda y Carthago).*

The House of Lords became a seething cauldron of impotent rage *(P36 Hidden Phase of American History).* The majority of citizens in England thought the Americans needed to be taught a lesson. They regarded them as being offensive, ungrateful, totally disloyal, and downright treacherous. The majority of Irish citizens were cheering them 100%. American freedom was the best news they had heard in 500 years of British occupation. So, it comes as a bit of a surprise that although the American Congress was incredibly grateful to them, American Generals, French Generals too; there was no place for them in the pristine well-shod history books of the New England armchair contingent. Sat in their chimney corners as Washington called this lot.

Many New Englanders looked towards England with nostalgia, fondness and the seed that was planted in America. The Irish and the Scottish looked upon England as a hindrance and a subjugation of their human rights and religious freedoms. To them England was an antagonist, they wished only to be left alone in America from British hegemony or selective law and apartheid laws. They looked upon England with the same respect and love the Czech and Polish population looked upon the German Wehrmacht and the Nazis. For Irish Americans, British rule meant British slavery of both Catholic and Presbyterian and to a lesser extent, Congregationalists. To this Irish element, this war was not about taxes, it was all about independence dignity, religious toleration, equality, and personal freedoms. Incidentally because the American congress had said the revolution was all about unfair taxes. The American congress was always short of money. Wars are extremely expensive things to run, and Congress was reluctant to impose much needed new taxes ostentatiously to fund a war it stated was about unfair imposed British taxes! Congress always felt it feet was tied about this matter.

One Irish teacher from Limerick a Mr. Sullivan was the father of a Governor of New Hampshire, a Governor of Massachusetts and father of the first Judge appointed in New Hampshire, an Attorney General of New Hampshire, and a General Major in the American Revolutionary army of liberation plus four sons who served as officers in the army of liberation. He was also a grandfather to Governor of Maine a United States Senator for New Hampshire an Attorney General of New Hampshire, a Judge of New Hampshire, Great Grandfather of Attorney General New Hampshire, and a great, great grandfather of a distinguished officer of the Civil War.

Irishmen were signers of the Declaration of American Independence and members of the first American Congress in 1774 and helped frame the American Constitution. Irishmen commanded brigades and regiments of the Continental Army of Liberation. An Irishman founded the American Navy, and they were Governors of American provinces in the vanguard of its army, indeed Irish regiments were repeatedly used as shock troops by American Generals, all stated they were the toughest and finest part of the full-time outfit even the French Generals admitted the same, as did all the British Generals on the opposing side.

An Irishman was the Governor of New York another for the Red Indians from the Hudson to the Mississippi, Governor of the Carolina's in the province of Maryland, first Governors of Delaware, State of Pennsylvania, and first Mayor of New York.

The first English speaking man on American soil was an Irishman. The Irish were in America in good numbers a full century before the founding Pilgrim Fathers, they were heavily embedded with the French colonials and Spanish. One of the Governors of Florida was an Irishman Arthur O'Neill 1781 – 1793. An Irish priest was in St. Augustine 1598 – 1606 so he too was administering to a large Irish population probably soldiers.

The Irish in the Spanish army defeated the Redcoats at Pensacola, Florida in 1781. Two more Irish priests resided in the parishes of Pensacola, Florida. Fr. Thomas Hassett and Fr. Michael O'Reilly to the parishes in Pensacola 1794 another Catholic priest was required Fr. James Coleman. All these Irish priests turning up in a Spanish colony! What was going on? They were there to administer to the Irish Catholics soldiers their families and Irish settlers.

The Pilgrim founding fathers arrived in 1620 a full half century after the church of St. Augustine was founded, built, and peopled by Spanish citizens, homesteaders, the Spanish homesteaders built up this successful Catholic colony. Mass had been celebrated for half century in America before even the planters had put their foot on any American rock or soil. It was the Catholics that demanded religious toleration for all. And definitely not the protestants who set about evicting each other's sects all across American colonies for decades. One thing for sure the early protestant sects claiming religious persecution sure persecuted each other's sects constantly. They could hardly be in the same room never mind the same states. Look it up read your history books it all there waiting to be discovered.

The French and Spanish people were all over America before the Puritans were even born. They had planted colonies in America in the mid-16th century, once again mass was being celebrated all over America a long, long time before the Puritans had placed their delicate wet feet upon American soil. By this time, the French were probably in every state in Eastern America. Americas real story began long before the pilgrim fathers ever set sail.

The very first colonials in non-native America to successfully live in America were free black slaves from a Spanish ship. They escaped or were left to settle with the Native Americans in Florida with which these black Africans did just fine. So, the historically correct; first Thanksgiving event was a black American Red Indian affair in 1528! A full 100 years before the Puritan event, this is factual history. When the Americans ordered all Indians to leave Florida, they stated all Indians and free black negroes are to leave Florida forthwith.

The African Americans had made a successful life with the native Americans a full 100 years before the Puritan festival was even started and yes, our black and brown brothers and sisters had turkey i.e., Florida turkey. So, but that in your pilgrim pipe and smoke it!

The first shall be last and the last shall be first in American history. Black slaves were all over southern America decades and centuries before 1620. Somehow the Puritans forgot that as they did those 1 in 4 volunteers at Yorktown were black/brown, that is another whitewash. The massive Irish presence in American history has been totally whitewashed ignored and cut out by the New Englanders. So too Americas vast penal colony history. A history relished in Australia. A lot of Australians are rightfully proud that their great Ancestors were rebels. Freedom fighters, Political agitators, and people not willing to be kicked around, or willing to bow down to his lordship. In America, the prudery prim and proper puritans who fancied themselves as proto-British upper class. To these New Englander brahmins America as a penal colony would not do; so that went out, along with black soldiers in massive numbers at Yorktown and large numbers on muster rolls or fighting for years as their slave master, all that history had to go into the delete bin plus the dirty Irish, racially inferior for sure they had to go too. H.M.G. insisted how the American revolution was to be taught. And the patriotic new Englanders were only too willing to write it...Viola!

Irish shipping predominates in shipping across the Atlantic to America by a long way. Irish ships were leaving weekly and many with immigrants from southern Irish ports all pouring into Virginia and Maryland. For decades! Nay centuries

---

(See P258/9 for whitewashing out early massive sustained Irish Catholic immigration into America from Ireland.

It was the Irish that kept America fed and provisioned, not British ports. Read *(A Hidden Phase of American History by (1909) Joseph O'Brien)*

for consummate details of shipping to American colonies. Indeed, when American colonies were starving because of Indian insurgents and it was Ireland that rushed food to New England colonies to feed them and keep them going, not England. England refused all help to burnt out New England, the whole colony could rot for all they cared. (For a better understanding of Britain's true and real intentions in early colonial America read, *How the Nation was won by H. Graham Lowry or see one of his videos on YouTube He's a fabulous public speaker*) Ireland fed these colonies and supplied them with all they needed to sustain themselves i.e., farming equipment, food, clothes cow's pig's sheep etc.

So much of American history has been whitewashed and prioritised that the fact that the avalanche of Irish Catholics emigrating to America Pre-Revolution has been systematically written out of the official history of its colonies and their development, is a historical disgrace by white Puritanical snobs too ashamed that Ireland and its people were so prevalent in America both in massive settler Catholic numbers and in its army of liberation.

For every ship from England twenty come from Ireland.

See   Chap XV Irish Immigration into Pennsylvania

        Chap XIV Irish Immigration prior to Revolution

        Chap XIII Irishmen flock to Standard of Washington (A hidden phase…)

When you read these chapters, you will soon see who was flocking to America in good numbers. Without the Irish there is no American freedom. No bloody wonder Washington said at the start of the American Revolution "if I had seen the New Englander's in action no amount of arm twisting, or persuasion would have ever got me to accept this command." Plus, he well knew they were talking up their role in the Revolution and its battles and belittling or ignoring other participants even when they carried the day. After the Revolution, the New Englander historians totally wrote the predominate Irish out and replaced them with their own little effort. Some Histories had as little as 40,000 Irish in America Pre-Revolution – what utter nonsense, lies and dog poop! No serious American could ever swallow this New Englander nonsense or take it seriously. Pure historical tripe.

This is history for white Anglo Saxons, for armchair patriots and total nonsense. Written by the chimney corner gang. Things only got worse as the 19th century developed. The New Englanders were ashamed and disgusted by the Irish. Even though it was the bloody Irish that paid for their freedom in bucket loads of blood, black blood, and German blood too. In fact, it is probably true that the German-Americans took more part in American liberation than the New Englanders. This 19th century history of the American Revolution should be gone with the wind.

Southern Ireland was a very big major jumping off point for immigration into America, the shipping records prove this fact. * All through the 17th and 18th centuries. *"The Irish in American Revolution"* by James Haltigan pub; Washington 1908... p/29 In 1728-29 the emigrants to Pennsylvania were as follows English and Welsh 267, Scottish 43 Germans 243 Irish 5655. The Irish outnumber all the others by a factor of 10-1 The Pennsylvanian historian goes on to relate that from Ulster alone Pennsylvania usually gets about 3000 emigrants. Catholics were being driven off the land and Presbyterians out of their businesses. Both disposed Catholics and Presbyterians were pouring into Americas mid colonies at a prodigious rate year upon year. This on top of Massive Catholics P.O.W.s dumped in the 16th century by Cromwell then old Sectarian promoter himself just

William and Mary. Heavy into Christian in toleration; an oxymoron for sure. Apparently, there were more Catholics dumped in America in the 16th century than protestant settlers. This penal episode will get well and truly written out of American History books for Puritans. Far to sullied for our pristine Christian anti papist intolerant pilgrims.

The colonists were so scared of the old faith that they instructed ships captains to administer oaths to emigrants to say they were protestants. So many Irish were pouring into America the Red Indians started to complain about them! Yet years later the New Englanders would insist they never existed. Americas so called Historians would go along with this ridiculous figure of 40,000 Irish Pre-Revolution; so too would American Institutions and government bodies repeat this nonsense. Wikipedia 2021 www Irish Americans. Subtitle "Irish immigration to the United States"; states 10,000 emigrants in total, for Catholics from Ireland to the United States prior to the American Revolutionary war in 1775. Since the Pilgrims arrived... what utter, utter dog poop. A hidden phase of American history "will show this pathetic number for what it is a complete historical lie. History for chimpanzees.

If we google the size of the American continental army a figure of 230,000 is suggested. Now if we take what all witnesses state under oath this army is 50% Irish so one could assume that a little over 100,000 are Irish volunteers in the Army, actually from Ireland never mind Irish Americans. Now that is just the volunteers. What about those men too old, their children, sisters, mothers? If we dare to include them then, for every volunteer in the continental army 3, or 4 or more could be back home so we could conservatively say the Irish population was 300,000 or 400,000 Any child of eight would know that if the American army was 230,000 and manned mainly by the Irish men and boys only, then; a figure of 10,000 Catholics in all of America is total Phish! Enough! be off with your New Englander looney bin history written to please the English and the keepers of the royal toothbrush. Be off I say and don't dare darken our door again with your chimpanzee history of America. Where in God's name did all these Irish appear from, to man your army, you fools? Ireland was the main supplier of goods and merchandise to the colonies every boat carried passengers many a lot! they were pouring out of Ireland and disappearing into its wilderness so much so the Red Indians Started to complain.

This is real history not the nonsense New England professors peddle, written up to please the English racial toffs in the 19th century. The Irish were pouring off these ships from Ireland willy nilly and being dumped in their tens of thousands throughout the 17th century. They were getting off boats read your history *"The hidden phase of American History"* would be a good place to start and open your eyes to real shipping lists quotas, passengers. And what the papers, printed at the time what the ships Captains reported at the time, open your eyes and ears. Scottish Highlanders P.O.W.s mostly Catholics were being dumped too after Bonnie's prince Charlies rising of 1745. Poor Catholics were imported into many colonies. Rich Catholics imported them into Virginia. The puritans were horrified that many large, landed estates were Catholic! And duly complained about this obvious threat to America as they saw it. Not to worry boy's, sectarian William and Mary will ban All Catholics and take away all their rights in America, just to keep America Hygienically clean as Hitler would say. The Protestant Volksland of the thirteen colonies was safe for another decade. A lot of Washington D.C. was built on Catholic Farmland god forbid where were the Klan when you need them? Rich Catholics in Maryland was another problem for the free enterprise puritans. More official complaints followed Catholics were getting into America Whether the Puritans liked it or not. They too were fleeing religious persecution of a kind that would turn your stomach and make what the Pilgrims were fleeing pure luxury, and certainly not worth a tin of beans; compared to what the Irish suffered for centuries.

The Irish wanted to be left alone to disappear into the wilderness or live quietly. Thus, thousands turned out to fight and enrol in areas that were thought to be old English Dutch, puritans or whatever. And what is more they did not run away when the going got tough or send a black man to represent them in their stead. Nor tarry with the English, nor refuse to accept continental money instead of English crowns for goods purchased,

Where New Englanders were outstanding was in their privateer enterprises i.e., American naval action in their own armed ships against British merchant shipping. In this they excelled no problem. The New Englander, fishermen and sailors were just as good as the Irish lads operating American privateers around British waters. The New Englanders were sweeping the Royal Navy and British merchant vessels from out of the north eastern Atlantic. "Manifest Destiny" and "Sons of Liberty" were Irish slogans, not Puritanical New Englander catchphrases. *(John Sullivan, United States Magazine Democratic Review 1845).*states New Englander Private Pirates under the stars and stripes would get stuck into British naval assets as best as they could and interdict commercial traders supplying the British army of occupation in America. Now no historians disagree with the proud and gallant performance New England seamen made to the patriotic cause on this issue they reign supreme. As do New England regiments, but militia no and as a population they were very, very loyalist. As stated earlier the New England patriots were most definitely in the minority.

The Irish in America were sold as slaves, worked as slaves, organised slave rebellions and fought in good numbers on both sides of the Civil War, built the Whitehouse on land donated by an Irish Catholic farmer and pretty much freed America from British rule. The first American Congress was offering Ireland, friendship, citizenship, and cheap land, passing resolutions about the Irish and stating that America welcomes Irish people.

When England tried to pen all settlers to America in 1763 with their proclamation line the Irish of course just ignored this official barrier to American settlement. Who was England to tell people where they could or couldn't live in on open wilderness? They didn't own this land yet seemed to think every tree, bush, river, fish, rock belonged to them and them alone

If Australian academics ever tried to tell the Australian public, that only true-blue bloodied Anglicans ever came to Australia, that they had liberated the land, worked it, explored it, they'd be laughed out of Australia or sectioned in the looney bin.

The bands of American freedom and population are intertwined; Ireland was the first country to recognise the 13 colonies as a country. When they placed Benjamin Franklin on a seat in the Irish parliament only for citizens from another sovereign parliament, not in the visitors' gallery. Compare and contrast how Ireland treated the founding father and how the British Houses of Parliament harangued, ridiculed, laughed, scorned, and rebuked Benjamin Franklin to much applause as the assembled Lords all gathered around him. Read up, that is how they treated that American Ambassador. As they scorned, clapped, and ridiculed the American founding father and egged each other on in insults to Benjamin Franklin to his face and badger baited him for over an hour. No bloody wonder the founding father preferred liberation, freedom and equality over scorn, ridicule and being laughed at like a child.

WHY WE FOUGHT

The British stopped laughing when the Irish opened up on them with dum dum bullets at Bunker Hill and shredded their line to pieces, not once but twice and left 1,000 of them screaming in pain or dead to this world. The American Eagle had set off and its talons were exposed for all to see. Its hawkish eyes flared, with anger and resentment. It would swoop down with speed and smite its foe. The eagle would strike a mighty blow to its enemies, who generally would not see it coming. The eagle would soar high and cast a cold eye over all its dominion. A symbolic guardian of American sovereignty and independence. The American Eagle had well and truly landed.

CHAPTER 7

"Smoked Irish"!

The Irish have a long tradition of rebellion wherever they ended up. In 1666 they fomented a slave rebellion in the Caribbean they were forever organising rebellions and a lot more slave rebellions went on in America and the Caribbean, than the popular history books claim.

Slavery to every Irishman and woman was an abomination to God, unchristian in virtue and kind. Unnatural and the work of the English *(P39 FFF)*. Richard Brown relates early American Irish sold as slaves 1651-1654. These "slaves" were Irish rebels i.e., partisan soldiers. This flow of Irish rebels and their families continued for all of 17th and 18th centuries. So, by the time rebellion came around in America from 1774 onwards the Irish and their descendants were all in, all right, right away.

One needs to know Irish history to understand the American Revolution. So heavy was Irish slavery in the Caribbean that many blacks spoke Gaelic in these Caribbean islands into the late 19th century. *

Many Irish were whipped as slaves and many of them inter-married with African women and many Irish women inter-married with brown African men, they saw each other as equals in an oppressive system invoked by

191

Britain. Many, many, Irish indentured servants, bonded men were worked into the ground. What did the master care, they were not their property, and the Irish had no value to them? But make no mistake no Irishman would ever want to change his place with the black/brown hereditary slavery. INDENTURED SLAVERY would be a more historically accurate assessment of their collective treatment. *See Wiki Montserrat*

They were sold, yes sold in some cases. Abused with brutal floggings worked to death these are uncomfortable facts. The Irish were treated as filth, detested, loathed; thought to be pretty near unbreakable and always ready to revolt at the drop of a hat, instantly. And to kill their oppressor. In whatever guise he took. The thought of revenge and revolt were constantly on their minds. And many slave revolts were started controlled and planned by them. The thoughts of blacks/brown slaves mixing with the Irish terrified the British plantation owners in the Caribbean. Just as the thought of illegal Irish settlers flooding into the wilderness and mixing openly with Scottish clansmen expelled from Scotland as P.O.W.s from bonnie prince Charlies' rebellion. These two highly cheesed of set of peoples were dreaded about in British colonial circles they regarded this mixture as highly explosive and a coming disaster for sure for long term British rule in America. This border must be sealed.

Tens of thousands, if not hundreds of thousands of Irish were forced transportation into America and the Caribbean, for sugar, tobacco, and other money enterprises. America was just as much a penal dumping ground as Australia *(See www.JStor The Irish in the Caribbean 1641-1837 Nin Rodger). Once again, this interesting part of America's development has gone missing America like Australia was a penal dumping ground. Only Australians take great pride in this fact of their history whilst Americans believe the New Englanders did it all, and they should know, well excuse me many, many early Yankees were Irish rebels dumped, sold, and indentured criminals in*

English eyes, and honourable rebels in Irish; all because they stood up for freedom and liberty from the Sassenach yoke.

The Irish nearly always made common cause with the brown slaves. They married the brown slaves which infuriated the English neurotic masters. No mixing was allowed, and they would go to church and call themselves Christians. Certainly, it was a very peculiar and funny sort of Christianity indeed. They took Christ out of Christianity and replaced him with you know who?

Irish children were forced into transportation. The English boasted about this slavery *(P147 FFF)*

After the Irish, indentured servitude began to dry up, Britain started up the enormous industrial scale of mass transportation of kidnapped African children. (When I first started to read about the transatlantic slave trade, the very first thing that struck me was that the white so-called Christian, slave masters preferred African children! What possible perversion was afoot? They preferred children because they would adapt to slavery much quicker than a fully grown adult male of the species.) Adult Africans were far more likely to rebel and needed constant watching over for the rest of their active lives. They needed new human beings' slaves to fill the growing Tobacco, and sugar, plantations now making vast sums of money for them, and they were greedy for more.

Children and young teenagers were preferred rather than fully grown adult males as they were harder to break than children. African children maintained a higher price at the human being auctions organised by the British commercial sector. This mass transportation of African children went on for decades, centuries and very popular it was too as much money was made this way. This is child kidnapping, and people trafficking on an industrial scale. This needs to be accepted as such. Also, it was a blatant crime against Humanity, conducted against African children by so called Christians. Who built many an English stately home upon these fabulously profitable mass kidnapping and human cargo. The only mitigating circumstance is that The Mass kidnappings were always carried out by Africans themselves. White Europeans could not live in the African interiors they quickly died of African diseases. Interior Africans soon fought other interior Africans for the franchise in human mass abduction, mass enslavement, and mass transportation. Slave wars decimated the African continent. More Africans died from slave wars than were taken as slaves to be. The Irish in the Caribbean were the ones to break the colour bar which really undermined the whole slavery premise.

There was a good mixing of Irish forced indentured population and the brown African slaves both wanted freedom and respect, both sought common interest especially where opportunities arose to free themselves from the British yoke. Britain re-enslaved free slaves: they disagreed with any freed slaves' policy. As a matter of fact the American administration had sought to ban slavery in America pre 1776 this was ruled out by king George, after the revolution some American states sought to ban slavery in America as per the Declaration of Independence Pennsylvania was one such state, not enough votes could be secured to carry this amendment. Same to for Catholic emancipation, even though they had liberated America and George Washington willed it full repeal of the penal laws had to wait another while. Congress was broke and the need to build up the country with scant resources was a nightmare. Once again congress felt it hands were tied when it came to the prudent policy to raise taxes. Always a very dodgy subject to broach

Although indentured servitude was for a specified time and involved being sold in many cases to a master and although they could be severely whipped, the abuse could be vile and sadistic at times. Our black/brown fellow humans had a lifetime of this, inhumane crime against humanity and black/brown children. And their children were born into this unchristian money-making machine for eternity. From birth till death and their children too. What unholy perniciousness and perversion.

England could not call itself a Christian country as long as their industrial enslaving of children went on and the abuse meted out to them; this was organised abuse, human trafficking on an enormous, industrial scale. Indentured servitude could be benign or sadistic and akin to slavery at its most vicious extent. Indentured servants could be whipped almost to the point of death for escaping and they could be placed in chains. This all sounds a lot like slavery to the victim. But no Irish man women or child would ever change places with those in chattel slavery.

Our black/brown brothers and sisters experienced a regime of sub-humanity. This was a disgusting and depraved way to treat children. The slave masters behaved as if the African children and very young adults were untermenchen. Some white slave masters enjoyed the power just as much as the Nazis in Treblinka, Balzac, Sobidor, Majdanek, Auschwitz. These white devils had sold their very souls for some earthly riches. White supremacism was promoted with all its devilish satanic nonsense to impressionable adult chimpanzees.

Many black/brown people and children died in the mass transportation programme and died in transit just as our Jewish brethren would die in their mass transportation experience. Some black/brown slaves were kept in good conditions and others resembled concentration camps. Children, brothers and sisters, mums and dads were split up upon arriving in America. The Irish experience was never as bad as this. Indeed, the black/brown slave children were born slaves into this white Christian regime.

WHY WE FOUGHT

All American Christian churches need to publicly apologise if they have not already done so, for their involvement and acquiescence in not condemning human slavery and mass child abduction, for child slavery. I'm not too sure whether a sitting American President has humbly apologized to those descendants of those slave workers, but essentially from my reading, the Revolution is in complete without it. Many wanted it banned as an aspiration and aim of the American Revolution. For it to appear in the constitution, many genuinely sought this as a revolutionary requirement.

Our black/ brown "volunteers" in the Continental Army after years of hard service, on successful completion of the American Revolution sadly had the heavy yoke of human slavery placed around their necks again. They returned not home but back to the slave camp with their slave wife and slave children Most African leaders and Presidents have now apologised for their involvement in enslaving their own people and selling them into slavery After the Revolution the country was broke, shattered, and heavily traumatized, and Americans could not live up to the beautiful document's ideals, aims and aspirations. They let their fellow citizens down in not living up to their stated ideals in the constitution of America i.e. All men are created equal.

Our black/brown brothers and sisters and their children made the southern States the fourth most profitable economy area in the world. The Irish experience was hard but not slavery *(P46 FFF)*.

We should remember many black/brown slaves lived amongst homesteaders not on plantations. Some plantations were benevolent compared to others. Some were outwardly very dutiful but you still were a trapped slave, under the whim of an overseer. Only a lash away. Outside the large Virginia plantations were the poor whites in utter wretchedness and utter dejection.

There are several sorts of power working at the fabric of the republic: -

Waterpower, steam power and Irish power. The last works hardest of all *(P46 FFF) citing Shannon, William the American Irish, a Political and Social Portrait 1966 (P26 McMillan & Co).* Some of America's no nothing wasps referred to the Irish as niggers turned inside out and the negroes as smoked Irish *(P47 FFF).*

Religious racism and exclusion were well practiced in wasp America. How these people can say they follow Jesus's principles is beyond belief. These people are no more Christian than an anteater or a packet of crisps! Sectarianism, bigotry, and white supremacism were all promoted by the Wasps, and we all know what big part they played in the revolution.

In 1881 W.E. Robinson refuted the claim that America was mainly Anglo-Saxon. Out of a population of 23 million he estimated the Irish element counted to 7,500,000. The *Irish world* claim that two thirds of Americans were of Irish descent. One New York paper estimated that out of the 23 million 14,325,000 Americans were of Irish origin see *(P49 FFF).* Certainly, many, many more Irish rebels were dumped into the 13 colonies than the Wasp historians let on. America was very much a penal colony like Australia, but this part was written out by the Pilgrim Fathers' white sect. The idea that America owes its freedom down to white minutemen New Englanders is a fairy story.

It was the Irish that built up North America into a world beating economy. Not New Englander Puritans: the black and brown brothers and sisters in work camps built up the Confederate States into the fourth largest economy in the world, based upon slavery; and the northern states built up a world beating economy on abundant cheap, very hard-working labour from peasant farmers from all over Europe.

America is just as much a black/brown man, s country, as it is a white man's country. Many many Europeans of all persuasions i.e., Greeks, Polish, Czechs, Slovaks, Spanish, Portuguese, French, German, Danish, Dutch, Swedish, Italian, Russian, Mexican and Asians; many, many more joined in to make America the most powerful industrial nation upon earth but also the freest nation by far on earth. All have added to the pot. The New Englanders did very little fighting in the American War of Independence - yet they played more than their full part in the Civil War. The foundation stories of the true, real America were laid a long time before the Pilgrim Fathers turned up.

Everyone here is an immigrant, and the puritan settlers would have failed without the red man's help and assistance. Freed blacks were living in America 100 years before the pilgrim founding fairy story. A surprising number of American Presidents have Irish blood in them including Barack Obama! Or should that be, Barack O; Bama for sure. His Irish Ancestors could show him the very house of his ancestor. Many, very many more Americans have Irish blood in their veins than know it or are aware of this fact. Americans over two hundred years in America are sure to have Irish blood in their veins. Sorry but true. The Irish changed their religion to fit in and their Irish names too. Many became protestant by default. There were no Catholic churches in New England, and if any Catholic wanted a Christian baptism, burial or wedding their only option was a protestant one. Thus, many grew up oblivious to their true ancestry or religious voca-tion. Yes, I know we were all Catholic in the past and that Protestantism is an outgrowth from a Catholic trunk and rootstock.

If you have been in America for over 200 years then your ancestors would have Irish blood in them for sure, even black/brown people. Because Britain maintained this sort of lobsided forced transportation and forced emigration against Catholics; males normally. Americas population was dying off and shrinking due to an extremely heavy bias towards males, Irish P.O.W.s Irish rebels (Criminals according to Britain) Dumping Catholic rebels into the colonies to work to death, meant the labour force was constantly dying. What they needed was more balanced emigration or just more females. America role as an active penal colony has been systematically written totally out by the New Englanders. The Australians revel in it; their American cousins whitewashed it out. America was a penal colony get over it! Irish women were mated with black/brown males indeed the transportation of women and girls had to be encouraged.

Never let Savannah celebrate St. Patrick's Day without the knowledge that many black soldiers fought with the French and Irish and local Virginians and Georgians to free Savannah from British rule. They failed but at least our black brothers turned up!

Most Northern regiments in the American Revolution recruited black/brown people to keep their quotas up. Northern states even resorted to buying slaves at human being auctions to fill up their quotas, so lax was volunteers to come forward. A large proportion of Irish and blacks were in the American navy because certain white soldiers did not want to mix with them thus a high proportion of blacks joined the navy. This is true for the Continental Navy and the Union Navy in the Civil War later on.

The American army during the Revolutionary War had many, many more black/brown brothers than has been usually recognised; large numbers sometimes appear on militia roll calls. As they were representing the white master? We know the New England patriotic homesteader did not want to leave their farms and homesteads over long periods, nor serve away from their locality and although black/brown patriots make up a smaller number than traditional whites, like the Irish they were usually on for the long haul. These white patriots came and went some stayed days some stayed weeks. Black/brown brethren in many cases stayed with the Revolutionary Army for years and years, just like the Irish. The American Army today; force multiplies their effort to nearly a 12%+ of the whole patriotic struggle see *(Americans in Revolutionary War). A lot more black/ brown patriots paid a pivotal role in the war of independence, according to Hessian accounts and muster rolls of the Continental army. Sometimes the Black/brown soldiers predominate these muster roll calls, so their real contribution was vastly larger by some measure than the white racist 19thcentury version still peddled today as American history.*

---

*WWW African Americans and the American War for Independence

**National Archives – African American History Revolutionary War and Early America, Dr. Grey Bradsher

***WWW African Americans and the Revolution, Jeffrey Crow Wikipedia

The siege of Yorktown was very hard fought and bloody by American War of Independence standards. James Armistead Lafayette was a poor well-educated black man and was an American army intelligence asset i.e., a spy. The British were so taken with this honest black man's demeaner that they decided to hire him as a way to gather information on the treacherous American patriots. Lafayette was an original American Army intelligence asset sent into the British lines to gather good intel on them. Ironically, the British were so taken with the cut of this African American they hired him to go back and spy on the American Army. American Army Intel Must have got a good laugh out of that turn of events. They duly sent Lafayette back with intel nonsense to keep the British more than happy. He played a good part in the victory at Yorktown. Certainly, his bravery knew no bounds as getting caught would have been a very nasty hanging offence at the least. This type of work called for nerves of steel and coolness under intense pressure, all alone in the enemy's camp never really knowing if his cover was secure. This type of work only suits very special people with ice cool nerves.

In the final stages of the assault of Yorktown two British Redoubts had to be taken. The French took one, the Irish took the other When the Irish overran their redoubt, they sent a signal where're here where are you? The French were still battling it out, eventually they were successful too. All American historians agree the French had the harder nut to crack. Yorktown lay open for a full-frontal assault. With the French fleet blocking them, the British knew the game was up. With no supplies or relief coming to their rescue, it was only a matter of time.

The victory at Yorktown decided the whole of the war, the fate of America and the rest of world history.

In White Plains, New York August 1778 the muster roll counts 755 black soldiers of which only 58 were free men. The rest were slaves sent by their white masters to fight in their stead and on their behalf. New Englanders sent their slaves to represent them in their thousands. Once again, these facts did not seem to make it on to celluloid version nor t.v. mini- series One quarter of the soldiers at Yorktown were black! Fact.

When the Continental army mustered for inspection in New York one quarter of that army was black/brown. The people actually mustering were black/brown in good numbers. We know the white homesteader had farms to run for their families. This is probably the cause of the numbers which crop up again and again. *

WHY WE FOUGHT

One German officer in 1777 observed "no regiment is to be seen in which there are not Negroes in abundance." * His words not mine.

These black/brown soldiers received no pay. That went to their white master on his homestead. Once the War for Independence of the white man was won, the yoke of slavery was once again put upon these patriotic soldiers' shoulders. But rest assured their white master would be proud and puffed up with their patriotic effort. **

Like the Irish the black/brown soldiers were written out and not on show in the film scenes. There is Irish blood in most Americans even in black/brown ones. Who would have ever thought that Barack Obama's distant relations were Irish? Many many American Presidents had Irish ancestry running through them. Most Americans born in America in the last 200 years were almost certainly have Irish blood in their veins a full quarter of the American population in 1776 was Irish. And Catholics were in the majority all thru the 16th century.

Yes, New Englander patriots could be very brave individually in small numbers, but they just do not make the large numbers. Most New Englanders preferred to sit on the fence after1776. Or send a black man in their stead if they felt patriotic. Many good regiments came out of New England but as a population they were staunch loyalist. The patriots were very much the minority. New England loyalists would be a more accurate description. As for the pilgrim fathers why not the pilgrim escaped slaves, or free slaves? Who made a successful life in America 100 years earlier!

Why not say here is the ground on which the first people settled in America. Yes, on this patch of Florida sand Black/Brown African Americans first made the successful attempt to live in America. In 1545. Soon black/brown African Americans can celebrate 500 years of Thanksgiving in America

and yes, they ate Florida turkey. This group was the first who were successful to form a village with people from the "old world". Africa is far older
than Europe and these Africans settled down with native Americans also
an ancient peoples thousands of years old too, they settled down together
in Florida in the early part of the 16th century, and apparently got on
quiet well in sunny Florida, thank you very much. The black/ brown free
Africans did not build stockades, they just introduced themselves and settled down with the native Americans, a hundred years before the Plymouth
pilgrims, escaping religious persecution. Well excuse me Irishmen too had
been escaping religious persecution and settled in America well before
the Famous Plymouth pilgrims ever set a foot on American soil. They
were apparently in Virginia when the pilgrims turned up and had been in
America for well over a hundred years with the Spanish and French. An
Irishman was on Christopher Columbus's ship in 1492. The first shall be
last and the last shall be first. Yes, British development of its colonies was
very successful but the French and Spanish beat them to American exploration, and settlement by 100 years!

St. Augustine was founded in 1565 with many Irish and black/brown people i.e., African Americans, long before the pilgrims set their precise ever
so gentle dainty feet or foot on American soil – fact!

Make no mistake; freedom is a hard fought and close-run thing. In the
dark days before victory seemed certain, many white folks sent their slaves
to represent them. The American army preferred the slaves because they
were usually troops who stayed around for a while and did not moan about
marching to distant pastures. For many this would be their first time to
view America, beyond their plantation work camp. The really big plantations must have been more akin to European concentration camps, as
discipline of hundreds of slaves must have entailed a large security appara-
tus. Certainly, protestant paranoia and neurosis was rife amongst some of

the plantation sect. To be honest some slaves were treated ok House slaves were the premier league of, American plantation slavery. They usually had good clothes and were the pretty ones. But the lash, abuse both verbal and physical always hung over their heads. Many ,many slaves were owned by small farmers who could afford just one or two to help run the farm. hopefully, without undue maltreatment So, for many young slaves tramping around America with George Washington and the Boys was probably a welcome diversion in some cases.

Once more see FN previous African Americans in Revolution, African Americans and the American War for Independence

** *www Black soldiers in the Revolutionary war United States Army.*

To these toughened black soldiers, it must have seemed ironic that they stayed whilst the white patriots came and went. White guys in America should remember that historical fact. Many, many white guys in their tens of thousands fled when the enterprise seemed on the brink of disaster, the black guys were going nowhere. Maybe I overstate the issue, but it evens up the historical narrative and the truth, the whole truth and nothing but the truth. Certainly, the accepted version of the American War for Independence has been crooked for far too long.

General Nathaniel Green was keeping up the New England side of things. Many, many New Englander insurgents fought well and hard, but too few to really change the course of events. The new Englander population as a whole were pretty much sit on the fencers, and outright loyalists to the auld country.

When Washington and other Generals saw the early New England militia in action Washington must have thought good God, these people are bloody useless. Send for the bloody Irish, I know that is not the chocolate box version of events but its damn near the truth. Maybe the New England militia came good later on. Washington thinks that with proper training and leadership they could become good soldiers but initially Washington thought no. For example, General Richard Montgomery to George Washington October 5th, 1775, he states privately in a letter to Washington that the new Englanders are the worst stuff imaginable for soldiers. Their regiments melt away there are very few among them in whose spirit I have any confidence. I do not see amongst them the zealous attachment to the cause. Washington replies January 1st, 1776, the account given of the behaviour of the men (i.e... New Englanders) is exactly consonant to the opinions I have formed of these people. They exhibit a lack of motivation to fight. Washington goes on to state that proof in abundance dissertations were rife and they all wanted to go home! And not one dead yet on either side! Lastly Washington states "if I have seen the new Englanders, I would most definitely not have accepted the commission of leader of the American Continental Army and no amount of persuasion could have convinced me to do otherwise". His words not mine, that needs to be remembered by the detractors.

They needed proper training and proper leadership; at the start they were a pathetic shamble. Washington feared a military disaster if things did not change drastically within their ranks. General Knox an Irishman transported the artillery, canons from Ticonderoga and Crown Point; 60 tons of cannon and armaments were hauled from Ticonderoga over mountains in snow across rivers to Boston to help with the siege. This is akin to what the

Viet Cong did at Dien Bien Phu to the western modern French army. The greatest soldiers ever fielded in battle beaten by a determined foe. This was typical Irish; I am not certain at that time the new Englanders would ever have thought to even attempt such a feat. The New Englanders were stuck in a militia mode.

The Irish were extremely heavily involved in the War for Independence on a large scale, even in New England. Governor Sharpe in a letter to Lord Baltimore states that Catholics were in a majority in Maryland, down to 1688. *See (P69 Catholic History of North America 1854).*

The Penal Colony of Virginia in 1625 had forcibly transported 1800 convicts to it (i.e., Irish patriots). Within six years 900 were dead and many were worked to death. The same was true in Barbados and Jamaica. In 1652 Cromwell's thugs were selling Irish women and probably Irish children too. In Virginia Sir William Petty mentions 6000 women and boys were mainly bound for the Caribbean. See *(P71 Catholic History of North America).*

Dr. Lingard, a very good British historian wrote correspondence to make it clear that 60,000 Irish were sold at these human markets. Anthony Borodin states 100,000. This is only for one tiny aspect time period over American Pre-Revolutionary history. Dr. Lingard is widely respected as one of England's greatest historians. He modernised historiography and insisted on the use of primary sources, on this small matter he was a revolutionary stickler

The first act of religious freedom in America was a Catholic Act in Maryland the 1649 Toleration Act. Protestant sects did not believe in religious toleration. Once in power they drew up laws to expel or disenfranchise the Catholic settlers, or all opposing protestant sects of which there were many.

True, most protestant sects were rabidly in tolerant of each other in colonial America. A sad unchristian true fact.

Freedom of conscience was a Catholic virtue in early America; it was brought to America by Catholics not Protestants. Catholics were banned from holding office in America and when the so called "glorious Revolution" happened in London England the vile sectarian religious intolerance reigned supreme in America.

Virginia slave code 1705 under just William and Mary made things worse again. Many Catholics sided with the African slaves for true freedom and dignity. Religious bigots and white racists burned down Catholic churches in America.

Church and State came together in Puritan America a bit like a Stalinesque; one party, one religion State. When the Catholics ran Maryland, Toleration was a key concept. When the Puritans arrived, they believed in a one party one religious state of religious intolerance. Religious intolerance was also a key concept to imposing slavery in America. White Anglo Saxon Protestants were superior to all and sundry. It was a short hop and skip from no Popery sectarianism and on into justifying slavery of fellow human beings. Keeping humans as slaves somehow became normal in Wasp land. Slavery being unchristian in nature never even entered these white people's heads. Protestant KKK activities mushroomed to groom adults into the racist party line. Priests in America now could be hunted down and killed. Priests who perpetually enact the Lord's last supper faced lifelong imprisonment. See *(P74 Catholic History of North America)*.

Old Nick was having a ball in all the 13 colonies running amok with religious racism intolerance and other brainwashing nonsense imported from England. All American colonies the British encouraged "no Popery" and hoped this would tie the natives to its glorious cause. When the English King and Queen brought laws out against the Catholic Old Faith; all 13 American colonies jumped on the auld sectarian bandwagon. In Georgia in 1740 banned the auld faith from living amongst them totally an unchristian act. Georgia was being turned into a white Protestant Volksland under British guidance.

All this nonsense about fellow Christians led directly to Protestant neurosis. The latent hysteria of Protestantism could be encouraged and worked upon and coaxed into manifesting itself in both 18th and 19th century England and 17th, 18[th,] and 19th century America. American masons were wholly involved in the witch's brew of white racism, sectarianism, religious elitism, and social nonsense.

Being a Catholic Rabbi in New York in 1741 was a crime punishable by death. Protestant sects along the American Eastern Seaboard became increasingly neurotic and psychotic. Hangings and burnings were seen as justice to imaginary plots running around in their heads. Much mumbo jumbo, penal laws of discrimination and plots for this and plots for that. American Protestants began to see plots everywhere and conspiracy theories, running around in their collective fevered heads. The root cause of all this nonsense was England. When the Protestants realised how they had been duped into believing nonsense, then they too began to promote religious toleration and the pursuit of happiness for white folks at least. Whenever and wherever the doctrine of superiority rears its ugly hydra head, and mankind denies his grip with common humanity as a whole; then usually some form of common madness or insanity is not to far behind in its wake. To lose one's grip on common humanity is to lose one's grip on common sanity.

President Washington after the hard-fought victory for America's independence stated to a group of American Catholics; -

> "I presume that your fellow citizens will not forget the patriotic part which you took in the accomplishment of their revolution and the establishment of their government *(P86 Catholic History of North America). Washington here is referring to the part Catholics made to American independence i.e., they won it hands down by far...*

Catholics had been systematically abused in America by Americans aping the British penal laws into the American psyche and laws. The original pioneers were Spanish explorers and French Catholic explorers, many, many decades before the so-called founding pilgrims. That is real American history, that is what actually happened and took place.

The Catholic Spanish were all over the western seaboard and southern states of America. The Spanish entered San Diego Bay in 1542. A full century before the famed Pilgrim Fathers. European Spanish explorers explored 42 of the States of America (as they would become known as). * Louisiana and Florida were heavily influenced by Spanish European colonisation.

The very first daily newspaper in America was the Pennsylvania Packet in 1771 issued by John Dunlop from Strabane Northern Ireland and it was the first to print the American Declaration of Independence. The very first person to read out the American Declaration of Independence was another Irishman, John Dixon, who read it out loud for the very first time.

Spanish Language in U.S. Wikipedia

---

to all the Americans assembled outside the window of Congress Hall. The first facsimiles of the American Declaration of Independence were made by another Irishman, John Binns in Philadelphia.

New England after the Revolution was targeted by English elite and government to separate this pro-British New England territory from the United States in 1812. This New England element and pro-British in 1812, H.M.G. hoped to coax out of the republic. New England was so British that Britain duly regarded and worked to separate New England from the United States they saw New England as fertile ground. H.M.G was always interested in ways to break up and dissolve the American union, they found their best results in New England. The New England soul and soil the British regarded as their most fertile ground with which their machinations could split up The United States. The New Englanders regarded Britain as their mother country!

At the very start of the first Congress opposition was voiced as to how the Irish were being written out of the Revolution. Certain elements wanted to ignore and rub out the heavy debt the United States owed to Ireland and its American Patriots. American freedom was won essentially by Irish Catholics in the main. (The biographer of General Reed) * This opposition was being voiced at the same time, as Roman Catholics ruled its army officer corps never mind that they dominated the American ordinary ranks *(P79 Catholic History of North America)*.

It was Irish merchants who supplied the Continental army when Protestant ones refused them aid. Which was extremely common indeed The Catholic merchants gave it and the heavily armed Protestants had to have it taken at gunpoint from them. These are the facts of the American Revolution. Protestant farmers refused to aid both Valley Forge and Morristown with food but were more than willing to supply the Red Coats who paid in acceptable English money. Washington would let the Protestant farmers fill up their wagons with goods for the British Army of occupation, and once on the road, American soldiers would confiscate the said wagons as legitimate illegal aid and sustenance to a foreign enemy. This is how they got their food. Read your good history books it's all their waiting to be discovered.

The Irish and Catholics gave amply to supply the American army in the field. Washington had to ambush the food convoys sent by Protestant farmers to feed the enemy. Out of these protestant farmers one can rule out the majority of Presbyterians, and to a lesser extent American Congregationists. The Presbyterians Irish and Congregationalist Irish can pretty much as a rule be exempted. from the protestant loyalists or people to afraid not to supply the British. Most American farmers in the north come what may; as rule would not accept American currency but would accept British money which they deemed would hold its value. Which was true. Catholics who had been persecuted by the Puritanical set in the colonies were the very people who liberated America and fought for it in massive numbers.

Lord Mountjoy no less stated to the House of Commons on April 2nd, 1784, that America was lost due to the Irish. Mountjoy went on to state: -

It was Irish valour and determination that lost us that colony." *(P159 A Hidden Phase). Marquis de Chastellux Major General of French army in America stated... Irish immigrants were fighting the battles of America by sea and land, an Irishman the instant he sets foot on American ground becomes ipso facto an American. Which is more than can be said for Americans themselves, many were in turmoil about what to do. The Irish had many scores to settle with the English and knew exactly what living under their rule as a man of the old faith would be like. De Chastellux went on "on more than one occasion Congress owed their existence and America possibly her preservation, to the fidelity and firmness of the Irish. Samuel smiles an English writer stated that it seemed as if Americans had mysteriously used the victims of Britain's cruelty in Ireland, as a means of their final punishment and humiliation on a foreign soil .p/256 Heroic.*

For Washington's and other American Generals' opinion on the New Englanders see *(P179 – 181 A Hidden Phase).*

British Captain Dugold Stuart, of Scottish Highlanders a good solid British regiment states: -

> "We come across an Irish line of the American army, their rifles were true and accurate, and a good body of our Scottish Highlanders fell in the first volley. A large tumulus ought to be in the vicinity where our dead lay buried."

He describes the Irish line in the American army as composed of American army marksmen. British Generals complain to each other that the Irish towns and settlements in America are hot beds of rebellion. See *(P200 – 201 Hidden Phase of American History).*

Not only were the Irish valued by the combat Generals but also another deadly foe was interspersed in the American Rank troops from the frontier country. Virginian historians call them the "choicest troops."

Augusta, Rock Bridge, Fincastle, Shenandoah Valley all possessed great and determined patriots who were lethal to the foe. There was just one large problem, there were not enough of them. They were highly motivated, could effectively work in a team, had a good rifle, and knew how to use it. Their hunting outdoor lifestyle made them good soldier material. Like the Irish who en masse needed no stimulus or incentive to fight. The same went for America's frontiersmen. American recruiting officers did very well in Irish townlands. American regiments are continuously finding a constant supply of good, committed recruits. General Washington once stated: -

> "Place me in Rock bridge County.........and I will get men enough to save the Revolution." (Rock Bridge County was heavily Irish and very Irish Presbyterian .in a word these guys were hotter than Hell all fired up and would march into the mouth of hell if their Minister so wished it. They were 110% all in for Independence against the Dirty British heathen swine as they saw them. They had every intention of putting proper manners on them and their hired swine)

Well, that is pretty emphatic from the man himself. The British would come to fear these frontiersmen; they appeared out of nowhere to create havoc in North and South Carolina, Georgia, Virginia, Pennsylvania. They acted like a ghost or invisible army. See *(P196 A Hidden Phase of History)*. *A little bit like the N.V.A.*

An English American or New Englander a Mr. Lodge declared that "Massachusetts was about 100~% pure English." Well, if that is the state where did all these Irish volunteers come from to man its militia? See (P320 A Hidden Phase of History). Massachusetts had 85 O'Brien's in the Revolutionary war. That is just for one Irish name. The author shows there are thousands of Irish names in Churchland's probate records; the vital records of Boston and all New England towns contain a veritable raft and Irish names come pouring out. See *(P222 A Hidden Phase of History) for examples of masses of Irish people in New England colonies. Massachusetts' Revolutionary roll has approximately 3,000 Irish names.* It was mainly the Irish and Germans in New Englander regiments after 1776. By autumn

1776 the mass of New Englanders were the most pro-British element in America with the exception of hot headed vindictive southern loyalists bitter to the core, and in some cases totally out of control. One American historian informs us: - "people of New England are singularly unmixed race. There is probably not a county in England occupied by a population of purer blood than they" (p/222 Hidden Phase)

The Irish were everywhere, even in New England; they are in its militia in good numbers, yet they cannot be expected with the frontiersmen to carry all the load of the Revolution. The average New Englander needed much training, more discipline, and a totally new attitude to sheer hardness to take whatever the weather gave them to march on half-empty stomachs, to be tired, but still operate on the switch of a whistle.

At the start of the Revolutionary war these attributes were totally lacking for the English stock at least. Maybe they had fond memories of England or really liked being part of the crown possessions; either way their start was pathetic from an American army perspective. **

It was the Irish in America that were agitating for full freedom, it was the Irish printing seditious documents i.e., in truth it was the Irish organising the military resistance.

An Irishman from Armagh distributes copies of Barre's speech in which he called the American patriots "Sons of Liberty" When an Irish vessel brought news that the Stamp Act had been repealed on February 22nd America exploded in excitement and bonfires were lit all across the land and church bells were ringing too. All of Ireland rejoiced at the "Sons of Liberty."

When the British came to realise that they could not win in America they began to offer the Continental Congress more and more concessions. Their concessions became so widespread that the Continental Congress; showed Britons good terms for a peaceful settlement to General Washington for his perusal. The Congress thought they were good terms for a settlement. Washington looked at the terms and said: ...."NO"!

We have come through too much now to turn back or not see it through. We can't accept them."

I do not know why or how Washington came to that consideration, but I would guess that glancing out from his military tent or headquarters and seeing the mighty Irishmen, half with no shoes, no uniforms and eaten away with starvation, a ragtag bunch but a very loyal one. Could he ever look them in the eyes again if he accepted a compromise – No! Most Irish would fear an English settlement.

They would fear for their own safety and the safety of their families. To the Irish this was all in or nothing. They totally distrusted any agreement with the British as they had broken every agreement ever made with the Irish population. They knew the full wrath of their anger would fall upon their shoulders and their shoulders only. Washington just could not do it to his comrades, they had been through too much suffering and sacrifice to compromise now. No! the Continental army would march on to TOTAL victory come what may heaven, hell, or high water. And on its own merits. Keep right on till the end of the road.

Independence from the British meant just that, not some watered-down New Englander compromise. Washington refused the British kind handsome paper offer. When it was unpopular to be an American patriot, the Irish flooded its ranks to overflowing. The Irish people could not care less about social standing. Unpopular or not the Irish Americans Wanted freedom from Britain in full measure.

Dr. Francis Allison from Donegal an American teacher taught three signatories of the Declaration of Independence. He did a good job; James Smith, George Read and Thomas McKean. The British population and government put the breakdown to diplomacy and military failures down to the Irish, see *(P158 – 159 A Hidden Phase)*. To a very large extent the Irish were systematically written out of the New Englander version of the great patriotic war; sectarianism, racism, anti-Catholicism, not like us, not true Englishmen. All went to systematically defraud the American public that in the true essence the American Revolution was a New Englander affair. Utter nonsense. It was a very Irish one as regards foot sloggers, grunts, leathernecks. Mr. O'Brien the author states that this written version historically writing the Irish out of the independence struggle was done deliberately! In the 19thcentury.

For how the Irish as a race were totally written out of the colonial phase of American settlement history, see *(chapter XIV Irish Immigration prior to the Revolution – A Hidden Phase P241 – 252 "vast Irish immigration to Pennsylvania" chapter XV P153-285, A Hidden Phase)*.

According to Wikipedia just 10,000 Catholics had made it to America over the first 150 years right up till the American war of Liberation. Just 10,000 what utter utter nonsense; why some years that would be just that year's annual amount. Just two words for this Historical nonsense and they are racist tripe. Well Wiki you really need to do your homework better. Half a million would be nearer to the mark, mostly Irish on a vast unreported scale and a good number of German Catholics. Too. The bloody Irish were all over every State in good numbers, all over the wild frontier too. For every ship that came from London, many, many more came from Ireland, *read chapter XIV, Irish immigration, a Hidden Phase* for a good analysis of the New Englander militia at the start of the war, see (P179-183 A Hidden Phase)

A captain in Dublin stated that 18,000 people had left Ireland for American in 1773 alone and that was January to August only. The New Englander, Brahmins, cut these dreadful uncouth Irish people out of American history. Two ships arrived about the about the same time with another 1,000 Irish immigrants. From March 1735 – 1737, 99 ships arrived from Ireland into Philadelphia alone. New England had a good trade with the Irish merchants, they sent to Ireland, Flax seed, lumber, and Iron. In return Ireland sent them passengers, Beef, Butter, and Linen (vast quantities of Irish linen was worn by Americans. It was comfortable, breathable, and much stronger than cotton Rev: Frank Reynolds reckons 11/12th of the American colonists wear Irish linen clothes'/161 *Ireland Heroic* part).

As I have stated earlier Ireland was the main trading partner with the thirteen colonies. Reverend Reynolds seems to think the whole colonial thanks giving's festival spread across the colonies as a direct result of Irelands feeding the New Englanders during the war of King Phillip. Much of New England was burnt out. Burnt down over a wide area... During the Famine most New Englanders wished to send food to Ireland to return a debt owed. Much like the Irish have done during the covid 19 pandemic to the Choctaw Indians in Southern states of America. Some snooty New Englanders refused to send aid to the Irish, during the famine holocaust. The good people of Boston chirped up straight away and stated any shortfall from any part of New England would be gladly made up by them in full.

The British elite heavily promoted the ridicule of the Irish race in America, a lot of snooty New Englanders believed this vile racist nonsense and possible still do till this day. It was as a direct result of this racist nonsense that

Irish Catholics and Presbyterians made such a pact of cold steel and determination to rid America of this vile Unchristian foolishness. Spread like muck onto the pristine green fields of New England, to contaminate their collective minds. Down into religious intolerance. One English army officer Sir, Joshua Pell stated in his diary, June 1st, 1776. Most of the rebels were Irish redemptorists and Convicts; for convicts read people who are willing to stick up against them for decent human rights for all, and redemptorists are Irish people indentured to serve as a worker for a master for a set period of time. (p/163 Ireland Heroic) Many were abused ill fed and worked like dogs. Many of these Irish young lads thought sod your indentured servitude without pay for 5, 6, or 7 years. I'm off to join the continental army. And that is exactly was masses of them did and George Washington could not be happier, nor the American congress. Their American master's personal loss was to congresses and America, s gain.

Let us be certain on one thing The Irish were determined to kick Britain and its rule out of America full stop, and that is exactly what they did and died for, over 7 hard fought years in an unpopular war. Fact!

In order to wear down the continental soldiers will to fight, the British distributed false letters pretending to be continental American soldiers complaining about how badly they were fed and clothed. And comparing that to the good care the British officers ensured their soldiers were looked after. The American officers do not care about us these letters would state. They are lying to you just look at your own raggy clothes they outfit you with. Look at how badly fed you are. Your cold, wet, hungry, and miserable because congress has abandoned you. You are all alone forgotten about in your dirty sordid encampments. At least the British look after their soldiers and keep them well fed. The British have not abandoned their soldiers, they care for them well. Congress does not care for your welfare one bit;

they only care about their own personal gain and reputations. They have abandoned you in your rags with no shoes to march in.

Such letters must have had an effect on some soldiers as their conditions were truly dreadful,

and their stomachs were truly mostly empty. Come and join your true friends who will welcome you with open arms the letters stated.

To the Irish they would know these were not their true friends and the conditions they complained and highlighted about; were the exact same conditions the British had reduced them and their families down too in Ireland. An entire country was kept in such a state, especially Irish Catholics no uncomfortableness was too good for them, no misery to extreme, no hunger too long to suffer. Half the names in the South Carolina rangers were Irish, 43% of South Carolina foot were Irish, 2nd Charleston foot 40% were Irish/ 173 *Heroic*. The Irish in the Southern regiments were usually 40%-50% some enrolments were as high as 75% Irish.

74,000 gave their birthplace as Ireland in the continental Army many do not even have a birth place recorded. This is a conservative estimate, God only knows how many Irish born in America actually enlisted to serve. Twenty-six Irish or Irish American Generals served in the continental Army of liberation. Both the French Army and Spanish army in the War for Independence had many Irish soldiers. Such was their need, numerous Catholic Irish priests had to be called for, to serve their needs in Spanish Florida alone. These priests were not brought over to administer to the Spanish their sole purpose was to administer the Catholic faith to the Irish soldiers in the Spanish army, and possibly to Irish settlers. Many Irish still only spoke the ancient Irish, a language three times older than English a language going back to 1000 B.C. If the Irish settlers or soldiers only spoke this very old language, then the Spanish might have brought Irish priests over who could carry out services for them in this very ancient language. A language two thousand years older than English. A European language that actually predates classical times. Many Irish soldiers in Service with Irish regiments of France and Spain in Irish regiments in America many may have only spoken ancient Gaelic, certainly that is the case during the American revolution. Many stated the ancient Irish language just as well spoken in the Pennsylvania line as English. Not only were the Irish in the crack regiments of Spain and France fighting the British Expeditionary force in America; but Irish citizens in the southern states along with southern patriots were making it very hostile for the British Army to operate in the southern states. From Pedee to Santee (South Carolina) the whole population is against us. British general lord Cornwallis to British General sir Henry Clinton would state (p200 Irelands heroic). Williamsburg township was described as a hot bed of rebellion... Wherever the Irish were settling down in the thirteen colonies these places would all morph into hot beds of rebellion. Even if the Irish had arrived decades earlier.

February 1729 the American weekly *Mercury of Philadelphia* wrote "Above 1,900 families had already sailed from Ireland to New England, and many more are daily sailing out from that place" The stupid idea that only 10,000 Catholics ever came to America Pre-Revolution is for the birds. Such phish dished up as truth. It is a hoax and a creation lie of criminal proportions Invented by racist ranters and ravers and people to Ashamed of the Irish to admit, they freed America ;especially Catholics, God forbid: For Wikipedia to even print such nonsense is pathetic and goes to only show how deep this anti Irish Catholic diatribe has sunk into the intellectual psyche of American wasp historians, who let us admit it have no idea what their talking about when it comes to Irish Catholic immigration in the States pre-famine. On that front they have swallowed the big Lie, hook, line, and sinker! John Rutledge from Co: Leitrim Ireland, the youngest signer of the declaration of Independence. Was a typical Irishman, He detested British rule whether in America or Ireland. Brigadier General Francis Marion of South Carolina noted that his Irish ancestry soldiers, soon spread their zeal and determination to beat the British on American soil p/200-202 Ireland Heroic... or read life of General Francis Marion p/60 by W Gilmore Simms. American General lee stated the Irish I believe will offer themselves in crowds, he seemed to think the Native Virginians would be reluctant to come forward to enlist. I do not think Washington would wholly agree, yes very many loyalists abounded in the Southern states, but they never rushed to serve the king as the British expected them to do. Indeed, the British seemed to think the war in the southern states would be a walkover It wasn't. The Shenandoah valley was like a lot of places in the south a hot bed of rebellion and the Shenandoah had a very mixed settlement. "Place me in Roxbridge county and I will get men enough to save the Revolution" So stated Washington himself. The Idea that every ship from Ulster was just discharging Presbyterians is erroneous. Catholics were being singled out for expulsion and loss of property and Land, in Ulster. Where do you think they all went to? This aspect of the Ulster Plantation in the 17th century and massive Continuous and perpetual harassment to Catholics in the 18th century. Their total loss of rights and being brought down to serfdom with no rights under British rule needs to be assimilated and incorporated into American Histography as regards Irish immigration into America pre-revolution. And the 19thcentury racially hygienic version of American Independence ditched. The facts speak volumes on this matter. Ulster in the 17th century was a catholic stronghold and had good Catholic numbers thru out the 18th century.

The landed Catholics lost out on an enormous scale in Ulster: English historian Trevelyan was another advocate of Irish ships only landing

Presbyterians. This pro-British racist history is no more accurate than Holocaust denial; again, racism abounds in that theory. Let's deny it ever happened. Washington's own adopted son after a massive survey into the War of Independence stated, "Ireland furnished 100 men to every single man furnished by any other nation".(Page 217 *Ireland's Important Heroic*) Reverend Reynolds Quotes the American official census taken on August 2 1790 just 7years after the war for independence From this census the Reverend Reynolds has the total white population of America as 3,172,000 ;... according to the census......... of that white population... 1,141,920 were Irish (yet wiki states only 10,000 Catholics ever went to America!) Anglo-saxons-841,800... Scottish, Welsh, French ....761,280 Dutch & Scandinavians.... 427,000 The idea that only 10;000 Catholics were in America is complete nonsense The British desire to rid America of it's true origins was done purely for racial prejudices of the 19thcentury. Dr: John O, Shea in his Life of General Reed Vol:1 States "The Catholics were to a man staunch and true which can be said of none of the other sects. For the Methodist Arnold{benedict} made his Protestantism a pretext to desert America" and I may add sell it down the river. Benedict Arnold thought the Catholics were too numerous. Benedict Arnold was an ultra-Protestant. He claimed that America was being overrun by dirty Catholics. Yet Wikipedia states only 10,000 Catholics ever came to America in all of its 150 years under British rule. There were probably 100,000 + Irish Catholics in the Continental army at one time or another. Minimum! Most decent Academic historians know this fact to be true. All those who actually partook in the war and all those sent over to inquire into why Britain was losing? They all insisted it was the bloody Irish every one of them! They all stated this to the British parliamentary inquiries, during the war and after it was over Everybody, everybody blamed the whole show on the Irish both Catholic and Presbyterian. The accepted Anglo-Saxon history of the

American Revolution is for the birds. It is racial tom foolery has no place in modern American history.

Some American Historians had noted that the British authority in America feared what the mix of Irish Catholics with Irish Presbyterians, would make for? Many noticed that Scottish Highlanders P.O.W.s and discontented Irish rebels were settling and mixing along the western frontier many purposely settled beyond the British Line of authority to escape their dictates. This may have been the root cause of Native Indian Complaints about to many Irish settlers. But hey, they don't exist - Wiki has it down to a mere 10,000 tops! Whatever Wiki states, the British authorities thought at the time that that mixture would auger badly indeed. They had learnt never to place the Irish with black slaves. And Scottish Highlanders mixing freely with the Irish worried them a lot. A lot! This dynamic concoction made for an extremely determined enemy on the American battlefields, all over the southern sector of operations. Only this time the highlanders didn't have battle-axes and claymores. Nor the Irish long pointy sticks with a metal spike on the end, no! this time they had guns too and a rifle that had a range of over 300 yards. This time they outgunned the "Sassenachs" and not the other way round. Once famous American sniper would drop two British senior officers in quick succession. That sniper was a young 19year old Irish sharpshooter. The British senior staff officers began to tear their epaulettes off for safety's sake. Really and honestly religion had little to do with it. It was more down to getting rid of an abuser that had abused both Christians and indeed promoted this abuse through all of its government agencies. Both Presbyterians and Catholics wanted this abusive trash off their streets, out of their communities and for them; this time to be forced out of their country! And not the other way round.

This steadfast desire cannot be overestimated when studying the dynamics of the revolutionary war. The Catholics and Presbyterians wanted rid of

British sectarianism their sectarian laws. Nearly all-American society and its denominations were divided on the nationalist cause and which side they should follow, all apart from the Catholics and Presbyterians and to a lesser extent Congregationalists. These three congregations especially the former two were 100% no quibble for complete independence, this is what was stated in British parliamentary investigations under oath, both during the Revolution and years later with the cold precision of dispassionate cool heads on reflection of the Revolution. Both American Catholics mainly Irish but a good show of Germans too and Presbyterians Irish with a good showing of their fellow Congregationalists were staunch for American Independence 100%. And they had been preaching sedition and independence from the pulpits nonstop. King George called it a religious war his damn Presbyterian war. A lot of American dissenters resented paying for the upkeep of the Anglican church and their Vicar wages. This dissenting voice would lead eventually to a pro-independence. Colonel Alexander Graydon of the Continental Army, stated in his memoirs p/122

"As to the genuine sons of Hibernia it was enough for them to know that England was the antagonist, stimulants here were wholly superfluous the only problem he states was in battle to rein them in". In honesty it was hard for ordinary American soldiers to emulate this visceral attitude to get rid of the English from off American soil. To truly understand where these American diehards came from you will need to understand their shared experiences. You will need to know what the British elite had put them thru. That is why they feared the Irish settling down with dispossessed Scottish Highlanders in the American frontier, beyond their reach. This unseen unobserved community of highly cheesed off American settlers disturbed their very restful sleep with all it could forbode. It was bad enough with the Irish mixing with the slaves never mind Scottish highlanders with a grudge and now with guns too. (p/220) in Ireland's *Heroic*....... William

Penn himself brought over many Irish. He had lived in Ireland for many years and had a large estate in County Cork. Many Irish arrived 1681/82; and 17 years later even more came over.

1729 "It looks as if Ireland is to send all her inhabitants hither for last week not less than six ships arrived and everyday two or more also arrive. *(P271 A Hidden Phase)*. The Irish were entering in their thousands each year. In 1727 1,155 arrived just in Delaware. The Irish far outstrip all other immigrants. See *(P270 A Hidden Phase)*.

Passengers Pennsylvania 1728 – 1729	
English/Welsh	267
Servants	68
Irish Passengers	5,655
Servants	230
Scottish Servants	43
Palatine Passenger	243

See page 231 *Heroic*.

In Newcastle, the government had been landed 4,800 passengers and servants, chiefly from Ireland. The Irish had been pouring into America since Cromwell dumped 25,000 to 35,000 slaves, indentured servants, "convicts" i.e., freedom fighters. 162 vessels from Ireland 1771 – 1773 landed in New York and Philadelphia from Ireland alone.

17,350 Irish passengers sailed from Ireland to America in just 1771 – 1772. Mr. O'Brien estimates that just short of 100,000 left Ireland for America in 1771, 1772 and 1773. From 1767 to 1774 32,640 Irish from Northern Ireland emigrated.

From 1766 Georgia attempted to entice the Irish to settle on its land. Many Irish came to Savannah and disappeared into the American interior.

WHY WE FOUGHT

Charleston was another port doing a good line in Irish settlers. *(P366 A Hidden Phase)*. The good city of Augusta was founded by an Irishman. The city of Atlanta was laid out by an Irishman. Dublin, Georgia is named after Dublin, Ireland. McDonough is named after an Irish American hero, same for Jasper, Georgia.

22 counties of Georgia are named after Irish American heroes. There you will find Limerick, Clare, Ennis, Killarney, Tyrone, Dublin, Blarney, Cork, Belfast, Newry, and Donegal. As well as 45 named after Irish settlers. *(P365 A Hidden Phase)*.

Not all were totally productive, but it still shows where the Irish put their roots down. 7,000 place names exist in America (1905) where the Irish people landed some are towns, cities, backwater wildernesses. 253 counties exist throughout America named after Irish people or Irish places. 25,000 acres near Queensborough Georgia were put aside for the sole use of Irish settlers. The Irish wanted to make America great for the first time. And yet American historians still peddle the big lie out of all these Irish settlers only 10,000 were Catholic! Shame on you and your powers of intellect and common sense. It's all 19th and late 18th century racist tom foolery spread by people with pointy hats and claiming that they really represent Christ on Earth.

With one wave of the magic New Englander wand "Hey Presto" all the Catholic Irish disappear. America does not belong to the Teutonic New Englanders who had to be coaxed to enlist and fight against their be-loved enemy. And in thousands of cases sent a black/ brown man to represent themselves. God knows they would have dearly loved to join up, but their farms needed tending to, animals to be fed, crops planted and harvested. Gods knows without these responsibilities they would be the first to join up. Well, Mr. New Englander writer of the unreal American Revolution.

Irish men in their hundreds of thousands all had farms and no slaves to help out all still volunteered their services why not you. Why not indeed.

In 1746 Penn wanted to recruit men for an invasion of Canada. 400 men were required and 55% of the men were actually born in Ireland itself never mind the American Irish or Irish born in America. Popular historians carry on the deceit that the Irish only came in numbers during and after the famine. About 500,000 Irish were in America in 1776-1783. Reverend Reynolds States in reality its over one million. He studied the census; he went over the data and his results speak with authority of one who has actually studied the data in depth. He could well be nearer the truth in reality, as esteemed ivy league academics getting the Irish catholic population down to 40,000 or in some cases 10,000; Gods only knows, what other trite nonsense has been successfully peddled into American history books and school texts.

At moaning times, in American New Englander history, the Irish settlers are all over the place, flooding in over running our pristine acres When complaints abound the Irish are everywhere and in good numbers, yet when praises are due not a papist is in sight nor do they exist! Funny sort of history that. Codswallop!

All those who fought against the Continental Army thought it was the Irish that gave them the toughest battles and that it was the very large Irish element in the Continental Army that was the vital ingredient to American liberation, freedom, and independence. The realities they endured in battle are at total variance to the New Englander account of the war. Esteemed American historian Phillip Thomas Tucker who wrote in 2015 his ground-breaking book "How the Irish Won the American Revolution." In Salon a preamble online magazine profile to his book Dr. Tucker states The Irish have become the forgotten players of America's struggle for independence. They made a significant contribution on a scale not fully appreciated by historians. Dr Tucker is one of Americas leading historians today He has written over 120 works of history both books and articles. And worked for the Department of Defence as a historian. He goes on in this article. "Unfortunately, what traditional historians have presented to us has been basically an inverted and severely distorted interpretation of the American Revolution from top down. He goes on to explain in this article that the hundreds of thousands (N.B Wiki not your 10,000 fig) of these Irish immigrants to America brought a with them a fierce determination for independence from Britain. "It was precisely these distinctive qualities and legacies that created the most ideal natural DIE-HARD revolutionaries in America." It was fortunate for the American Revolution that it contained and possessed a large population of settlers who were already militant agitators and rebels before they ever migrated to the New World. He continues "for more than two centuries what has been most forgotten about America's stirring creation story were the crucial and disproportionate contribution that the Irish people played in winning the American Revolution." This fierce die-hard attitude to kick the British out of America Dr. Tucker puts down to Irelands dark legacy of early subjugation by England.

He states a mythical portrayal of Americas struggle for survival has overlooked the Revolutionaries most important players. For two centuries one of the greatest mysteries of how America could take on a global superpower and win has intrigued and baffled American historians. Many explanations have been offered to explain this enduring mystery thru out the past, but none are entirely satisfactory. He asks Can a more accurate answer be found at this late date? i.e., circa2017. Well, I'd like to think this little book goes some way to addressing the mystery of how America beat the mighty British without a standing army of its own.

He calls the Irish effort for American liberty and freedom as leading the vanguard of resistance. Thru out the entire war for independence. He states the massive Irish effort has been generally unrecognised. The average Irish immigrant came to America with a deeply embedded tradition of rising up against an abusive authority. In their hearts and minds this was always a paramount virtue, they never needed to read pamphlets to become fiery revolutionaries for America's cause. They saw Americas cause as their cause far more than any other American group. The fact that America was fighting the British was good enough for them. Dr. Tucker states what has been created is a highly romanticised view of Americas creation story, that is exclusive, congratulatory, and self-aggrandising. Dr. Tucker calls the accepted version of the Revolution as mythical a made-up story, to suit an Anglo-Saxon version of events. He states the Irish were the heart and soul of Americas resistance and it was to them that made the dream of Americas Founding Fathers come true. He states the accepted version of events is an Anglo-Saxon one promoting a false narrative.

He also states the Irish and the Irish Catholics especially were systematically written out of American history, as regards these events. This was all done deliberately to promote a selfish interests, semi racial culture, and national prejudices. He goes on" generations of Americans never understood a fundamental reality that without the important contribution of the Irish… thru out the Americans Revolution tortured course a new nation conceived in liberty would have almost certainly succumbed to an early death." The Irish he says were more than willing to fight and die to create their new nation. These fundamental facts have disappeared from popular Anglo-Saxon revolutionary interpretations of the American Revolution. By far he states the Irish contribution to America's liberty was second to none. He goes on THIS INVALUABLE IRISH CONTRIBUTION TO AMERICAN SALVATION HAS BEEN FORGOTTEN TODAY BECAUSE

WHY WE FOUGHT

AMERICAS REVOLUTIONARY STORY HAS BEEN SO THROUGHLY RE-INVENTED. The Irish in America not only changed American history, but these foot sloggers consequently changed world history. These Irish Soldiers sacrificed so much to deliver the American dream, for themselves and all Americans and all those who came after them to live and settle upon its shores.

All this from an eminent American Historian as he debunks the popular history told today. See www The Irish have become the forgotten players of Americas struggle for independence. "SALON" March 17th 2020. I could not have put it better myself. When you go back and read what actually happened. Who actually did the fighting, you realise the common every-day version is for the birds. The white Anglo Saxon birds and we all know what birds do. It's simple not based in any way or form on what actually happened. But let us not waste any more time on diversions let us get back to our story of what actually happened in America at that time.

CHAPTER 8

The Bloody Irish

The battle for Long Island and New York took a decisive turn for the worst for the Continental Army when Fort Lee was lost along with a vast amount of equipment. Most assumed the war for independence was lost too. Many in their droves began to flee, desert, and give up in this crazy independence scheme which was getting nowhere and only resulting in indurated hardship and casualties. As the British pulled out of Dunkirk in WWII, so too the Continental Army retreated from Fort Lee and abandoned all its precious equipment.

The only people who stayed in good numbers were the Irish. They were not going to give up on independence from British rule. 99% of the Irish were 100% for liberty as compared to 33% of Americans in general *(P100 FN73 How the Irish won the American Revolution by Phillip Thomas Tucker)*. One American John Randolph from an elite Virginian planter family stated I have seen a white cow and heard of black swans: but an Irish opponent of American liberty. I never even saw or heard of. Same footnote a respected Episcopalian in Philadelphia calls the Presbyterians the most radical anti-king religious faith in all of America. The list goes on and on and the foot notes detail in minute observations, the vital dynamic element, the steadfast Irish, as a full community made to the hard struggle for American independence, in hard-line volunteers in the continental army when most others looked the other way, or were too scared to get involved, indeed with much rightful judgement. No one knew who would win and most expected the British to carry the day.

The New Englanders as a population, just looked on the American continental army as dirty, rough uncouth, tough tramps with guns. An absolute shower and a disgrace to America, just look at that catholic Irish dirty rabble, parading thru our streets. Historian Mr Tucker also relates the important Irish role in crossing the American Army over the Delaware. Many Irish lived near Sam Mc Conkeys ferry. The men helped the crossing whilst the women got down to tending and feeding the sick. They as a community in whatever part of the United States gave 100% effort in money, food, volunteers, and civilian backing to the American rebel insurgency. Irish townlands were always regarded, and rightfully so, as hostile enemy territory sympathetic to the American cause.

The most dangerous part for Washington was the Crossing of Delaware and already the Irish had been called into action to get across the Continental Army as quickly as possible.

British officers were struck by the large number of Irish captured in the New York campaign and very few "Americans". It was the same story in the Southern States; the British officers were once again struck by the vast amounts of Irish in their prisoners.

Irish Presbyterians were being reported all over the show. King George called the American War of Independence a holy war *(P101 FN79 IBID)* and renamed it that damned Presbyterian War. Another British officer in the Southern States called it a "Scotch Irish Presbyterian Rebellion" *(P 102 IBID, FN82, FN 83).*

Horace Walpole a famous British art historian and politician called the American Revolution in H of C nothing more than a revolution run by Presbyterian parsons and that the Irish Presbyterians were deciding America's future and that their fate was total independence see *(P102 FN83).* One observer in 1775 stated that it was the Irish Presbyterian and not the N.E. who were really running the show and were giving the revolution its energy, vitality, and stubbornness to win. *(P103 FN85).*

Thomas Sullivan saw how the American people were arming themselves in Boston and how the energy was being driven by British misrule. Thomas was a member of the British army. He switched sides in 1778 as an Irishman he saw only the justice of the American cause. If captured, he was sure to hang but he swapped sides anyway.

Admiral Richard Howes, Royal Navy, was attached to the British effort during the war for independence. His personal secretary Ambrose Serle stated that the Presbyterians were behind the whole American fiasco that Presbyterians and the Irish were a terrible combination. *(FN88 IBID).* Serle noted that the Irish and Scottish are dead set against us while the English are mostly for us …. A Captain Johann Heinen noted in 1776 "that the American Revolution was nothing more than a Scots Irish rebellion."

George Washington Parke Custis, adopted son of George Washington, after an extremely exhaustive study of the American Revolution stated upon completion of his study: -

"The shamrock should be intertwined with the laurels of the revolution". *(P108 FN91)*.

On reading about the American Revolution, one quickly concludes that without the Irish you have no revolution – without the Irish, you lose! The two are totally synonymous with each other. You cannot have a revolution without the Irish. They make up 50% of the army during good times and 90% during bad times, when all others fall away. The British knew this and so did George Washington.

British General James Murray a senior British Commander stated that Washington's only reliable men were recent immigrants from Ireland, see *(FN94)*. A British physician who traversed across both lines stated to the H of C that the Continental Army was mainly an Irish one. Another soldier – Captain Frederick McKenzie of the Royal Welch Fusiliers stated: -

> "The only sure reliable strength of the rebel army consisted particularly of (Irishmen who made up a preponderance of many regiments) – see *(106 FN97)*.

This list of eye-witness accounts, written accounts, diary entries and letters home all state that the Irish make up the preponderance of the rebel American army and that they are its backbone and the most stubborn and vigorous element in the whole of the army and able to withstand conditions that other Americans fail to take. Most if not all British Generals agreed with General Murray as to whom they were actually up against. Most simply saw the Continental Army as essentially an Irish one. This fact was well and truly perceived and understood at the time. See *(P106 FN 94 and 98)*.

Dr. John Berkenhout wrote to George Germain British Secretary of State for America that: -

"The Continental Army consisted chiefly of transported Irishmen i.e., Irish felons or people the British didn't like i.e., people with funny and dangerous attitudes, like equality, Christianity, Catholicism and Presbyterianism."

"If defeated everywhere", Washington wrote I will make my final stand at Virginia amongst the Scots Irish" *(P102 FN)*. Scots Irish is a term used by Americans for people from Ulster Ireland and not from Scotland. Too a large extent the New Englanders purloined the American revolution and created a false myth that New England was more patriotic than the Southern states, who actually carried on a guerrilla war against the British Army for years. All alone! This created a false dichotomy in the American cultural and historical psyche and divided the Urban patriotic north from the rural backward southern states. New England claimed a kind of smug sovereignty over the Independence struggle and fight. It designed and declared itself as the cockpit of the revolution; it was no such thing. If the story of the revolution were shifted towards a southern axis, one could see the civil war perhaps no ensuing. As the southern states could rightly claimed the American Revolution as a fight they won. And thus, be less likely to break up a union they themselves had created and were extremely proud of. Instead, the New Englanders claimed all the kudos, glory, and cojones. The very people who did so very little and were the staunchest pro- British loyalist element in the whole of the United States!!

Not to be finished with the United States; Britain attempted to cajole New England from the United States. They saw them as the best bet to secede from the Union So unpatriotic were they and still so pro-British. When that did not work Britain got down to sowing division in the rural south, from urban America.

WHY WE FOUGHT

General James Murray Senior British Commander regarded the Irish as fit for battle, the rest were not, see *(FN 94, 96)*. So, one should get a pretty good picture from the above of who were all there and those actually involved in the fighting. Who it was that they were up against, and they <u>all</u> replied – "The Irish"!

Washington mulled over the idea that if things got rough, he could always retreat west to the borderland frontier full of Scots Irish and full Irish. This area would have created a safe haven in which to spring from, a safe rest and recover area dominated by Irish settlers. *(P109 FN103) Kindle version. A little bit like the same roll Cambodia and Laos played in the Vietnam war. Only in the war for Independence the frontier was not another country, but according to the British elite; an area out of bounds, "beyond the pale" would be a very good Irish analogy.*

When all the others fled, Washington sent Colonel John Armstrong into Irish townlands near Philadelphia to gather up more Irish recruits. When all the New Englander's had departed as when everyone else was deserting the star-spangled banner, the Irish were rushing to its rescue some in their farm clothes! *(fact)*. Armstrong came back quickly with a hundred fresh Irish recruits on horses see *(P109 FN 108)*.

Washington loved the Irish like no other and hoped that America <u>would not forget</u> the vital part they played when all others fled. Well George, the Irish did not get to write up the story of the American Revolution as they were way too busy fighting for it!

American General Horatio Gates was advised in his advance south to go through Charlotte, Mecklenburg County, Salisbury Raison County, North Carolina i.e., to go through mainly Irish areas and to pick up fresh recruits for the cause. General Gates decided to go through Piedmont

Camden Town, South Carolina to pick up new Irish recruits there instead. All American generals used Irish townlands as reserves for quick enlistment into the cause see *(P111 FN111)*. One English officer – a top Calvary Commander described the Piedmont in the southern theatre of operations area of North Carolina as the most hostile to the British Army in the whole of North America. Woo-hoo! Go Piedmont.!

North and South Carolina especially where the Irish settled would cause many headaches for the British forces and many recruits were ready and willing to fight on short notice in achieving American freedom, ideals and the setting up of its own government see *(FN112)*. Many people in North and South Carolina were acting like flies and gnats upon a large force constantly sniping and firing from concealed places and stopping the whole British effort of occupying North and South Carolina *(FN 113, 114)*. The British remained exhausted and dilapidated by these guerrilla tactics employed by the Carolina patriots.

The main British Commander of land forces in North America, Lord Cornwall stated that Mecklenburg County was: -

"A damned hornet's nest of rebellion *(FN111)* which I am sure that will make everyone in Mecklenburg County mighty proud of themselves, even today."

If North Carolina was bad, then South Carolina was just as tough. Here a vicious asymmetrical war waged against the British military forces and their loyalist kin. This was not a pretty war, it set American against American, and many American patriots' homes were burned down by the British soldiers and loyalist militia. Reprisal followed upon reprisal. Many loyalists became quite nasty in their tactics. British officers noted their sinister side, which in some cases only made them less human. Some British officers were disturbed by the loyalist lust for vengeance.

The American revolutionaries had become American partisans under British occupation and over years they would keep up the struggle for independence and house, home and farm buildings being set alight only made this worse for the British. It did not cow the Americans as it was hoped; it only inflamed them into more resistance. North and South Carolina quickly turned into places the British Army feared and they became impossible to govern effectively. North and South Carolina and their frontier men and accomplices showed much true grit against a professional force. The British Army became bogged down in the woods and wilderness of North and South Carolina. Their pacification programs were as effective as the American armies in South Vietnam.

These patriotic partisans insisted that they would only hang their guns up when Britain had left them alone see *(FN 117, 118) and departed from America.* Man for man and pound for pound the Southern partisans of N & S Carolina were well armed, well-motivated, used better tactics and were more determined than the British redcoats to stick it out and achieve a win. They would only be drawn into battle on their own terms and eventually made life unbearable for the British Army of occupation.

One Scottish Highlander in Fort Morris, Georgia, a Colonel Lachlan McIntosh, even though surrounded on all sides by a large British Army presence, was offered the reasonable request to surrender the Fort, his reply was "come and take it" see *(FN119).* They didn't! A (little bit like the "Nuts" episode in Bastogne WW2 When the American 101st Airborne was surrounded by a large mechanized German army detachment far and away bigger than the lightly armed American paratroopers dug in around this vital town The German Commanders offered the outnumbered America good surrender terms, warm food "Hot Chow and Safety only 300 yards away. The American commander very briefly replied: - To the German commander, from the American Commander armed forces Bastogne "NUTS". It took the Germans a little time to understand that the Americans weren't asking for food but telling them "You can go to Hell" see www.army.mil The Story of NUTS reply Article *The United States Army*.

The Irish in South Carolina joined up in prodigious numbers. One elite regiment the South Carolina Rangers had more recruits born in Ireland than born in South Carolina *(FN123)*. The British may have taken Charleston, but South Carolina still remains defiant and a hotbed of republicanism. Many American soldiers were sent to British prison hulks, and many would die of starvation in them. Welcome to the Hanoi Hilton!

The British assumed that the Southern states had many loyalists which was true but the expected loyalist uprising to aid the British army never materialised and the southern patriots rose up in numbers and made a British victory impossible though they controlled the main towns and had defeated the regular contracted army in Charleston and captured a vast amount of military hardware and supplies. They may control the towns and highways but just as in Vietnam once off these highways and out in the boonies they got jumped on.

Washington noticed that the Irish were his most fervent supporters. There were enough Irish Presbyterian and Catholics and people of Scottish origins in North and South Carolina to make British effective rule impossible. All alone behind enemy lines they kept up the partisan war for years and pretty soon the British came to slowly realise that they could not contain the North nor dominate the South even if they held Savannah and Charleston.

The type of asymmetrical war in the South made a victory impossible. The British responded with house and farm burnings, and this only provoked a very toxic and inflammable brew even more to resistance.

South Carolina Santee to Pedee were staunch republican areas where the term "sons of liberty" was worn with pride on their Irish linen hunting shirts. First phrased by an Irishman Isaac Barre in the British House of Commons.

<u>6th February 1765 HOUSE of COMMONS London England</u>

Before the American Revolution broke out, the situation in America was deteriorating politically. The British wanted a heavier hand in American affairs and wanted the right to increase taxes at their discretion. During a debate on America, Irishman Isaac Barre stood up. "We are working in the dark and the less we do the better. Power and right, caution to be exercised lest the power be abused, and right subverted and two million unrepresented people mistreated and in their own opinion [made] slaves. The tax intended is odious to all your colonies, and they tremble at it."

The Rt. Hon. Charles Townsend responded: -

"And now will these Americans, children planted by our care, nourished by our indulgences… will they grudge to contribute their mite to relieve us from the heavy weight of that burden which we lie under?"

Isaac Barre (An Irishman) immediately stood up and responded: -

"They planted with your care. No!! Your oppression planted them in America, they fled from your tyranny to a then uncultivated and inhospitable country where they exposed themselves to almost all the hardships to which human nature is liable…. They met all these hardships with pleasure compared with those they suffered in their own country. From the hands of those who should have been their friend (Barre is talking about the Irish and Ireland here and not English immigrants). They nourished up by your own indulgence. (sarcasm) They grew by your neglect of them, sending persons in one department then another, sent to spy on their liberty and to misrepresent their actions and prey upon them. Men whose behaviour on many occasions has caused the blood of those "sons of liberty" to recoil with them. And believe me, remember I this day told you so; that same spirit of freedom which activated the people at first will accompany them still, but prudence forbids me to explain myself further.

The people I believe are as truly loyal as any subjects.... But people jealous of their liberties and who will vindicate them if ever they should be violated, but the subject is too delicate, I will say no more.

Here Barre, the Irish politician is warning the British House of Commons to be on its guard against abusing Americans and their rightfully hard-won freedoms of local government. "Mark this day" Barre warns. Barre had lived with the Americans and knew them well. Another Irishman Edmund Burke, a famous orator, philosopher warned the House of Commons in 1775: - as American resistance to British control was becoming armed and openly hostile.

"In this character of the Americans a love of freedom is the predominant feature which marks and distinguishes the whole...."

"Whenever they see the least attempt to wrest from them by force or struggle from them by chicane [try]. What do they think the only advantage is worth living for? This fierce spirit of liberty is stronger in the English colonies probably than in any other people on earth and this from a great variety of powerful curves." This is Edmund Burke the same man who tried

241

Warren Hastings at his impeachment which is an extremely rare form of trial under British law.

Britain decided to take no heed of Burke's warning and decided to send to America not solace or words of wisdom, but the biggest armada ever constructed in world's history at that time. *(William and Marys invasion of England in 1688 was actually a far larger military amphibious operation) This vast amphibious undertaking was meant to subdue and cower the Americans; it did neither. They would fight and defeat the massive British army in the field of battle.

After Barre's speech the Americans took up this Irishman's phrase and repeatedly called each other the "sons of liberty". All across America towns are named in this Irishman's honour. "Barre Massachusetts, Wilkes Barre City Pennsylvania, Barre in Vermont, Barre New York, Barre Wisconsin plus many streets in America named in this Irishman's honour.

By the fall 1776 a vast majority of Washington's troops had left the army and defeat seemed inevitable. Many saw the writing on the wall; even Congress deserted and must have drawn up at least an outline of what they would tolerate and consider, as they gave General Washington the Power to seek peace terms if he thought it advisable. One would presume they must have most likely informed him of the outline congress would wish to follow in such matters. General Washington wrote that the "game was up, all is lost." And indeed, it was for any sensible man.

The Irish, to a man, were hyped up to high doe. The Presbyterian ministers were preaching pure sedition. The Irish, both Catholic and Presbyterian had combined to rid America of the British and that is exactly what these total diehards intended to do forthwith. In order to understand this intense commitment, to die for this cause, by the whole Irish community one needs to take on board the centuries of British violence in Ireland and its sick Sectarian agenda, heavily promoted by them. Its special discriminatory laws, its apartheid system, and its segregationist laws of total exclusion. Its spasmodic outbursts of extreme violence against the Irish people and their communities. Its programs, of death and destruction and massive land confiscation on an industrial scale akin to the Soviet Union under Stalin. Britain's special segregationalist laws and special unchristian laws were far worse than the Nuremburg laws against the Jewish Faithful in 1930s Germany. Only these special laws lasted in Irelands case, over hundreds of years and not a few years as the Jewish community experienced. But sadly, and tragically, eventually a thorough highly organised total elimination process not just of exclusion in law but of exclusion off the face of the Earth on an enormous industrial scale was practised and implemented against our Jewish brothers and sisters, fathers and mothers, babies and kids too. A development never before seen or experienced; not in Roman or Greek times, nor Babylonian or Sumerian, neither the Dark Ages or Mogul hoards, only the extremes of the Aztec civilisation would predate such human inhuman debauched vile evil satanic activity against people of the Jewish faith, babes and children too.

The Catholics were sharpening their bayonets they had never had it so good. The Catholic Irish always fought outnumbered and surrounded and with no guns, now they had guns a plenty, now they had an army of 2,000. This, in Irish eyes was a mighty army and now they could hit the British just as hard as they hit them, when all they had were sticks with metal blades on the end. Now too, they had cannons and from an Irish perspective thing had never looked so good or pleasing. They had every intention to smash the British Redcoats into the ground.

The British Redcoats had complained about the American rebels' use of dum dum bullets at Bunker Hill. The Irish and Americans had used nails, metal balls and broken bits of metal to fire at the British. When they came up the hill the Redcoats all lined up military style and got unceremoniously shredded at 50 yards. They were shocked and cowed, they retreated. Their officers ordered another charge and this time nothing happened as they stepped over the dead and dying, now they got to within 30 yards, maybe they had scooted? They must have hoped so, as they got nearer and nearer, nothing had happened! all of a sudden, the inevitable happened when the Americans (half Irish) open up and re-shredded the Redcoats. They retreated yet again, and their officers had a hard time getting them to mount another full-frontal offence. They called in an artillery barrage from the royal navies guns to soften them up. The next time they advanced; the Americans had bugged out...

The Redcoats were shocked to find few Americans dead and their Generals now all feared a frontal attack upon well dug in Americans. These Redcoats had learned their lesson alright; the Americans were not cowed they could fight and knew many tricks too.

The true history of the American Revolution is one of an Irish story. They made up the vast part of its army and more than that, they were in it for the long haul, death or victory was their only name, no parlaying with the British.

This true history of the American Revolution and how it actually happened did not suit the New Englander who revelled in their English heritage. No! Having the Irish win the American War of Independence was not the most suitable story. No, the story that stout-hearted New Englander won the war was more Protestant to their liking and WASP, prejudices. These people hated the sight of Washington's ragtag army. No! only well-dressed and pressed uniforms for these armchair sunshine and fair-weather patriots. If blame was been attributed the Papists abounded in colonial America. The dreaded and feared papists were everywhere. But when praises were being sung and delivered to one n all "Hey-Presto" they disappeared not a papist was to be seen in revolutionary America. Only 10,000 tops! Only 10,000 ever came to America in total between 1642 and 1776. Honest ask Wiki.

See *(P124 FN145)*.

By early winter 1776 the resistance was all over across America and so too the Revolution, it was only down to a diehard army of mainly Irishmen and frontier hard liners who were still in the fight, on the field sharpening their bayonets. Nearly all to a man Irish, and some Germans too were in good reasonable numbers. To this band of Irish diehards, they were looking forward to giving it to the dirty Redcoat Army, tramping looting, burning, and molesting its way all across the state of New Jersey. See *(P124 FN146)*.

"This was a rich man's war but a poor man's fight." *(P129)*.

This branch of ragtag ill-shod dirty Irish did not fit the picture of well-dressed patriots. The truth of the story is that the armchair New England white Anglo-Saxon armchair runaway patriots were ashamed and disgusted with the Irish and the real story. They preferred soft soap and snappily dressed square jawed patriots. And they got down to writing the history from the safety of their chimney corners and hey a little poetic licence was needed and the armchair chimney corner patriots turned into Teutonic storm troopers in snazzy outfits.

Rogers Rifles an elite frontier crack American fighting unit was mainly manned by Catholics. This was just one crack frontier unit; the frontier supplied many such units. The western frontier was littered with these ad hoc hard-hitting and hunting units who used the "Indian" methods of fighting i.e., not all lined up in a nice, neat line. No, they shoot and scoot, use cover and fire and move up and back. When you think you have them licked, they hit harder again and again, they will kill you, but they make it awfully hard to get a good line on them. These frontier men used a long rifle which apparently could kill at 300 yards much further than the 50 yards the British Redcoats were used to.

One such sharpshooting American sniper was a young Irish teenager of nineteen years who used his long rifle to snipe and kill British officers. He used to climb trees and shoot at the officers only. This was a mighty powerful and effective way to defeat the Redcoats, take out their officers and they would all collapse without leadership at all.

A ghost army or invisible American Army existed in the western wilderness; the British only saw a vast empty wilderness. Where did all these frontier men come from? Many Irish and Scottish settlers had pushed on illegally into the vast wilderness. They had freedom and plenty of land, they loved it and they had every intention to hold on to this lifestyle, they had not travelled half-way around the world to be lauded it over them again by the dreaded Sassenach Redcoats. It was in many cases Irish settlers that broke into the wilderness, thus the American Red Indians complaints about them to the British. Irish settlers had no respect for arbitrary British lines drawn on American soil and indeed would have been more drawn to the wilderness as British writ did not run that far. Sweet music to them and their children for sure.

This is the real story of the American Revolution. Those who fought and those who did not and those who actually turned up.

The New Englanders have written a version of American history which bears no relation to historical reality. Some American generals were snobs who looked down upon the vast Irish contingent and some American historians still peddle those lies and write about battles to suit themselves and their own image. General Washington knew all about this nonsense from New England "patriots". The chimney corner gang.

For example *(P156 FN57 IBID)* author Philip Thomas Tucker gives an example of how Colonel Morgan's Rifles contributed vitally to the victory at Saratoga in October 1777 yet in the reports to Congress by General Gates they are snubbed and in their place the victory was all down to General Gates' superb leadership. Colonel Morgan a fine American leader of a crack unit was not even invited to the victory dinner after the battle. These rag tag army could fight alright but they just would not do for the boys' history picture books. The New Englander would write up from their cosy warm armchair with a well-dressed uniform hung up and a black slave representing them on the front whilst they got his army pay.

Homesteaders made far more contribution than New Englanders to the American Revolutionary Army. Some homestead children! turned out for battle at Yorktown. A full quarter of the American Army at Yorktown was black/brown, get over it! Seek some therapy, if need be, but get over it! Don't rub them out of the story of the real Revolution. Most volunteers were poor, ill-dressed veterans. Others were hard-headed frontiersmen who were half-starved and half-shod, they looked more like a rabble than an army, yet these rough looking men would kick the English fancy pants up their royal asses. Major James Robertson informed the British House of Commons that half of the American Army was Irish *(Chap 4 FN15 IBID)*. Yet another British Army lieutenant William Fielding wrote to the Earl of Denbigh that above half the rebel army is Irish and Scottish with the former being in preponderance. [The Scots could be Northern Irish]. As Americans call the settlers from Northern Ireland Scotch Irish *(Chap 4, FN16)*. American Generals and officers would come to relish their Irish patriots for their courage, ruthlessness, stubbornness, tenacity, and sheer resilience *(Chap 4, FN46)*.

General Clinton, the British head honcho of the whole British campaign in America regarded the Irish as his strongest proponents. Colonel Banastre Tarleton regarded the Irish settlers in South Carolina as the "most adverse of all other settlers to the British government in America *(Chap 4, FN53)*. Not to be outdone the Irish in Georgia, North Carolina, and Pennsylvania all harried the British to death and made sure this was a hot area for the British Army to operate within.

The Irish of course would have been helped by their neighbours, those strong and tough enough to get involved. Getting involved could cost you your life or your home and farm burnt down. Let us be serious, to the Irish in America this was just old tack. They had lived under such conditions for years, decades, centuries and they had emigrated all the way to America to escape this nonsense and were in no mood to take it over there. British terror tactics did not faze them one bit,100,000 Irish immigrants came to America in between 1771-1773(chap4 fn56) A massive inflow of Irish immigration started in 1770 and carried on up to 1776. An extremely large element of these Irish were indentured servants for servitude over many years. 66% of all servitude immigrants were Irish Catholics from the very start in the 18th Century. Massive amounts came after the famine in 1740-41. (See page68-70 Ireland Irishmen& Revolutionary America 1760-1820) No one truly knows how many Irish came to America many came surreptitiously and were dropped off up rivers. Many got off at minor ports. These were not passengers' ships as they were in the 1840s, they were cargo vessels primarily with passengers secondary. Many ships called into minor American ports firstly and then larger ports secondly, these ships were then classed as internal American maritime traffic and cargo. Most Catholics fleeing would have been instructed to declare themselves protestant. Many ships

Captains classed them as such as they liked the trade. Once in America Catholics were strictly banned from owning a firearm once again a vast imperative and incentive to declare protestant and get armed. Owning a gun was vital to one's survival in the wilderness, where thousands decided to live away and free of British religious and racial oppression.

Luckily for America and its independence and liberty and self-determination a vast multitude of Irish began to enter America from 1770 to 1776, They were being evicted due to excessive rents demanded for tiny plots of land allowed to them and their families. It was to this gang that upped its penal servitude and massed into the Continental Army to kick their oppressor out of the New World. It was to this lot that Britain blamed the whole show and the loss of its thirteen colonies. As one senior British observer noted; as soon as an Irishman, any Irishman steps foot upon American soil he is ipso facto – an American rebel and 100% for the cause – all in. 20 Irishmen became Generals – not bad for a despised people, looked down upon by others, even Yankee Generals at the start of the Revolution.

One third of all active chiefs of the Continental Army were Irish born or Irish Americans. New Hampshire was prevalent with not New Englander's Anglo-Saxon stock but Irish and Irish Americans. Recruiting for the Continental Army was always brisk in Irish towns and townlands.

In the summer of 1775 Continental Congress ordered the raising of several regiments from Pennsylvania and the Irish fill them up in droves. For example, one small town Bedford in New Hampshire, the Irish raised 1 Major, 1 colonel, 1 lieutenant and 68 volunteers all from one small Irish townland. These people are Irish people, many Catholics in a New Hampshire regiment, not good auld Anglo-Saxons pro-British farmers and tradesmen, they to a tee were all in for Britain and godly king George. Fact!

The area of Concord where the Revolution started had a lot of Irish in its townland. It was apparently called Concord because the Irish and German settlers were disputing the neighbourhood, others say it was named after a peace agreement with the local Indians. The Germans arrived first and the Irish later so to please all they named the town Concord (meaning good natured, cordial) as a place to settle these settlers land disputes. Because Concord had a lot of Irish around it, the arms stored there did not go to the Loyalist Americans, but stayed safe in the arms of the American patriots.

Many, townlands supposedly Dutch and English fielded an awful lot of soldier volunteers in the American Army with Irish names they are an absolute plethora in many supposedly non-Irish townlands. The Irish were all over America in good numbers right from the start and duly written out of colonial history, the Irish arms speak for themselves. Also, many muster roll calls contain a plethora of black/brown brethren. Are they representing their white masters or just being written out again in the New Englander 19th century version of the revolution? They are there on the muster rolls. Are they representing white masters? The muster rolls show large numbers.

Washington himself noted this prevalence among the New Englanders to talk up "their" victories and their supposedly patriotism. The very first Continental Congress had Congressmen openly stating that the official version of the American Revolution was rewriting it to suit the New Englander fancy pants and obliterating the Irish contribution. At the Battle of Lexington 174 Irish were present (Ancient Order Hibernian Irish role in American Independence AOH Florida State Board). At Bunker Hill half were Irish 698. A lot of the Michigan Concord Militia would have been made up of Irish Americans.

Most of the American population was neutral or loyal to England. Most American historians state that one third Loyalist, one third Patriots and one third neutral. The American War of Independence was a dirty war, a civil war, especially in the south. The British thought they could take the South with a Loyalist uprising, it never occurred. The same too in New England; many were unsure, and many New Englanders were downright hostile towards the patriots.

"These are the times that try men's souls. The summer soldier and sunshine patriot will in this crisis shrink from the service of their country but he that stands by it now deserves the love and thanks of man and woman. Tyranny like hell is not easily conquered"; Thomas Paine's opening lines to "The Crisis" dated 23rd December 1776. Many in New England became disillusioned with this dreadful war dragging on. American regiments one after the other used Irish towns to refill up their depleted ranks as the war became more unpopular and dragged on and on and on. By 1780 the war had become very unpopular, in many cases lots of decent Americans just wished it over. War weariness and horror at the sacrifices, death and destruction of towns, homes, farms and livestock, and people all went to a re-evaluation of the struggle.

The British Generals and administration stated that two thirds of America was Loyalist in the House of Commons. Certainly, this is what they thought and had bargained on. American General Lee an anti-Irish American General stated to a congressman: -

"I do not believe that many of the native Virginians i.e. [non-Irish] will offer themselves [to save the Continental Army]. The Irish, I am persuaded, will enlist in crowds. This disappointed him as it would the New Englanders. The Irish were enlisting in droves whilst the "native" good American stock were not forthcoming, such a desperate disappointment, I'm sure. I mean after all, just look at them, not one wearing a proper uniform, what an utter disgrace!

WHY WE FOUGHT

Well to this ragtag hardy non-stock hungry mob, you owe your freedom to. They would follow Washington to hell and back and never desert but keep right on till the end of the bloody road. The Continental Army to many New Englanders was an absolute disgrace to look upon.

Washington liked the Irish, their prowess, keenness, stamina and above all their will to fight on no matter what and under the most dreadful circumstances that no other humans could tolerate. He only had one vice against them and that was that he was deadly scared they might get drunk. Whatsoever, this thought was always on him. I get the Strong impression he was bloody glad when St. Patricks day was over, he always seemed to fear the worst.

At either Morristown or Valley Forge the Continental Army was in its winter quarters. Over St. Patrick's Day (March 17th) his Irish soldiers took umbrage when a German detachment made an effigy of St. Patrick or an Irishman and began to mock it. This caused a melee amongst the ranks. Washington himself rode up to set the matter out. He was informed by the angry Irish of what the Germans had done. General Washington asked the Irish contingent to point out the responsible Germans to him. They could not specify which German individually was to blame. Washington could not therefore discipline any individuals. He instructed the Germans that they were to take full measure and join in the St. Patrick's Day celebration. Next, he turned to the Irish and "you are not to get drunk"!

Whenever the Continental Army celebrated St. Patrick's Day Washington always cautioned his officers "one drink only". Like the Duke of Wellington, he was scared the Irish might get out of control. He worried about this every St. Patrick's Day even during the bloody war!

General Washington was sworn in as an Irishman. He attended full dinners with his Irish officers, at the Friendly sons of St Patrick in Philadelphia after the war was won. During the war itself Washington seemed to fear the demon drink more than the Redcoats. For New England fears that the Irish were taking over America see (Chap V FN).

At the Continental Army's first encampment in Cambridge, George Washington was shocked to see that the lowly Irish were present amongst its officers. Irishmen demanding independence in America precedented the Declaration of Independence. The "Paxton boys" Declaration and Remonstrance 1764 Lancaster West to Barton County, fair play system 1773 Pine Creek Declaration of Independence from Britain 1776.

Westmoreland Declaration Pennsylvania 1775

Mecklenburg Declaration of Independence 1775

These Declarations of Independence were all heavily driven by Irishmen and women. See (*Irish Won American Revolution P192-195 Chap V*).

Scottish American Patrick Henry summed up well the Irish and Scottish planter desire: -

"Give me liberty or give me death."

It was the Irish in America who advocated early for American independence, even before it was rubber stamped by Congress. The Irish were at the vanguard both politically and militarily. The movers and shakers of the coming revolution were holding clandestine meetings in Irish warehouse and offices. What they were talking about, was definitely not the weather. Under Masonic influence, with Irish presbyterian zeal and Irish Catholic muscle and manpower. the bloody masons might pull it off… They did!

WHY WE FOUGHT

The birth of a nation was very much an Irish mother pushing out a baby blood an all. The New Englanders worried about a "Mac ocracy" as they said and feared *(P195 Chap V)*. ... "Mac-ocracy" is a play and pun as the Irish were known as Micks or Paddy's. and "Mac ocracy" means they will run the country because they are in the majority. But eh relax neurotic New Englanders theirs only 10,000 of them officially ask Wiki.

Most patriotic Americans should go down on their knees and thank God there were hundreds of thousands of Irish Catholics in America and its down to these hard-line Irish Catholics that America won its freedom or had it won for them more accurately. The Freedoms virtues and values, they all enjoy; was bought with much Irish blood and guts. And eventually much frontier blood and American blood as they all rowed in together to kick the British out of their land. Including the Germans for some unknown reason the Germans were the only ones who could stick it with the Irish, when the going got very tough, very, very tough indeed. The Irish in massive numbers with their fellow Irish Presbyterians and their fiery ministers had every intention of kicking the British out of America come what may thru heaven hell or high water. Like Washington they would go down fighting all the way than ever give in or bow down to the British. And that is exactly what happened.

All comers were welcome, all non-Irish were watched. American patriots fought hard once they too had learnt what the heavy hand of Britain was capable of. To be honest it must have been exceptionally hard for American patriots to go from talking to fighting. The Irish all had many Grievances and had suffered much under British rule for centuries, to them it was easy to fight. For the Americans, they had no bitter memories to exercise or scores to settle. To the Irish getting the British off their land and their abusers to be ejected was pure music to their ears. Americans would pretty quickly come to learn what it was like to have farms burnt to the ground, fathers shot, young sons shot and the death of their loved ones who starved to death in British hulk prison ships. And I am sad to say in some cases much, much, worse.

To a large extent the New England Ivy League would have welcomed an accommodation with the "mother" country and their cousins across the water. The Presbyterians and Irish Catholics had had more than enough of British elitist government, misrule, ridicule, and apartheid laws.

The Irish Presbyterians regarded the British royalty and all its regalia as Egyptian Pharaonic madness and unbecoming to any committed Christian. They felt enslaved under British rule as the Israelites hold in captivity in Egypt. Indeed, the Irish had been held in captivity far longer than the Israelites in Egypt Indeed they had suffered far more persecution, extermination discrimination and torture than the Israelites ever had under the Pharoah.

They had persevered and survived and made it to America, so do not feel too bad if it took the American Army sometime to fight with tough guts, determination, and vigour.

The Irish Americans believed wealth should not be a virtue or pre-requisite to good governance. So, the egalitarian aspects of the Declaration of Independence meant an awful lot to these oppressed folks. Indeed, the American Declaration of Independence was to them equivalent to manna from heaven.

In Irish dominated Pennsylvania, this State government passed laws to abolish slavery a British institution in their eyes. The Irish radicals in America wanted the rights of man to include all Catholics and Protestants, black or white, rich, or poor and to rid America of human bondage. The

Irish wanted those things in word and deed and not just some abstract goal to be observed in the breach and not in the observance. To the Irish the Declaration of Independence was hollow without its deeds being put into practice.

The Irish Catholics and Presbyterians on the whole were pushing for independence from Britain from Delaware to New Jersey, from New Hampshire to Georgia. The Irish and Scottish were pushing America to demand freedom from Britain. The Irish and Scots had no warm feeling towards the "mother country". Unlike the New Englanders who revelled in their Anglo-Saxon heritage, the Irish and the Scots had no qualms about cutting these apron strings. To the Irish and Scots those apron strings were chains. The Irish did not suffer any conscience of what to do or loyalty to Britain, its own folks, or its institutions. Both the Scottish settlers and the Irish who dominated, they viewed Britain as a tyrannical enemy to be resisted.

The Irish made up a full quarter of the American population and not the 40,000 some wasp historians claim. The Irish were at the vanguard of the revolution both militarily and so too politically as in agitation.

When American Army revolutionaries needed to take Stony Point Fort in 1779, a vital and strategic outpost on the Hudson River. This heavily defended British outpost had to be taken at all costs to the war and revolutions success and continuance. Who did Washington pick for

this most delicate mission? He chose an Irishman "mad Anthony Wayne" according to Wiki: - "In a well-planned and executed night-time attack a highly trained and select group i.e., Irish. This professional elite wing of the Continental Army advanced quietly at night up towards the well and heavily defended rocky outcrop.

This heavily defended British fort had earlier been reconnoitred by fellow Irishman Captain Allan McLane. McLane had escorted a mother who wanted to see her son a militia man in this impregnable fortress. He was dressed as a backwoods man on his charitable effort. As the mother visited her son McLane had a good dander about the place. He noticed the cannons were naval and could not be turned easily. He noticed a gap in their field of sight. He noticed enough to crack this very tight nut. McLane presented his intelligence and plan of attack to Washington at a vital intelligence gathering meeting with General Washington. This would be a very tricky mission indeed. Washington chose his best troops; Mad Anthony Wayne and his Irish die- hards. General Wayne told Washington: -

"General if you only plan it, I'll storm hell".

Washington replied with his typical humour: -

"Perhaps General Wayne we had better try Stony Point first."

This would be a most tricky mission and only the finest and most dedicated soldiers could carry it off successfully. It would be one of the most difficult assignments of the Independence War. Washington was for a night-time attack on this granite fortress. The Irish would have to scale up the rocks in complete silence; they were led by Lieutenant George Knox an Irish American. To achieve this fantastic military feat, mad Anthony Wayne ordered his Irish troops selected for this very special mission to have no ammunition with them; so that even the chance of shooting at the British was a nonstarter. The only way they could hit back was to close up fast to them and use their bayonets. Any thoughts of shooting from the cliffs was thus ruled out.... This particular American revolutionary military action would resonate to the Fantastic American special forces, Army Ranger Assault Group, attack on Pointe du Hoc, Normandy WW2.. The

Continental volunteers had to scale the heights at Stony Point Fort, in complete silence and then swiftly despatch their guards. The elite troops scaled up the heights without a sound. Colonel Richard Butler from Dublin was also in the vanguard. "Mad Wayne" had decided upon a two-pronged attack upon the fortress.

As the Irish troops neared the top of the rocky outcrop all hell broke loose. An avalanche of shots screeched out all along the fort. The hidden Americans were lit up like a Christmas tree. Mad Wayne's battle-hardened troops reacted instinctively under very heavy cannon and musket fire the Irish as usual closed up to the British very fast. The Americans with rage and venom tore up the rocks over the castellation's against all the odds and they quickly tore into the British Redcoats. Their cannons and muskets did not intimidate this crack outfit. Mad Wayne was shot on the head himself but carried on. The British Redcoats quickly surrendered.

British General Henry Clinton thought the attack was a remarkable achievement. He had already stated that Washington's Irish troops were his best soldiers *(P246)*. This victory was a shot in the arm to the Revolutionary Army. These types of operations could not be achieved by any militia, they needed seasoned professional soldiers which was what Washington was pressing the Continental Congress to produce and support in the field.

American General Lee stated: -

"The troops rushed forward with a vigour hardly to be paralleled and with a silence which would do honour to the first veterans on earth. A spirit of death or victory animated all ranks." *(P246-247)*.

This type of commando stealthy assault would do any special forces proud. The British garrison surrendered itself, its cannons and all arms and ammunition intact.

What most Americans need to understand that it is the Presbyterian Irish and Catholic Irish who regarded this war as very personal crusade against their collective abuser at large. They had had many hardships thrust upon them and their kin for decades even centuries. They had not crossed to the far side of the world to let them lord it over them and discriminate against them, no sir! Thus, this gave them an edge that other Americans found hard to emulate until their homes or homesteads had been burnt down by Redcoats. Then it too would be personal to them also. Many Americans would come to feel British oppression, especially in the South. North and South Carolina both had many scores to settle, this guerrilla war would be most bloody and nasty indeed.

British General Clinton felt he needed to hand in his resignation, after this daring American raid upon a supposedly impregnable British fortress, it was turned down. *(P247 FN31 Chap 6) incidentally the British red coats would emulate this Irish American tactic. Successfully themselves only the British officers would insist every British commando hand in their flintlocks just to be sure.*

After Stony Point, Senior British Commanders began to think the unthinkable maybe, just maybe the bloody Americans might win. Brave and daring American attacks were becoming more common. Washington was now producing really good professional battle-hardened soldiers in the field of operations. The days of the American "pushover" were long gone. American General William Heath called the Stony Point attack "a most brilliant affair" *(P247 FN30).*

British Generals began to realise that no ultimate victory was achievable just as the Americans would in Vietnam many years later. If Washington was retreating, he usually chose an Irish regiment if one was available to cover his retreat. The first American General to die for America in battle was an Irishman, General Montgomery from Swords, Dublin; See *(FN41 – 46 Chap 6), he died late 1775.*

Many many Irish recruits were indentured servants who had been sold in auction by any purchaser and set to work straight away. They were kept alive on a cheap diet and treated cruelly and sometimes viciously whipped like slaves; see www.jstor Colonists in colonial Maryland, Richard J. Purcell. No bloody wonder all Irish indentured servants jumped at the chance to enlist in the American Army and sod their overseer.

Many Irish had been transported against their will and sold to American colonists by Cromwell. Cromwell used America as a penal colony, a history which has been left unwritten about. Between 1718-1776 H.M.G. transported 50,000 convicts to Virginia and Maryland alone! In 1750 Scottish landlords started evicting Scottish highlanders off their land. Many highlanders emigrate en masse to America. These highlanders like the bloody Irish would seek revenge on the British Army come the glorious revolution of 1776.

CHAPTER 9

Countdown To Victory

Prior to the Revolution in 1773, British journalist and parliamentarian John Wilkes was arrested for writing naughty things about British royalty, and he was repeatedly expelled from the House of Commons because he held uncomfortable views. British soldiers even killed his supporters. Once again, the Masons in America were taking note of how dissenters were being badly treated under Briton's heel. The clock was ticking down towards Rebellion, Revolution, and insurrection; like so much sand endlessly falling on towards a date with destiny.

The leading masons in the revolution were extremely broad minded when it came to religious affiliation, protestant sectarianism or puritanical tyranny were totally absent from their thoughts. Unlike a lot of the protestant sects in America they were not intolerant of other people's persuasions whether Catholic or Protestant on this issue they were thankfully broad minded from the start. They were more humanistic and thoroughly enlightened too much for religious Protestant supremacy or puritanical Protestant nonsense. An ailment many sects suffered from towards each other whether it was Presbyterians kicking out Catholics or Anglicans kicking out Presbyterians. Or Episcopalians intolerant to Quakers or

Congregationalists. The original experience for many colonies was religious intolerance towards each other especially amongst the Protestant sects towards each other. The only people to espouse religious freedom were the Catholics in Maryland. Religious toleration is the normal mode for Catholics and highly contrary to Reformation lies.

Anyway, the Masons involved in the American Revolution were way ahead of their time. Most were humanistic not interested in one's religion only ones demeaner and moral code. Washington wanted the American Congress to do right by the Catholics and repeal all English penal laws against them in the United States, whether they did or not I am not sure about {on further exploration the penal laws were sadly not fully revoked} and thus, cannot discuss this matter. But these particular Masons wanted religious freedom, humanistic rights for all, whether they could deliver on those promises remained an issue even down to today!...... No one can ignore. "We hold these truths to be self-evident, that all men are created equal, and that they are endowed by their creator with certain unalienable rights, that among these are life, liberty and the pursuit of happiness."

What an absolutely beautiful document. Very Catholic in its premises. Unfortunately, Congress was too small to pass these revolutionary ideas. "The pursuit of Happiness" what a beautiful dedication for Mankind or common humanity. All men are created equal what a totally, totally revolutionary idea. Very, Very Catholic and one worth dying for; as indeed many would on the beaches of Normandy Omaha, Bocage, Hurtgen forest," Nuts" Iwo Jima, Saipan, Tarawa, New Guinea, on the seas and in the Air, many young fellas gave their lives, so that others after them, could enjoy life to the full. These young, British, Russian, and Americans all sacrificed their lives so that those who came after them could live in a descent Christian, or humanistic society.

When Winston Churchill came to America both troops sang hymns and attended a religious ceremony, and America was not even in the war then! Before D-Day president Roosevelt had a special Christian prayer composed for the occasion. You would never see Hitler ask for special prayers to be composed for a coming battle, The allies under Churchill especially wished to save Christendom from the devil's brew of Nazism. President Roosevelt was all for Christendom, but he most earnestly wanted to save the world from the abuses of the British Empire. Americans would die for liberty and justice but not sacrifice their sons for the English Empire

Certainly, the Declaration of independence was ahead of the American people. Slavery was successfully sold into their collective minds as being okay when it totally goes against the beautiful document. It was a document the people after the revolution could not live up to or accept fully its wonderful principles. Certainly, many of the revolutionary Masons had no trouble with Catholics though many still did. And in New England they would Promote protestant supremacy. Somehow being Protestant was more American Than Being a Catholic Even though many Armchair New Englanders fled the field, and left Washington all on his own with mainly a catholic force of Irish Catholics and Presbyterians and 800 Germans. Everybody else had up and left. It was the Catholics Irish that did most of the fighting, most of the supplying with goods, it was the Catholic business community that took Government I.O.U's and Continental money. It was the Catholics that supplied most new recruits, and finally the Catholic business community in Philadelphia that bankrolled the whole revolutionary effort full stop.... Yet those that failed to turn up and were openly described by Washington and his Generals as not, up to much, on the soldier front. They then write American History a version not even fit for banana eating chimpanzees.

One has to ask who made the New Englanders the cockpit of the revolution? Apart from themselves. One could effectively argue that more patriotism was shown, by Virginians, North and South Carolinians, Pennsylvanians and possibly, Georgians. Certainly, the southern patriots carried out a war on their own without the American Army to help them or back them up. Just because the Continental Army had left them, did not mean they could not carry the struggle on. This asymmetrical warfare was extremely dangerous for those involved and their families. In many respects the southerners showed far more patriotic zeal and sheer commitment to the cause. Yet after the 19th century, somehow the New Englanders Protestant families came out on top as the very epitome of revolutionary America. Nothing could be further from the historical truth. Southerners and belittled blacks, massive Catholic and Irish commitment on all fronts, massive Irish Presbyterian military commitment and many others acts of bravery by many others, were somehow, just not as on par with the military prowess of the famed New Englanders, The all-American patriots. I'm sorry to say this but New Englander loyalists would be a far more historically accurate description of the New England population as a whole. Yes, some were patriots but the vast majority by far were Anglo-Saxon stock 100% loyalists/. Indeed, New England was by far the most predominately pro- British part of all America. A shock I know, but one that is true to history. About 20%- 30% were patriots. Some very much so but they swam in a sea full of loyalists for sure.

American frontiersmen gave many a British Redcoat an unhealthy surprise at a safe 300 yards from the battle. One famous American sniper 19-year-old, young Timothy Murphy, an Irishman. He liked to pick off British officers, easily recognised at the back in very smart distinctive uniforms. With the frontiersmen long rifle, American frontiersman, militia and the regular American Continental army snipers operated possibly the first such army tactical use of rifle development, much to the surprise and ill health, of senior British officers. Most military soldier actions took place within 60-70 yards. Thus, British Army officers were shocked to discover that the American Army could kill them at that distance. Timothy dropped General Simon Fraser and Sir Francis Clerke in quick succession. Sir Francis Clerke was General John Burgoyne's aide-de-camp. From henceforth British officers began to rip the embroidered epaulettes of their uniforms. This may well be the only time that the British Army would come up against a superior weapon, deployed by any adversary over the next one hundred years.

The Americans soon learned to aim for the British officers first as this on many occasions led directly to the British Army losing momentum in the attack or indeed gaining momentum in retreat. The British regarded an Irish detachment the Morgan Rifles as the finest in the world at that time. *(FN68, Chap 6).*

As the war dragged on and on becoming increasingly unpopular which each passing year. War fatigue set in with the American populace, the South was increasingly, especially South Carolina morphing into Germany at the end of World War two. Empty burnout farms, a countryside denuded of people animals and birds. A really eerie place to operate in The Southern hill billies, and homesteaders could take the pressure but the general American population began to become totally disinterested, and indifferent to their soldier's plight. (Yet another Vietnam Veterans analogy) This public apathy shocked General Washington and his fellow American officers, they as a cadre became ashamed of how the country treated them. See page 357- 358 "The Unknown American Revolution" By the esteemed American Revolutionary Historian Professor Nash. Here Professor Nash lays it all on the line

The American soldiers are sick of starving to death, they describe the American populace as not caring about them. One American officer a Yale graduate relates to his brother how the soldiers are insulted and neglected by Congress and his countrymen. He has become most upset and is now ashamed to call himself an American. Washington is worried sick about the state of his neglected Army. He writes to fellow Irishman Robert Morris about his troubles and chronic despair.

"It would be well for troops if like Chameleons they could live upon fresh air, or like the Bear suck their paws for sustenance" American soldiers had already taken to eating their shoes for sustenance winters earlier! The American population was indifferent to their suffering, or suffering themselves. Fathers, brothers, sons had died, many maimed. America and its Army was on the wrack with no end in sight. The New Englanders called the Rhode Island Regiment "The ragged lousy naked regiment" (see p/229 "Unknown American Revolution)

Towards the end of the war American troops were down to sharing one lousy ration between two troopers and one lousy blanket between two freezing hungry Americans soldiers. But still they refused to give in! The American Army had been in tighter spots before, and its men did not buckle under. David Ramsey the Earliest authentic voice of the Revolutionary Historians, had described succinctly the American Army in Late November 1776 as annihilated! The physical hardships the Young American Army suffered year upon dreadful year can hardly be imagined. All suffered this agony Irish, Germans, Hillbillies Frontiersmen, South Carolina troopers North Carolina Troopers, men from Virginia, Pennsylvanian and every other American colony. Beggars' belief. The Army as Trevelyan states should have collapsed, Long Ago!

As the American War of Independence dragged on more American soldiers became more professional, better trained, and led. They became more seasoned battle hardened, more tactical, more aggressive, and more determined and with more true grit, in a word the Continental army became more like the Irish, they had to be willing to fight and die for the cause. The Irish both Presbyterian and Catholic had at the start of the campaign every reason to be the above Americans. At least one third of the American population acquiesced to British rule and regarded Britain as the mother country. Another third was indifferent, they wanted the war and killing to stop. The last third were becoming deeply committed to independence and American liberties as espoused by the Declaration of independence. A document that set Irelands hearts on fire with its aims. Not only Ireland but the Whole of Europe was electrified, by this document aims, and what the new country was trying to establish on this earth. Most ordinary Europeans were rooting for America.

The story of American prisoners of war being abused, kicked, thumped, starved to death began to appear in the American press and to be reported on. Some American prisoners of war were transported across the Atlantic to Britain.

As the war dragged on and more towns were burnt down, the indifferent third started to evolve towards the patriots and the militia became more professional. The Morgan Rifles was a typical Irish outfit during the war for independence. Frontiersmen with long rifles and much antipathy towards British rule. Morgan their leader had been whipped by the British officers for giving cheek whilst in their army during the French Indian war and striking an abusive British officer he got 499 lashes and a deeply scarred back. He would describe beating the British in many battles as giving them a "damn good flogging".

British officers were extremely abusive to their men. Private Thomas McMahon received 1000 lashes for having stolen goods in his possession while his Irish wife Isabella McMahon was whipped 100 times for the same offence see *(P189 FN63 Chap 4)*.

Flogging Irish men in the British Army was two-a-penny as was hanging Irish people, young lads too. In Ireland every old Irish town or old Irish bridge would, as likely or not, have hung Irish people on or about it at some time or other in its past. Sir Walter Raleigh had a camp with its entrance towards it lined with Irish heads on poles. A nice calling card, I am sure! A little too much like the Montagnard village from *Apocalypse Now*.

This type of activity was meat and veg to the Irish it neither cowed them nor frightened them, it only made them more determined to get rid of the British war machine. From 1169 onwards. This type of satanic military show much on offer in Ireland was the main driving force behind their prowess, and military aggression in America against the dreaded Redcoats. Not much talked about in American history books of the revolution, but vital to understanding why the Irish fought so hard for so long, come what may and could keep this activity up for decades, centuries if need be! If the American Revolution was still on today, they would still be fighting, the fight would be passed down from generation to generation. Each Irish volunteer even those not born yet in America, all would know the true story of Ireland and British rule over them.

A sordid perverted twisted story of occupation, hunting down Catholic Rabbis and chopping their heads off was another English sport in Ireland as too were the public shows of satanic torture on a human body that would make Montezuma blush and was heavily practised in Ireland. The public torture shows were designed to spread fear and trepidation, they did no such thing. The British policy in Ireland of extreme torture shows was a complete failure. It always and only produced a violent backlash year upon year, decade upon decade, century upon century.

It was the sons and daughters of those tortured and hung people who made up the American Army of Liberation. The British encamped all along the American East Coast was more akin to Vietnam than Waterloo. In the southern States the British and Loyalists resorted to a campaign of terror and house burnings. The Americans (mainly Irish) responded in kind.

Irish generals littered Washington's Army; Knox, Morgan (who could have been Irish or Welsh some state he was born in Northern Ireland), Wayne, Hand, Sullivan, Lewis, Thompson, Butler, Irvine, Stewart, Maxwell in all 22 "Irish" Generals who were either born in Ireland or America to Irish parents or parentage.

June 1777 as the British advanced toward Delaware, Washington relied mainly upon Irish regiments commanded by Morgan, Sullivan, Maxwell, and Wayne to guard his rear. Whenever the British offered an opportunity Washington ordered his Irish regiments to fall upon them. Maxwell and Sullivan attacked the British flanks whilst Morgan went for the centre. The British Redcoats had no option but to reorganise and all the time the Irish kept the pressure on.

Within 12 months after the Long Island American debacle, the Continental Army could now hold its own against the battle-hardened Redcoats and Hessians. Within 12 months the American Army had come such a long way.

Now it was the turn of the British to retreat. The British had learned that the Americans were too stubborn to wear down in the north of the country. They shifted their strategic tactical position and tilted towards the southern states in which they hoped to get tremendous support from the Loyalists in the south.

Down in the south, with or without an American army and the southern-ers helped by Frontiersmen pouring in from the wilderness, the Redcoats found they could take the towns but once out in the open, just like in Vietnam, nowhere was safe. The British could hug the coast, but the elusive hardy southern patriots had no intention of giving in. There was a problem in the north, the American politicians tried to micro-manage the war there. General Stark was so annoyed with the fancy-pants politicians he resigned. The politicians had their view from the seclusion of Philadelphia or were ever they resided. Political backbiting was common and petty jealousies were arising and other nonsense from the political swamp of Continental Philadelphia. The northern politicians were dragging the war down into the quicksand of political intrigue.

General Stark returned in summer 1777 as the entire New England front was about to collapse. This time General Stark would only offer his services if he had total control of the battle area and freedom of movement and total tactical independence. This was granted, reluctantly! Stark marched off to cause much chaos amongst the British ranks and turn the tide in America's favour once again.

Irish General Stark went on to deliver Congress one of its most spectacular successes. General Stark in one day defeated two independent large contin-gents with his mainly Irish Scottish (Northern Irish) but not exclusively so. Stark had militia in his ranks, but this was well trained militia a long, long way from the Long Island debacle the previous year. These militia could now take on the British regulars. The fact that American militia could hold up its own end against British regulars boded well for the Americans but ill for the British. This was summer 1777, in autumn the Americans would smash the British at Saratoga in October. Saratoga was the Leningrad of the American Revolution; the Americans surrounded a British army with no way out and no help on the way.

The massive British army was floundering in America the easy push-over had vanished. One German General stated on his death bed that the Americans under Stark "fought more like hell-hounds than soldiers" (FN126 Chap 6).

The role of the American masons cannot be ignored. They seem to be very influential in the lead up to the revolution and in its carrying out. Masonic meetings were incredibly held in the field. Some Masons combined as officers to instruct the volunteers into the ideals of the Revolution. One American Commander waiting to be dispatched to the Grand Lodge in heaven showed the Redcoat his masonic ring. The Recoat left him alone and moved on to bayonet other American soldiers.

Washington himself was a Mason and a member of the St. Patrick's Fraternity like the pact of steel the Irish Catholics had with Irish Presbyterians. So too the small masonic outfit had to rely on Catholic Irish muscle and mass volunteers to achieve their aims in the American Revolution.

One particular American outfit known as Washington's "Immortals" or "Immortal 400" was a Masonic trained group of volunteers from Maryland. This regiment like the Spartans at Thermopylae (before Athens) this regiment held the line against the full force of the British expedition force at a New York bottleneck. They gave up their lives for a better tomorrow and not only did this regiment show tremendous raw courage and discipline, but their replacements from Maryland were just as good as the originals which is always a sure sign the training regime has got its act together. (See Washington's Immortals by Patrick K. O'Donnell). O'Donnell is most definitely not an armchair historian. He was embedded with the United States Marine Corps in Iraq as their official historian which really is going above and beyond the call of duty.

At this battle at Long Island, New York, most of those captured were Irish volunteers. This surprised the British as they expected Americans to make up the ranks. See *(P18 FN 13 and 14)*.

Ambrose Serle; Admiral Richard Howe's personal secretary was shocked by the sight of the vast numbers of Irish "in Washington's ranks in the Southern States" too.

In the South when Charleston, South Carolina was captured four years later, the British were astounded by the mainly Irish ranks of captured soldiers. See *(Chap 1, FN14)*. *How the Irish Won the American Revolution* by Phillip Thomas Tucker.

The Irish off the field of battle were voting out all Loyalist representatives. Most American patriots were not New England Anglo-Saxons; they were vastly predominantly Irish and Irish American, Germans, Scottish and English Roundheads. In the southern sector the Irish once again dominated in sheer numbers to volunteer.

According to the English the average American soldier was usually Irish, badly fed, badly clothed, badly paid, badly shod, they had in some numbers the long rifles. They had hardy frontiersmen who made ideal soldiers of all persuasions. They were mean, lean, hungry, and as hard as nails able to take great punishment in all-weather above all other strengths to see it through to victory. The British, on the other hand, were well fed, clothed, shod and supplied but morale was waning, and most could not see an ultimate victory on the horizon, like the Americans in Vietnam they were bogged down clinging to the coastline and the big cities.

The Irish volunteers knew full well that if captured they could be hung. Britain attempted to do this on a number of occasions. American Generals to a man all backed up their Irish soldiers and made the British well aware on a number of occasions that if they carried out these threats, the American Generals were more than ready to start hanging British officers.

Washington himself warned his British counterparts that he would not hesitate to string up British officers if they carried out these sentences against Irish/American soldiers. King George of England heard about these goings on and quickly instructed his military that he would hang dozens of Americans.

Washington saw the English King down and made it known he had hundreds of British P.O.W.s. and would hang dozens of British officers' man for man. King George backed down. This was a good job, because Washington was not joking, and was more than willing to carry it out in full.

No American soldiers were to be hung, born in Ireland or not, the British called the Irish people traitors. Traitors to what? - oppression, mass slaughter, mass starvation mass hangings, apartheid, deportations? The Irish were never British subjects. It was the elite British that were the traitors – traitors to Christianity if the truth be told. These so-called Christians would go on to be the biggest mass enslavers of children in all of inhumanities history. Bigger enslavers than either Rome or pharaohs Egypt

The idea that a well-dressed Anglo Saxon freed America is a pipe dream. It is American history for the birds or the chimps. You might as well state that the British Redcoats in America were beaten by the Zulus. The vast Irish element in the American army has been written out of the historical record or New Englanders approach to American historiography

The original White House was based upon the Irish Parliamentary House i.e., Leinster House, Dublin. The White House is on land given to America by an Irish Catholic and the only Catholic to sign the Declaration of Independence.

The Irish shamrock could well be intertwined alongside the olive branch clasp in the Eagle's talon. George Washington was well aware of that fact. The Irish not on their own, but by far the majority of the effort, liberated America from the Sassenachs. America was made in Ireland with much Irish blood and guts.

If you do not know the history of Ireland it is truly hard to understand how the Americans won their liberty. This has been the conundrum American Historians have been trying to undo for two centuries. Without the Irish element the American Revolution makes no sense. With it, it all fall into place nicely. The Re-Writing of the American Revolution to fit Anglo-Saxon sectarian foibles, prejudices both religious and racial. This hygienically clean 19th century Anglo-Saxon version of American history might suit racial theories so abundant in Victorian times, but it is a travesty and a concocted lie.

The British at the time all stated it was down to the pesky Irish 100%. The French considered opinion was that without the Irish you lost. Somehow this accepted historical fact got lost in the New Englander nice, sweet uniform version of American history – American history for the chimps for sure. The Irish were the first to muster and the last to leave. Most signed up for three years or the duration. There were no minute men here. More like three yearly men! To be true, some in the American Congress were fully aware how much of a debt America owed to Ireland.

On 4th October 1778, whilst the war was still raging, the American Congress addressed the people of Ireland: -

> "The misery and distress which your ill-fated country has been so frequently exposed to and has so often experienced by such a combination of rapine, treachery and violence as would have disgraced the name of government in the most arbitrary country in the world, has most sincerely affected your friends in America and has enjoyed the most serious attention in the Congress."

For a very long time America has been Ireland's only true friend in the whole wide world. It is American industries that supply Ireland with its wealth, and it is to America that Ireland looks for lasting friendship and help. It was to America, De Valera went to, while Ireland was struggling against the British, to plead and insist America help establish the Irish Nation. It is also to America that Ireland owes its freedom and for the first time in 800 years, peace in Ireland, and a blessed future. Ireland owes all this down to American influence and political fortitude and commitment, over the last one hundred years.

Benjamin Franklin went on: -

> "I have in my commission to report to you my good friends the candid concern that Congress takes in everything that relates to the happiness of Ireland."

Happiness in Ireland – what a wonderful remark, what wonderful words. America was not only looking to make and create the pursuit of happiness in America. American Congress whilst still fighting for its survival, wanted to know that the Irish were in their hearts, just as much as the vast majority of the Irish were fighting to achieve American identity and a new country.

Benjamin Franklin also warns Britain that if it does not treat Ireland well Congress, the American Congress will impose tariffs on British goods. America was sticking by Ireland as the Irish were fighting and dying for America and it goes all the way back to the bloody start of the Revolution.

On 28th July 1775 the American Congressional President, John Hancock: -{who we must remember was holding clandestine meetings in a Irish commercial premises with other high ranking American Revolutionaries before the Revolution was even declared, and I hardly think they were talking about roses} President of the American Congress states:-

In the Congresses' address to the people of Ireland: -

"That should it occasion much distress (the coming war with England) the fertile regions of America would afford you a safe asylum from poverty and in time from oppression… also, an asylum in which many thousands of your countrymen have found hospitality, peace, affluence and become united to us by all the ties of consanguinity (same blood, kith and kin) mutual interest and affection. The first "President" of America and the first Congress address the people of Ireland as "fellow subjects"."

Here at the very start of the Revolution, the American Congress is offering Irish citizens asylum from hunger and oppression to its fellow "Irish subjects". Ireland was important to the Congress; it was treated well by the Irish parliament.

Here the Congress is making it well known that they like the Irish and would wish them well and if they are in need of refuge in their fight against Britain that America would always be a refuge for them. This whilst America and its Congress was still fighting to be born, and in a bloody battle up to its knees in the blood of its own kith and kin. Yet the American Congress still found time to address the people of Ireland, actively struggling with them for America's freedom The true and real American Revolution is bound up with Irish America 100%, and to a lesser extent with Ireland and its peoples as a belligerent in these proceedings. These are historical hard facts!

When you consider how the Irish Parliament treated Benjamin Franklin giving him the full honour of a representative from another sovereign country, and the way the British lords and parliamentarians collectively abused and gang up and ridiculed, laughed and scoffed at, rebuked and scolded Benjamin Franklin in their House of Commons, no bloody wonder, the Continentals had had enough of British panto politics!

Benjamin Franklin knows full well the debt America's existence owed to Ireland. With its military effort to establish American sovereignty, how the Irish take up the main part of the struggle, either die in America or die fighting for America, was an attitude that prevailed in the hearts of all those Irish that made it alive to America.

The Congress's address to Ireland goes on: -

> "Accept our most grateful acknowledgement for your friendly disposition, you have always shown us. We know that you are not without your grievances.
>
> We hope that the patient abiding of the meek may not always be forgotten and God grant that the iniquitous schemes

of extirpating liberty from the British Empire may soon
be defeated."

Signed John Hancock "President"
Philadelphia July 28th, 1775

The young American Congress had not finished yet with its deep concerns
about Ireland.

October 2nd, 1775

The Continental Congress passes a resolution that in fighting
Britain it recognises the deep Irish sympathy for its cause and
respects Ireland's much needed friendliness towards America,
it states: -

"The Continental Congress are of the opinion that great kind-
ness and attention ought to be paid to such of that oppressed
nation as have or may come to settle in America and that it be
earnestly recommended by this Congress to the good people
of these colonies to let them have lands at cheap rate and easy
terms and that several conventions and assemblies and committees thru' out these Confederate countries afford them aid
and do every friendly office."

Here the American Congress is once again making it clear that should
things get too bad in Ireland; America will always offer them a refuge, now
and into the future. The two countries are duty bound to each other especially America with its vast expanse of land.

This is struggling American giving aid sustenance and citizenship to the
Irish people. They are more than welcome to come and live with us. This

was probably the nicest, decent-ist thing that Ireland had ever heard of for 600 years. Here was a fellow country that was offering refuge and succour to the Irish, truly a blessing at that time.

These declaration addresses by the Congress State assemblies, conventions and committees throughout the United States meant a lot to the Irish in America and those in Ireland. The Irish were all in with the Continental Congress, come what may, even to the bitter end. They would fight and die for American freedom, liberty, and the formation of a new country with forward thinking ideas, even if other Americans would not.

Irish Americans and recently arrived Irish enlisted in their droves into the Continental Army. Totally unlike any other denomination or ethnic group, the freedom loving Irish dominated the American army.

From its inception the destiny of America was in Ireland's soldiers' hands, mainly a fact! I know some will find it disappointing or hard to imagine. The two countries were intertwined. Some historians noted that the Irish shamrock deserves to be intertwined around the Eagle's olive branch. They were in this together from the start. After the two battles of Trenton and Princeton. The Irish/Americans made it safe to Morristown, on the very last day of Christmas. The new year looked somewhat rosier that it could have been expected. The American revolution had lived on into see another year, it was still alive and kicking.

Nollaig Shóna agus áth Bhliain faoi mhaise daoibh

Am a briseadh amach an fuisce agus an rum. * agus bia, te anseo l'aibe i do shiúil d'fheicfeadh Mheiriceá 1777. * {Merry Christmas and a Happy New Year. Time to break out the whiskey and rum and hot food. Here's mud in yer eye the American Revolution will see 1777} Samuel Smiles an English writer stated: "That it seemed as if the Americans had mysteriously used the victims of Britain's cruelty to Ireland; as the means of their final punishment and humiliation on a foreign soil... so true, so true.

A list of the Friendly Sons of St: Patrick

George Washington, Andrew Jackson, 3 postmaster Generals, 1 secretary of the Treasury, 2 secretaries of war, 1 secretary of the Navy, 1 attorney general, plus various American diplomats based abroad.26 American generals (not including G.W) 20 Colonels, 5 lieutenant Colonels, 6 Majors, 5 Captains. 4 Lieutenants, 1 Admiral, 3 commodores, 5 Captains, 2 army surgeons, 2 directors of the Mint, 10 Attorney Generals, 6 state Governors, 4 members of Congress, 29 Representatives, 3 District court Judges, 3 Chief Justices of the Supreme court, 5 Justices of the Supreme Court.

All FROM AN IRISH ASSOCIATION OUT IN THE OPEN, OPENLY SUPPORTING THE REVOLUTION AND WILLING TO FIGHT AND DIE FOR IT AND ITS PROCLAIMED PRINCIPLES.... this was open revolt.

The Masons were the hidden hand. The Irish, the open clenched fists. Openly showing defiance. Irish merchants were all 100% in for the American Revolution They gladly accepted its money as most Protestant merchants refused it with the great exception of presbyterian and Congregationalists'. Whether Irish or American, they too were all in. Death or Liberty three small words but meant from the heart mean massive consequences. The friendly sons of St; Patrick, and Irish Merchants in Philadelphia were instrumental in setting up the Bank of Philadelphia the bank to finance the Revolution this was another predominately Irish merchant venture......
For one small Irish association, founded just five years before the declaration of Independence that is some achievement when it had its annual

280

dinner you had all of the American military, a lot of its senior people in government, law, and civic administration. That is some achievement. A whole gamut of the friendly sons were running the young country. "Ask not what your country can do for you but ask what you can do for your country" ...... The friendly sons of St. Patrick had done their duty and achieved their open aim full unequivocal American independence They seemed to have gone into suspended animation for a time and The Hibernian Society was formed, a society more akin to Ireland and Irish America and one for a peaceful open American society. But you cannot hide the enormous historical part the Friendly sons had to support both financially militarily and leadership and pure bloody determination to see it through; no one no one comes anywhere near to achieving American Independence as much as the Irish without the massive military effort of the Irish community you have no revolution. Just New England talk and masonic machinations. Only the Irish could put into hard military achievements all their talk and blather.

When the signees of the American Declaration of Independence were placing their signatures to this important piece of legal rebellion, a hanging offence for sure. The only catholic to sign it was Charles Carroll possibly the richest man in America at that time. The White House was built on this Irish man's land and the White House is designed along the same plan as was used to build Leinster house the Irish Parliament. Indeed, the Architect was an Irishman. So, when the American President receives a bowl of Shamrock in the White House there's an awful lot of significance involved in that gesture of goodwill and kinship Going back all the way to the Declaration of Independence, and the work up to it, pamphlet printing, fighting, dying, organising feeding, supporting, and paying for the whole revolution. Many Irish businessmen went broke paying for the revolution and its half fed clothed and shod soldiers. Mostly dirt poor Irish American settlers! The real die-hard patriots, who would not give in, or surrender on the American cause and revolution come what may... "NUTS" to the British.

Those who signed; the declaration of Independence signed their lives and property away. One jolly swag joked to Mr. Carroll; they might not know you, as there are so many Carroll's about town. No sooner said, than the Irish man Mr. Carroll added next to his signature his address". "Charles Carroll of Carrollton" "Well they will know who I am and where to come looking for me". You can look up his signature with his accompanying location on google images, it is still there for all to see and witness. He used to sign his official documents even before the American Revolution was declared as "The First Citizen".

If half of the army in good times was Irish and probably well over that in bad times; if one in four volunteers was black at Yorktown; are these black people being counted as New Englanders all because the white New Englander a large landed settler had loaned them to the American army to represent him? If a quarter are black/brown, half are Irish, an incredibly good contingent of German Americans; just; actually, how many genuine Anglo-Saxon, New Englanders actually fought at Yorktown in 1781? Considering a good proportion were French Catholic how much did the New Englander Puritans actually contribute in manpower to this decisive vital battle. Oh, their slaves are there alright representing them. A lot of local black slaves probably turned out for their masters.

So how many from the Puritans in New England 5%, 10% or 15%? If the Irish and Blacks make up 75% and the German Americans had good numbers, what was left? Certainly, the French had good numbers when you take out the American Germans and the French and the local southern regiments in good numbers. Were there really any bloody actual New

Englander Puritans at this decisive battle? Any righteous historians must consider in the true light of day the historical facts, as observed by those present at the time. George Washington himself was totally flabbergasted at the New Englanders ability to blow themselves up to high dough about their non-existent bravery, bravado, and self-importance as regards battlefield wins. Many other active American generals came to the same conclusion as what Washington had. These are historical facts as on the ground at the broken bottle end of the revolutionary American war; uncomfortable facts I am sure for some, but historically accurate.

I would be surprised if there were one hundred actually born in America New Englanders, white Anglo-Saxon Protestants, at the battle of Yorktown. Sure, there are New England regiments manned by Irish Catholics, Presbyterians, Congregationalists, Germans and other groups, but white Anglo Saxon protestants were pretty much one hundred percent all for king German George, and deference to the "Mother country". As far as England was concerned America was to provide Britain with raw commodities, and in return buy British finished goods. America was to be an appendage of the British mercantile system, nothing more. Any industry which threatened British merchants were to be targeted for shutting down, just as they had systematically paupered Irish Industry every last one.

The New Englander militia were totally against being ordered away from their homesteads and businesses. God knows they complained ad nauseum about being away from their farms. They only wanted to fight for six months or a few weeks at a time. But boy oh boy could they write up a mighty fine version of how they, yes, they, had won this battle or that battle. Washington was shocked to hear about their poncey reports and lack of vigour in the fight. God knows from reading about them you got the impression they were dynamite troops. Washington's observations and it has to be said the same observations were made by many American Generals actually doing the fighting.

When New Englanders can get the dreadful dirty Irish down to 40,000 in 1776 (*Famine Fenians Freedom – Richard Brown published 2011; Population of America 1700's published by Clio 3,100,000 of which 500,000 were Irish*) and get American historians and government officials' years and decades later to accept this number, its nuts. Half a million Irish people have just been written out of American puritanical history. Joseph Stalin would have been so impressed with such revisionist rancid history of America which was totally at odds with the true facts.

One in every three houses in Savannah was Irish, actually born in Ireland, by 1860. Never mind the Irish born in America to Irish parents. The largest St. Patrick's Day parade outside of New York is in the southern State of Georgia. Both Charleston and Savannah acted as entry ports to Irish settlers arriving in their droves even early on in American History, 1729 (*See P39 F.F.F.*).

In Montserrat in the Caribbean, their biggest festival is St. Patrick's Day. All the Montserrat native women get dressed up fancy for this one day. The Irish were all over the Caribbean and South American countries and southern American colonies. Possibly more Germans came in larger numbers than Puritans from England. The Germans are another massive set of immigrants, washed down the proverbial plug hole of Anglo-Saxon Colonial America. The Irish helped liberate nearly all of the South American countries; and made good with the Caribbean brown people and married many, much to Britain's absolute horror and disdain. They were forever making sedition and rebellion with the black slaves from British oppressive slave rule. The British soon learnt not to put the Irish with the Slaves as usually a rebellion would ensue, at some time.

We must remember St. Patrick was a white slave, kidnapped and sent to Ireland to work as a slave. So, St. Patricks day is the celebration of an English slave who returned to Ireland, the land of his oppressors, to spread Christianity and the Irish took to it like salmon to water. The very first slaves to be shipped to the Caribbean were Irish slaves sold at markets.

Virginia militia and local militia volunteers alone would have outnumbered any N.E. Puritans at Yorktown. Yes, there were troops from New Hampshire, New Jersey, Massachusetts, New York, and Connecticut but what percentage of them was Irish, Scots, or German or even black, especially with regards to Rhode Island. I am not putting their efforts down but how many New Englander Puritans actually enrolled and fought over a long period needs to be put into perspective. 40,000 Irish people in America in 1776 is history for chimpanzees.

Two thirds of all medals of honour, the highest medal the United States can bestow upon a soldier have been awarded to Irishmen in America for outstanding feats of bravery, above and beyond the call of duty since 1776.

*Merry Christmas and Happy New Year, time to break out the whiskey and rum and hot

food here's mud in yer eye. The American Revolution would see 1777 agus in a dhiadh sin {and beyond}.*

CHAPTER 10

The Irish, And The Foundations Of The Continental United States Navy

No institution in America has more of an Irish pioneering spirit than the American Navy

The very first shot of the embryonic Continental American Navy; was made by Jeremiah O'Brien and his brothers when they captured two British merchant ships supplying the British crown forces. The Continental Navy was off to a grand start compliments of Irish American Patriots. The newly formed American Navy would go on to encapsulate a daring commitment to stand up against the Royal navy who presumed that the seas belonged to it. And sang songs to encapsulate that message, that Britain ruled the waves, all of them, apparently!

A Gallant Irish American: Captain Boyle in the 1812 War, single-handedly created havoc with the British Navy in the Caribbean. On his very first sortie he captured four British vessels. On his second sortie he captured 5 British vessels but unfortunately the Royal Navy recaptured all 5 again. On his third patrol he captured 20 British vessels. Up till then Boyle had patrolled near the Eastern Sea board of America's Atlantic and Caribbean coast. Next, he set sail for a patrol around the British Isles themselves.

Around Britain itself he sank or captured 18 British vessels, he even had the audacity to proclaim an absolute embargo and blockade of all British vessels operating in their home waters. "Lloyd's" coffee house listed his declaration. One must say you have to admire these Irish men's Bravado, the Dublin lads knocking hells bells out of British vessels in their home waters, and now an Irish man declaring a full blockade on all British shipping around the British Isles. That would wipe the smile of the good Lords faces. Possibly now they might treat an American Ambassador with more grace respect and hospitality, next time one visits their houses of parliament. Captains Boyle Proclamation was sincere he explicitly told all vessels to stay away from Britain, just as British Naval vessels had a total blockade on the Eastern coast of America. His last patrol of the 1812 war around the Caribbean, saw Captain Boyle take on a mighty Royal Navy cruiser H.M.S. St. Lawrence in just 15 minutes she was captured These Irish men, as we shall see and read, Dublin latichos, and young fellas certainly weren't daunted by the mighty Royal Navy or British home-waters. If Britain placed an embargo or blockade against America, they duly responded with the same hospitality in kind. If the Royal Navy patrolled aggressively off the American coast, they would return the compliment with aggressive patrolling around Britain's home waters, indeed two Irish Captains sailed into British ports to have their American Warships repaired and then sailed out again to do more damage. Now the Royal Navy never did that!

Irish Captain Johnson Blakely captured one British ship, "the Reindeer" in 19 minutes flat and would go on to capture two more British ships. Irishman Captain John Shaw captured in six months 8 French Privateers in 1798 during America's quasi-war with France.

During the American War for Independence the newly formed American Navy got off to a grand start, shoving it up to the British Navy, who thought they ruled the waves. Donegal's Gustavus Conyngham an Irish born Captain in the American Navy; escaped twice from British prisons and even had the gall to sail into a British port to have his rebel American ship refitted and repaired by the British in a British harbour! A true Irishman, with the balls and the affront to do that! The British ship builders were totally unaware that this was an American enemy vessel and not one of their own from the Royal Navy. When the ship was duly repaired Conyngham, and his crew departed in good faith to sink more ships. British ones for the record.

Conyngham captured 24 British ships, many of which were in the English Channel under the Royal Navy's very nose and in their home waters. Irishman Commodore Thomas Macdonough fighting in the American Continental Navy beat the British on Lake Champlain in the 1812 war. A war in which the British burnt down the Whitehouse in a naval raid. When the local Washington militia fled three Irish civilians defended the Whitehouse, they manned a cannon and retreated to a nearby nail factory. See below for more details. The British as per normal wanted to hang the Irish patriots the American General nearby let it be known he would not hesitate to start stringing up British P.O.W.s officers, if need be, none were hung. These threats were two a penny, all American Generals saw down these threats every last one! Irish Stubbornness' was a virtue in wartime but could be a hinderance in peace.

A Major Grogan an Irishman with 160 men and one six pounder beat off a British Commander with 700 men and a full supply of artillery! Major Grogan had been invited by his superior U.S. Commander to burn the fort down and retreat. He stated that he thought he could hold the fort and requested to stay. The American Commander left him on his own to face the British and their consequences. The British with their native Indians tried several times to dislodge this isolated stubborn Irishman and they failed on all occasions.

Thomas Macdonough was involved in a daring naval raid on Tripoli, he also was involved in the revenge of James Decatur an American naval officer who was killed when a Tripolitania ship feigned surrender only to kill Americans when they boarded it. After chasing the ship down the American Navy boarded this vessel and although outnumbered 5:1 the Americans boarding party killed its Commander and took over his vessel. Macdonough was also placed in charge of protecting New York with his small force of U.S.S. Saratoga, Eagle, Ticonderoga and Prebble. They took on a full British squadron and although outgunned, in just 4 hours Macdonough had totally defeated this British squadron. The American Congress struck a coin to celebrate this heroic victory for a new American Navy over a heavily armed global supremacist outfit with centuries of history.

John Barry from Wexford was the very first Commodore of this new vigorous attacking navy, taking on a naval superpower. All four Commanders of the Continental Navy were Irish. The New American Continental Navy captured a massive 1551 British ships.

After a terrific fight and sea battle valiant& victorious, American Captain John Paul Jones, watches his own ship sink beneath the waves from the captured British vessel H.M.S Serapis.in British home waters North Sea 1779

Hang em High

As previously stated, the British attack on the Whitehouse was personally defended by a Mr. J. O'Neal and two others who faced down a British force of 400, the local militia had abandoned the area. O'Neal and the other two operated a small American battery for a while; they then retreated to a nail factory and carried on the fight from there. British Marines finally captured O'Neal. They wanted to hang him as a traitor, he was Irish. American General Miller, like George Washington faced down this threat with gusto. He let it be known to the British that if they hung O'Neal, he would immediately execute two British P.O.W's in retaliation. King George of England let it be known that any American soldiers born in Ireland would be hung. On all occasions every American General, and Captain stood up to the mighty British with regards to American patriots born in Ireland. Everyone on every occasion bar none, let their enemy know in no uncertain terms hangings of Irish people would directly and immediately result in British service men swinging from the rope, officers too.! The Irish pledged allegiance to America and its fight for basic human rights and freedoms; and not to their oppressor or torturer, which got right up the English elite's royal noses. They seemed to think that they could systematically abuse kill, murder, ethnically cleanse Irelands population, repeatedly over centuries bring in a racist regime with social and economic strict apartheid laws. Treat the Irish like filth and that Ireland and its peoples owed them allegiance what total depraved way to think! Bonkers! "Nuts" to that arrogance.

President James Madison like Washington before him would not be intimidated by such threats. King George wanted to keep Americans anxious and harassed; the British King was determined to never acknowledge American independence. Madison let it be known that any hanging would be reciprocated.........King George backed down.

The 1812 war ended when Andrew Jackson who had been mutilated in his own home as a child (he was staying at a friend's house actually for the finicky) by a British officer. In the war of Independence when the young Jackson refused to clean his boots the officer lashed out with his sword at young Andrew for his cheek and insolence, scaring the young lad's face and slashing his hand. Next the officer moved on to Jacksons brother and told him to clean his boots. He too refused this demand; Jackson's brother was heavily attacked by this obnoxious rogue in a uniform with his sword. Jackson's brother would die from his wounds. The two young brothers were locked up in a prison hulk and both young fellas nearly starved to death.

Andrew's brother died as too did his mother who was exposed to bad weather and constantly visiting the young lads. His brother died on his way home in terrible weather, his mother died shortly afterwards. Andrew Jackson never forgave or forgot what happened. Years later the young Jackson had matured into a dedicated American General. Jackson got his revenge when a large British Army attempted to take New Orleans. Jackson and his Militia were well dug in. Jackson intended to well and truly revenge his brothers and his mother's premature death. Jackson let the British task force advance upon his position; an entire British taskforce was systematically wiped out by a force of militia led by Andrew Jackson who totally annihilated it. The British dead lay everywhere, it is estimated up to 2,000 British soldiers were dead, never mind the wounded. The American militia lost just 7 men! {some documentary makers say 70 plus}

"In 1775 before the United States had come into existence, before her star had lighted her to glory or her stripes had been felt by her foes; before the voice of independence had even been heard on her mountains or the shouts of victory had echoed through her valleys; her statesmen and patriots assembled at their seats of government in their future hall of independence and by a public address made known to the world, her grateful and affectionate sympathy and respect for the parliament and the people of Ireland, kindly inviting her people to come and inhabit the fertile regions of America. Alderman Binns on hearing of the Irish Famine (P138 A history of Irish Settlers in N. America, Thomas Darcy McGee published 1852).

Well they heard the call and came to America. Those Irish already there filled up the ranks and offices of its new Continental Army and Navy. Many thousands accepted the invitation and by their toil and their suffering the sweat and their blood assisted to make great glorious and free America, the United States of America."

There can be no doubt the American Congress knew from the start the Pivotal role Irish men and women and families would play in the coming struggle. They knew the Irish would fill the ranks of its new American Army. They knew Irish people, politicians, and businesses back home in Ireland would support the American Revolution in any way they could. They would not know, nor could they, of the enormous and gallant and brave show the Irish lads would display when they began to sink British ships in their hundreds around the British Isles and English Channel right under their very noses. This was all done by Irish men who had never been in America. Benjamin Franklin oversaw the whole operation by Irish men, manning captured British boats, and now flying the American stars and stripes. And going out to sink and take on the British Royal Navy. No one asked them to do this, nor was there a recruiting depot they could go to, to enlist. They just saw America's struggle for freedom as an Irish one. Without Irish gallantry and military bravado, commitment to the long military struggle ahead, without that, the Revolution was a nonstarter. Without the Irish there was no American Revolution. The British crown forces knew this; and made strenuous efforts to stifle commitment. They failed to stop the Revolution. They failed to dislodge Irish commitment to the cause of American freedoms for all. All British commanders stated at the times and years later, that America would still be ours if it were not fore massive Irish commitment to free America from British Despotism or as they would say enlightened rule. The very names American Revolution, American war for Independence, these very titles could easily have, historically the monikers Irish-American Revolution or Irish-American war of Independence, because let's be truthful that is exactly how they were perceived at the time by those involved.

During the Irish Famine, the American Navy, flying the stars and stripes came to feed Ireland's children and its starving millions. To do what the English crown refused to do. Washington knew the Irish had delivered American freedom and independence; Washington's adopted son George Washington Parke Custis stated about the Irish: -

> "Washington loved them for they were the companions of his
> toils, his perils, his glories in the deliverance of his country.
> (FNH Chap 1 How the Irish won the American Revolution).

The Baltimore Irish and Scottish (Northern Irish) to a man were hell bent on sedition, the whole lot are fanatics. (P72 H 1 War) In Order to Understand that Irish fanaticism, one needs to be aware what Britain had systematically put them thru for centuries. On hearing that Americans wanted freedom from Britain, that automatically made every granny, grandad uncle, sister, brother, father, mother child all in all the way for life, until the hard struggle was won. Come what may. Full stop! And those yet to be born would carry on the struggle. And any Irish person not all in would be regarded as pure dirt *and filth and totally ostracised. That was how wars were fought in Ireland for centuries, against the sassenachs.*

Baltimore became the place appropriately where the national anthem was born and Baltimore was also the place the Continental Congress retreated to in winter, 12th December 1776.

After the war for independence, the Irish were well represented in Presidents and on the economic front Irish labour substantially helped to build up America.

Joseph Galloway to the House of Commons committee stated with regards to America: -

> "The Irish fiercely independent in the manner and action and that they are in a continuous state of agitation and independence in Pennsylvania and Maryland."

He describes the Irish as being responsible for refusing the Stamp Act. He refers to them as dangerous people with regards to American Independence. See *(P98 A Hidden Phase of American History).*

Michael Joseph O'Brien the author of A Hidden Phase of American History makes the case that it was the Irish that agitated on the ground in support of independence and not the New Englanders, see *(P 74 – 97 Chapter VI, Ireland's Share in America's Fight for Freedom).*

Ambrose Serle, private secretary to Lord Dartmouth in a strictly confidential assignment. Was sent to America at the behest of the British cabinet no less, to personally review the situation with his own eyes and report back personally to the British cabinet with his strictly private findings answering directly to the British cabinet only. Serle was a stickler for first-hand accounts. He was quite rightly regarded as "the" authority on America. Serle followed the British army all over America. He states: - *(P107 A Hidden Phase of American History)*

> "Great numbers of emigrants, particularly Irish are in the rebel army. Irish political prisoners' "felons" abound its ranks

> (Irish felons were people who wanted Irish independence from Britain. Britain always criminalised those who stood up against their abuse in Ireland).

> Believe it or not during the enormous Irish famine in the mid-19th century Britain made it a crime to say disparaging comments about their Queen as millions starved to death, children and babies too! That was British rule in Ireland, completely crackers.

> Incidentally Queen Victoria comes out on the Righteous side of that sick, wicked and perverse mass starvation programme. So too does her relation Lord Bentinck. Not one person would have starved to death in Ireland if that man had his way. The Irish Embassy in London should lay a wreath of thanks at that man's statue in London, Every Christmas. He was a giant for Ireland. So, too Lionel & Myer Rothschild, and the city bankers of London. They too make it onto the Righteous list, as do the fabulous Quakers. Millions upon millions of Irish people are alive today, due to Quaker perseverance and determination not to cross on the other side of the road, as everyone else did, when others looked on smugly, derided their efforts and chastised them for doing Jesus's work. Eternal Shame on you.

And let us not forget the proud and honourable part Britain and all its people played in saving the world from final damnation. The Nazi horde. The enslavers of whole societies what a dark dreadful era. An era and civilization nice on the outside but full of the dead and decaying on the inside. The heavy stench of rotting flesh was always in the air to those who wished to smell its essence. Like the Devil himself Hitler offered the British a very tempting offer. Bow down and accept me, and the world is ours to rule over A very tempting offer, especially when your down on your knees. All alone... Britain told the monster to get stuffed, and a righteous battle ensued, between the forces of Darkness and Evil, and those of common decency for all. Common decency won out. But just look at all the harm we inflict on each other today Our shared world isn't perfect, but it is shared, people still suffer and the fight of the righteous goes on, into another generation. But alas as they say, these revelations are for another book and another time and place, another story. Back to Mr. Serle and his acute first-hand observations.

Serle wanted the transportation of these Irish "criminals" partisans' rebels really, stopped. He stated "England must stop this transportation as it only goes to make American arms stronger, here they enlist freely"."

Another British observer Joshua Pell, British army officer wrote in his personal diary on 1st June 1776: -

"The rebels consist chiefly of Irish redemptioners (indentured servants) and convicts i.e. (Catholics). Most of those prisoner's taken in battle are Irish. *(108 A Hidden Phase of American History)."*

George Washington was a member of the friendly Sons of St. Patrick. St. Patrick was the watchword for sentries at the siege of Boston. The British government put the loss of America down to the Irish per se. America WAS made in Ireland.

American agents in France equipped many ships with Irish volunteer sailors to raid British home waters and set the English home waters ablaze. Dunkirk was full of Irish seamen, each one with a plan to attack the English ships. No one asked these Irish people to become American privateers i.e., pirates They heard America was at war with England and that made it an Irish fight. They simply got boats struck up the stars and stripes and started to attack the British navy and sink its merchant fleet on behalf of America.

One Irishman sailing for American liberty captured 120 British ships in just 18 months – that Captain was Patrick Dalvin. All Irish and Americans were sworn in as American subjects of the American Navy. To the Irish born this was a mighty gamble as if captured they could be hung or even tortured to death. Many P.O.W's were kept in dreadful conditions, and many starved to death under British tutelage. Many were kept in chains for weeks aboard the British vessels some were handcuffed. *(P70 A Hidden Phase of American History).* No matter the gruesome ending or the threat of hanging if captured, the Irish born still volunteered in droves to join the American navy – no matter what the awful consequences. Better to die fighting for America and against tyranny and cruelty and famine than live as a slave under British rule at home.

Another Irishman had a very fast cutter built for himself in Boulogne with the intention of doing much damage to British shipping. He hoped

Benjamin Franklin would grant his request to help the Continental navy and be sworn into the American Continental navy. The vessel was named the "Fear Not". Whilst waiting for official word from Benjamin Franklin that he could fly the stars n stripes, the French navy offered, to immediately take him on board and allow him to fly the French naval flag as one of their navy, but the Irishman thought he should stick it out for the American flag as he saw that was more his fight than a French flag. Eventually the "Fear Not" was accepted into the American navy to wreak havoc in British home waters and bring the fight to their doorstep. To see how they liked that!

These Irish captains and crew had every intention to make the British pay for insulting Benjamin Franklin; the British would not be clapping now or jeering and laughing at Americans when their ships were at the bottom of the sea.

When British naval ships entered Ireland with American prisoners of war. With a lot of the American P.O.Ws chained down below. The Irish would insist on feeding the starving Americans and buying them new clothes. Many were in a bad shape and semi-naked in strict confinement. Horace Walpole English writer wrote "all Ireland is America mad" June 1776. The Irish burned down a Cork factory because it sold clothing and footwear to the British army in America. *(P66 A Hidden Phase of American History)*. Arthur Young on his tour of Ireland says…. "A large manufacturing for army clothing and shoes at Cork 1773, it was burned down by a mob. *(P64 A Hidden Phase of American History). This predates open hostilities, but it goes to show even before the war started that the Irish population would fight British organised abuse in America. If they were openly doing this before hostilities started god only knows what they did during the war that has been censored out.*

The Irish were boycotting buying British goods in support of the American rebels. The Irish were also selling gunpowder to the American rebels by a very circuitous route (*P64 AHP*) also firearms from Dublin were sent to America (*P66*). Irish sympathisers with America were attacking and burning down wagons on Irish roads with stores for British vessels bound for America. When the Revolutionary war broke out, many skilled Irish fishermen and boat builders some very wealthy indeed seeing as they were not wanted in Ireland under British rule jumped at the chance to hit the British back. Most ships into colonial America were Irish ones these Irish Captains made good Privateers. They re-flagged their ships with the stars and stripes and set sail into the well-known Atlantic to sink and destroy British ships whether commercial or naval. Lots of Irish men set to work destroying British ships. One Irish man Was Captain of a vessel named the "Gamecock" his name was Capt. Nathaniel Tracy, his father was from Wexford, Tracey was born in America, The Gamecock had the honour of being the first American Privateer, i.e., a private vessel kitted out with arms that sailed under an American flag. Tracy got down to work straight away. Tracy oversaw a massive commercial fleet of 110 vessels all of which he put at the disposal of the American Navy. Twenty of his vessels were massive cruisers with 298 gunners between them and with a compliment of 1618 crew. With this unofficial American navy, he captured 120 British vessels worth $3,950,000 he also captured 2,225 British P.O.W.s. The founding Father of the American Navy was an Irish man called John Barry, from Wexford. His duty was to get the American navy up and running and sinking British ships. Which he duly did.

The fact that the Americans should turn to an Irish man should come as no surprise to those who have learnt the true history of the American Revolution and not the New England Anglo-Saxon version, Ireland was the main provider of the 13 colonies as such its sea captains knew the

American waters very well. Yet another daring Irish man Capt. Hugh Hill of Carrickfergus. He sailed his American flagged ship right under the Royal navy's noses. He ploughed Irish waters sinking British vessels as other Irish lads would do to tremendous effect to the Revolution and tremendous damage to British interests, reputation, and commercial acumen. Capt. Hugh Hill was a wanted man by the Royal Navy which, far from ruling the seas, was in desperate straits with Irish Ships under American flags knocking ten bells out of them. Capt. Hill ship was boarded by a royal Navy vessel His ship was flying an English ensign to throw them off his scent. He was informed by the Royal Navy Capt. That he was desperate to track down the Notorious Capt. Hugh Hill. Hill cheekily replied that he too was on the lookout for the same individual and hoped to meet him soon! Days later the Irish saw the same British royal Navy vessel, this time the British ensign came down and the stars and stripes were hoisted. Battle ensued with the result that the British Capt. Did indeed catch up with Mr. Notorious Hugh Hill as a Prisoner. His ship became a prize booty!

Reading about early colonial America one is staggered to see how many wealthy Irish Catholics lived there quietly. p/75-85 "Irelands Important and Heroic part in American Independence" Edward O'Brian built 39 ships in his own docks in America. Many American states early on in the colonial period set much land aside for the exclusive use of Irish Farmers. Whom they hoped to entice over.

In 1780 Britain allowed trade to flow freely to Americans from Ireland, large amounts of gunpowder were exported secretly. It was the Irish that did most of the trade with the English colonies in America and not British ships out of London or Bristol. In 1676 the New Englanders were starving to death. The British government refused to send any aid to the starving Americans in Massachusetts, the New England colony was devastated with an Indian war. Many homesteads had been burned down and whole towns were burnt and deserted, the New Englanders were in a very bad way.

New York refused to send them aid. The Massachusetts colony had been overrun by Indians on the warpath; the colony was a shambolic mess. Ireland had heard of their dire straits and sent aid immediately. *

Even today the Irish still donated money to Choctaw, Navajo and Hopi nations during the pandemic. *(www.Irish people donate €2.5 million. www. homenews An Ocean Apart Irish donate $670,000 to Navajo and Hopi. See Irish donation 1676 wiki, or Irish Donation 1676 en linkfang.org).*

Rhode Island was in ruins and half of New England's towns had been attacked. England gave them no succour; only Irish people came to their desperate aid. In 1847, 200 years later the Massachusetts people donated two fully laden ships with aid for Ireland. Ireland had sent them one fully laden with food stores in 1676. The know nothings, New English elite canvassed for no aid to be given to the Irish! See *(en linkfang.org. www Irish donation of 1676)*. When snooty New Englander's refused to send aid to Ireland's starving people, the good people of Boston took up their slack stating that any money short from the New England element would be gladly made good by the good people of Boston.

The chained up American sailors during the war of liberation knew about the Irish donation and aid to the New England colonies in 1676 they wrote about it in their thank you letters to the Irish who insisted they come aboard to feed the American P.O.W.s. When the Irish got down into the bowels of the Royal Navy vessel, they were shocked to see the desperate state of the half-starved, half-naked chained up American P.O.W.'s, the Irish party were disgusted. They quickly supplied every American P.O.W. with food and new clothes. These American P.O.W.'s were lucky they landed in Ireland and not in Britain see *(P70-71 A Hidden Phase of American History)*. The English captain was away whilst all this was going on. When he returned, he was shocked to see Irish "rebels" feeding, even feasting American rebels. He soon put a stop to it. Whilst this was going on a small boat arrived and came to halt next to the British warship. When the captain asked what their business was, they stated that Dublin men had supplied them with food for the American P.O.W.'s, he soon chased them away.

When a British ship pulled into Madeira carrying American P.O.W.'s an Irishman heard about this and insisted he be allowed to bring food to the P.O.W.'s Madeira was a Portuguese possession, this was not a British port. It seems no matter where a British naval vessel tied up if it had American P.O.W.'s the Irish insisted on feeding them and being allowed to see them.

By the second year of the Revolution, New Englander sailors were creating havoc all along the New England seaboard and at that they excelled. At the same time Irish born American John Paul Jones was bringing havoc to British home waters. Britain was well and truly getting sunk all over the place by the American Navy. British ships were going down like nine pins.

Benjamin Franklin the man whom the Lords had laughed at and ridiculed and clapped his ridicule. Was now busy hiring Irishmen to man the new American navy. He was busy converting merchant ships into American fighting ships and getting these fighting ships to give the snooty Lords a bloody nose. The American Navy was now heavily involved in sinking, burning, or capturing British merchant vessels. Soon these Irish/American navy vessels flying the American flag were clearing the British merchant ships from their own home waters, and off the oceans.

Two shifty Dubliners had quickly brought captured British ships into the French port of Dunkirk. They had netted a total of 38 British ships. The two chancers were joined by yet another chancer from Dublin and all three got to work sinking any and every British vessel that they came across. Soon the three Dublin lads had netted 34 more British vessels. The Irishmen, manned what Winston Churchill would later describe as "Q" ships i.e., ships pretending to be merchant ships but when alongside, the flaps come down to reveal a heavily armed American navy vessel. London merchants began to demand that all goods must now be carried in any ship *but* a British one!

Captain Patrick Dowling operating on his own captured 16 prize British ships off Scotland. The Irish lads would change their hunting grounds to fool the Royal navy as to their position of operation. Like Conyngham, Ryan one of the Dublin chancers unbelievably pulled his damaged ship into a British port, he held up the port authorities and the townspeople until his American ship was fixed up and sailed out again to cause more havoc!

These Irish people must have been mad or something; nothing seemed to phase their operational activity. The Dubliners threatened to destroy the warehouses unless their ship was patched up quickly. These men were playing fast and loose and if caught they would be hung as traitors if they were lucky and tortured to death if not.

733 British vessels were taken just by these three Dublin latchico, s £2,000,000 worth of goods valued at equivalent today to £361 million and that does not include the cost of the ships: that is just the destroyed goods.

At the end of the War for American Independence the American navy and the French fleet had cost the British merchant fleet £8 million in damage which today is worth £1,199,263,157 that is 1 trillion, i.e., one hundred and ninety-nine million. That should teach the good Lords for laughing at Benjamin Franklin, American ambassador. Nor does that enormous figure take into account the massive Royal navy losses to Irish Americans who sank them left, right and centre.

The Irishmen were so good at sinking British naval and merchant vessels that they began to become an embarrassment to the Continental Congress, as their successful sprees in British home waters were upsetting the money markets of Europe and the London bankers. The whole European financial market was starting to buckle under this concerted naval intervention against British Maritime trade and shipping. A bit like an embargo or enforced sanctions against free British maritime commerce. Indeed, it was fair game for Walter Raleigh, Captain Drake, and the rest of the British privateers to attack Spanish merchant vessels; but it was all crocodile tears when Irish privateers under the American flag began raiding their home waters and destroying their merchant fleet. They did not like that then. As usual for Britain it was do as i say, and not as I do. Complete hypocrisy and British blarney and humbug!

Britain could not take much more of the punishment that these three Dubliners were dishing out to them on a daily basis. And many Irish captains of fishing boats, and Trans-Atlantic Irish Ships, were playing their heroic part as essentially latter-day Irish pirates flying the American Stars and stripes and knocking the Royal Navy for six here there and everywhere. As stated earlier Irish merchant vessels were the majority of ships that sailed into American harbours. Ireland was the main commercial trading partner with the pre-revolutionary colonies. Thus, these Irish Captains new American waters, Harbours, and the Northern Atlantic intimately and offered their services to build up the American Navy from scratch. As American privateers the New Englanders excelled in that service to their country

On this *one* issue of armed privateers the New Englanders excelled in good numbers. So, bad had commercial trading for Britain become, their manufactures began to demand concessions be made to end this senseless war. H.M.G. began to seriously consider giving the Americans good favourable terms. By now, our three Irish Latchicos had built up a considerable fleet of armed vessels, and they had Q ships tactics down to a fine T. Their crews were not well dressed, and the crew were ordered to look dishevelled and lazy, as they would approach an enemy vessel, in a lazy, haphazard, amateurish, sailing style which was obviously not a well-run navy ship. But obviously one badly sailed by land lubbers. Obviously, this ship was more of a nuisance than any real threat. As this nuisance sailing ship, got dangerously to near for comfort, the sailors were more likely to shout at it and tell it to keep away than ring battle-stations and when up close it was all to late.

The Irish crew had all their cannons lit on a slow fuse, all burning and loaded and when they came alongside the flaps suddenly went down and the lazy crew quickly morphed into a very heavily armed no nonsense large boarding party. As armed men quickly came out of concealed spaces or emerged en masse from below decks. If need be, the Irish crew could within a split-second fire the cannons; and an almighty power would be released to destroy the enemy ship at awfully close quarters in seconds. For the captured ship, the game was most definitely up before it had even got started. Any resistance was met with immediate sinking!

The Irish lads next began to raid British ports. Benjamin Franklin refused to let them be part officially of the American navy, but they were entitled to fly the American flag. In essence they were privateers, or American pirates if you like. Benjamin Franklin instructed the Irish lads to get him more British prisoners which he needed to exchange for American P.O.W.'s.

The Royal navy was now under extreme pressure to bring this privateering in its home waters, to a halt. The Irish boys had been busy buying up full French navy ships which were extremely well-armed with crews of up to 250. The boys pushed their luck too far, come 1781 just off the Firth of Forth, Scotland April 1781 they had captured a British brig which they wished to ransom. Whilst loitering about the area three royal navy ships came into view, one of which was a massive 74 gunner plus two 36 gunners.

The Royal navy ships did not hang about they opened up straight away. For about an hour the Irish lads slugged it out with the Royal navy and eventually they surrendered as a "French ship" of war. The British became suspicious of this French ship story. All three Dubliners were sent down to London for trial. All three captains claimed they were French born. If they had been born in France, they could not be hung.

One must say that the British revel in Raleigh and Drake but when it was against them, they cry foul. if they were British, they would be described as swashbuckling, but when they are Irish it is felons, fiend, monster, an extreme miscreant total humbug from Britain the hypocrisy of their legal system is astonishing. * One was hung the other two got away. Alas when the two freed Irish Latchicos went to retrieve their swag money kept in English banks believe it or not! Their massive bank accounts had been cleaned out by British cunning. When one went to collect his swag, his, "Wife" had been in earlier and took the whole lot. The British were not foolish enough to let them get away with their haul.

*www Murder Mystery Mayhem, Joe O'Shea- O'Brien Press

I could go on, with daring do stories of the Irish in America, how one Irishman Thomas McDonagh was tasked with Protecting New York from a massive British fleet. First Lieutenant McDonagh had the Saratoga, Eagle, Ticonderoga, Preble and ten galley ships in total. First lieutenant McDonagh of the United States Navy fielded in all 86 guns. Ranged against the New York squadron were the British Royal Navy with the very latest in ship design and with 96 guns in all. The royal Navy clashed with the New York Squadron at 8am. By 12am midday, first lieutenant McDonagh had either captured or sunk all the Royal Navy big boats a few smaller ones managed to slip away. But enough... time is money, and our story must continue on.

There can be no doubt that the amount of Celtic blood in the American people is very much greater than they themselves would like to allow. Circa 1851 The Irish World claimed 2/3rds of the American population had Irish blood flowing through its veins the "Irish World" a New York paper, claimed in 1851 that 14,325,000 Americans were of Irish origin; out of a population of 23 million. During the American Civil war, the know nothings of the Union Army would jeer the Irish regiments and non-Irish Regiments;

still containing very large, Irish contingents and the Jewish boys thrown in amongst them. Yes, one Irish regiment, the 69th Pennsylvania accommodated our Jewish brethren. Both were mocked by the know nothings, as they moved up the line.

The know nothings still, by 1861 and all throughout the American Civil war until 1865 still hated the Irish in their ranks who bloody well fought for their bloody independence and now fighting for the bloody Union. These patriots need showing up for what they were, white Anglo Saxon protestants who would write the history books in their own favour for their own selfish advantage by their own myopic self-serving historians. History of the wasps by the wasps and for the wasps.

The more I read on the War of American Independence the more it becomes obvious that the Irish stuck by Washington when all else left the field would be a nice way to put it. Both Trenton and Princeton were mainly Irish victories for America the Irish never deserted Washington when the new Englanders did en masse before the battle of Trenton directly after the Continental defeat in New York. A massive 90% of Washington's army up and left and went back to their warm homesteads. American independence was just a silly idea; not worth dying for. The Irish thought otherwise and hung about Washington in the freezing cold god forsaken depths of winter.

No bloody wonder that President Abraham Lincoln loved the Irish and was surrounded by them 24/7. No bloody wonder President Washington loved them because he knew when all else failed, when all else deserted him, the bloody Irish would not! – come hell or high water, victory, or defeat. They nailed their colours to the American flag and fought like hell not to dishonour but to achieve its aims. General Washington's personal guard was mainly Irish Catholics.

Without the Irish there would have been no independent America. The Irish won two thirds of all-American medals of honour that were awarded in the American Civil war. During the American Revolution, they rallied quickly and en masse to the call of the bugle, no fear. If it came to a fight, they would stand with George Washington no matter what, through thick and thin for all time not part time soldier patriots, minute men or New England part-time patriots. They would march whenever and wherever to beat the deadly foe. Who all said it was the bloody Irish who lost us America, and won American freedom and liberty, two things which were near to an Irishman's heart, freedom, and liberty?

To be honest and fair to our wasp element, the Irish were going nowhere and to them this was personal. The British had treated them very badly, so they were all fired up ready to go from the off. They had nowhere else to go, the British would never accept them. There was far too much religious discrimination and they would hang the Irish as traitors.

This was never the case for the Wasps, they could always change sides, and many did avail of this opportunity, when it presented itself. Many chose to send their slaves to represent them; thus, ¼ of the force at the final battle of Yorktown was well represented by the slave owners of the colonies, if they could not be there in person to free America from tyranny; then by hell they were going to be at least represented by their slaves....... Also, they got their pay; after all they were their "property" risking their necks and blood on behalf of their truly patriotic slave master, who just couldn't find the time to serve in person. Washington used to call these New Englanders people of the Chimney Corner. They would sit out the war in the comfort on these sturdy warm houses in the warmth of their Chimney corner, and God bless them one an all.

The Irish loved America, it was a land full of good cheap land and if any man wanted to work hard it was the place of dreams, the Promised Land to every Irishman and his sons and daughters, it was a land worth fighting and dying for, for sure 100%. You bet your cotton dollar on that one. America and its people had many hard years of trouble and strife ahead of them. Not all would make it to the promised land. Many would be maimed, tormented, and broken, by the momentous struggle for survival of the American dream. Some battles would be won many lost. The vagaries and fortunes of war would swing this way then, back again. Each side would suffer, and Americans would seem nearer to defeat than schoolbooks like to admit. It was a gigantic struggle in which many came of worse than they entered it. Many many times people would give up with this unending war, which was ripping the country apart. Was it worth it, to struggle on endlessly? Washington and his die-hards thought so. when Congress passed on to him Britain's latest good offer and asked for his opinion, it was. We have come to far, suffered too much, borne every burden a man can take, starved, and struggled thru to give up now, we soldier on to the bitter end, if need be. We will brook no compromise; we will not give up the dream nor dilute it down.

If you are reading this in America then next time you wander about your town, city, or pleasant green land, remember all your freedoms were hard won. Very hard won. Your civic and federal representations to serve and represent your beliefs, your civic rights of fundamental freedoms, freedom of speech, religious thought, representation, no matter your colour creed or wealth. One man one vote.

The poor American down on his luck gets equal representation to the mega-rich mogul. Equality of justice for all. No fancy titles or kingly garb curry any favour here. This is your land, a land in which freedom of expression is enshrined in law. A land in which each individual should be honoured and cherished as an individual with inalienable rights which no one, no judge, no political party, no sheriff, no mogul, can take from you as an American citizen. Equal to all other citizens no more no less. When the good men of America stated that they wished to produce a country in this land for all comers, in which life, liberty and the pursuit of happiness was a goal. It was one small aim and sentence for one man to write, but one giant leap forward for all mankind.

At the start of this journey, I quoted Dr. Phillip Thomas Tucker a respected American author. One who has written well on colonial times its struggles and its people and has been a historian for the United States of America's Department of Defence. Now that our journey is coming to its end and conclusion, I would wish to return to these historians, writings, views, and analysis and have you take heed of them.

Dr. Tucker states in an article he wrote for" Salon. Com. "an online magazine of news, politics, culture, science and food. Dated 17 March 2020. Dr. Tucker states the Irish have become the forgotten players in America's struggle for Independence. He relates todays historical interpretations...." One of the greatest mysteries of American has revolved around the intriguing question of how general George Washington and his revolutionaries could have possibly prevailed over a mighty British Empire. Many explanations have been offered to explain this enduring legacy thru out the past. But none are entirely satisfactory. Can a more accurate and correct answer be found at this late date to better explain how and why England lost its thirteen colonies forever.... fortunately for America, it possessed a large population of colonists, who were already militants, agitators, and rebels before they ever migrated to the New World. It needs to be remembered that America went into this titanic struggle with no standing army. It was going up against a well-trained well-armed professional seasoned Army.

The best in the whole of Europe at that time. America did not even have enough gun powder for Christ's sake.

For more than two centuries what has been forgotten about America's stirring creation story were the crucial and disproportionate contribution that the Irish people played in the winning of the American Revolution. Largely because of Ireland's dark legacy of early subjugation by England, and {the} difficult economic times that caused a mass exodus of immigrants to colonial America. I take a little issue here with American historians historical reading of historical events. Irish Catholics came in good numbers. before the Revolution. see "Irelands Important and Heroic Part in Americas Independence and Development" by Rev.Frank L Reynolds, Circa 1919? And especially "*A Hidden phase of American history Irelands part in America's struggle for Liberty*" by Michael Joseph O'Brien [a giant of American true colonial history, a researcher of intrepid tenacity a historian who rightly tackled the snobbery of the New England Brahmins & was duly derided for it. But History I believe will prove him right and them wrong] pub 1919 see also book bibliography and further reading list. Americans historians had traditionally thru out the 19th Century, had a heavy bias towards Non-Catholics immigration from Ireland, out of a predominately Catholic province in the process of being cleared out of Catholics as truly an historical perversion of the facts, by Americas New England elite in the heavily racial 19thCentury. This Historical Hogwash was peddled and disseminated widely for purely racial and religious supremacist reasons and bears no relation to the historical record. When prestigious periodicals, peer reviewed online encyclopaedia Wikipedia states that only 10,000 Catholics ever migrated to America, pre -revolution. Then that is balderdash of fine variety.

Where in God's name did the 100,000 Irish volunteers, come from to free America? Everyone probably had some children. So, 100,000 comes

400,000 quickly. The contortion of mathematical gymnastics, the putting thru the wringer of demographic figures, is astounding. And all for racial and religious biases from white supremacists, the W.A.S.P. elite, in the 19th Century. The marriage, birth certs, paper articles, ships captains all pertain to the Irish both Catholic and Presbyterian coming off many Irish ships continuously over the 17th & 18th Centuries. Indeed, for only 10,000 over the whole of those two centuries this tiny number of people of the auld faith sure caused a stink. Complaints of Papists running amok, taking over this place, that place, even the Native American Indians got in on the act complaining about the Irish taking over. These letters, articles in papers must all be then part of some historical conspiracy to blow out of all proportion the tiny few, handful of Catholics who dot America as very noisy individuals. This is historical rewriting out on gigantic proportions a group of people and their communities who freed America pretty much single handily but not quiet. Why in God's name did George Washington make Every St. Patricks day whilst operating in the field, a holiday for the Continental Army? Why did he distribute papers amongst the troops, an unusual activity! And then sit back and wait as an eruption of joy and shouting came up from its massed ranks. Inside the paper was an article. The Irish Parliament had recognised America as an independent country! The troops went mad with joy. Why did American generals use Irish townlands for rapid troop enhancement if these Townlands according to Wikipedia did not exist! Why was the Continental Army called the popes Army? Why does Benedict Arnold deride it as such in his confession to entice more protestants to leave? Why did the British Army use psychops to encourage Catholics to join its ranks? Especially when only, a few exist or have ever existed in the whole of Americas colonial history.? Why did British Forces see the Sectarian division of Catholics and true honourable protestants as a main strategy if as so-called historians state a mere handful of Catholics only exist, or even ever existed in pre-revolutionary America. What utter, utter, utter nonsense.

This bare handful are sure making it awfully hard for a mighty army to even march anywhere unmolested. Its all-hogwash history made up and invented by a clique of wasp elite who did bugger all during the Revolution. A virulent form of religious racism which needs addressing. Everybody is complaining vociferously about the Papists being everywhere, yet historians say they don't exist! They don't exist for praises but overflow the place as regards vociferous complaints. Somethings wrong there, I think. Take note those peddling this monstrous lie are the very people who did little at the time, yet now write they did a lot, if not all of it! The facts are the Continental Army was half Catholic, it used Catholic townlands for rapid recruitment. The Catholics and Presbyterians all over America funded the Army, Fed the Army, paid its wages, took its Continental money, when true blue blooded New Englanders sat in their "Chimney Corner" and refused point blank to trade with it, join it or support it in any true fashion. What these elite were willing to do was write a false narrative of the Revolution which incredible made them the "PATRIOTS"!

I also take issue with the term Scotch Irish for people from Northern Ireland as many were Catholics. This lazy or indeed convenient way to make Catholics disappear is not true or accurate to history. To make out every boat from Northern Ireland or Ulster was jam packed with Presbyterians *only* is Jabberwocky and foolish naivety.

Dr. Tucker goes on. Irelands leading role in breaking into the frontier and going westwards is widely recognised in America; yet the leading role of the Irish in being America's vanguard of resistance during the Revolutionary war from its start all the way to its finish, is not fully appreciated

315

He states the Irish made a fundamental contribution in shaping America. But that this contribution both on and of the Battlefield has over the years been heavily sanitized out, for racial and religious reasons. This goes for the black/brown skinned Americans one in four soldiers at Yorktown on the Continental side was black/brown get over it. The Hessians who were there also wrote home that not one regiment exists without a sizeable proportion of Negros in it. What happened to these Negro soldiers? Where is their history? It too went in the heavily sanitized version of white elite history. "The Patriots" for sure. This New Englander school of historical interpretation still so widely accepted as truth, is a myth. This anglicized version for wasps by wasps is not the real history at all. The real and accurate history of America and its momentous tough hard struggle by the people for the people, contains many Catholics and more Blacks/brown involvement than the New England version allows for or is or was willing to accept or allow. Dr. Tucker calls the Irish the most important players and does call out the New England school for essentially writing them out. He states the Irish were leading the way in Agitation for independence, sustaining the war effort, and leading to an ultimate American victory. Dr. Tucker states the Irish fought in far larger numbers than the Anglo-Saxons or New Englanders. He calls the Irish "The most sturdy core foundation" of the American Army. He calls them the "reliable Backbone" of Americas resistance from beginning to end. These were no minute men they signed up en masse for years

He goes on the standard interpretations of "America's long and hard revolutionary struggle." Have obscured the undeniable truth of the all-important contributions of the Irish "and its peoples. Dr. Tucker calls the Irish highly motivated to take up arms and join the fight in any way, militarily or economically. In order to achieve independence from Britain. Indeed, they were as a people more motivated than most to take on the British

Army... One French officer on manoeuvres with his detachment of troops come across a lone straggler he is a recently arrived emigrant from Ireland. He joined the fight right away. He got injured. He was now on his way to re-join the Battle. The French officer stated that just about sums up the Irish in America during the Revolution. Dr. Tucker accurately states the bare facts of the matter."

This significant Irish contribution has been long obscured because the mythical revolution has presented America's struggle for liberty as primarily an Anglo-Saxon triumph won by colonists of English descent. Dr. Tucker rightly calls the Irish the" Die-Hards" of the American Revolution. These are not the words of some light weight, American historian, but the writings of a mainstream one. These findings cannot be ignored or dismissed because they tackle some outdated national shibboleths. They are the truth long hidden and ignored for purely racial reasons. Dr. Tucker states that this New Englander version has unfortunately prevailed. America was lucky to have a sizable population ready and willing to take on the British. And mentally prepared for the hardships that followed He calls the widely accepted version a "severely distorted interpretation" of the American Revolution. He goes on "generations of Americans never understood a fundamental reality that without the...Irish... the Americans revolutions tortured course; a new nation conceived in liberty would have almost certainly succumbed to an early death... {say about December 1776 it would all have been over; done and dusted, a veritable footnote in British American history little studied by American scholars of British history}.

You can read Dr. Tuckers little essay at www salon.com "*The Irish have become the forgotten players of Americas struggle for independence.*" It certainly worth your while. He speaks with good academic analysis of the history of the American Revolution so far. He states the American "revolution story has been so thoroughly reinvented" one needs to peel back

the distortions to get to the true core. He calls the Irish "the heart and soul of American resistance". Second to none." It was the Irish people's belief in Freedom and liberty and the American cause, and their deep-seated gut-tural stubborn belief to never give in, and sheer stamina to fight on no matter what, that saved the day and the Revolution time and time again. It was Irish arms that were pivotal to winning the American Revolution......
But before we finally leave the battlefield of American freedom, and New England all alone with its favourite cousins departing across the sea in their boats

Let us walk along that New England shore in another American epoch, a quieter time, the mid-19th century., America has been free for some time and is doing well, its cities are expanding and America and its peoples are growing into a strong prosperous nation, equal to the mightiest nation, Britain. America will soon have its peace disturbed by British machina-tions in the southern states, to rip it asunder., but for now the wind is free, and a fresh spring air is coming in from off the New England coast.

It is 1849 and the Irish are fleeing Ireland once again in massive numbers, this time its not only mass evictions, this time its massed hunger on a scale to terrify any sane Ethiopian

Mass starvation has gripped Ireland for three horrific years already; and no end is in sight. Mass starvation encroaches like a devouring beetle hungry for more skeletal human bodies. An ever-hungry monster scours and devours the land, towns and cities, and their collective inhabitants. It infects Europe and Russia too.

The French and Russian Armies are mobilised to bring food into the Starving areas, In Ireland and only in Ireland Troops are brought in to escort the vital food *out* of the starvation areas! Across the whole of Europe governments rush to buy food from America's bulging warehouses and larders. In Ireland, emergency food depots are kept mysteriously locked, bolted and guarded! The largest richest trading nation on the planet goes scurrying about trying to buy up food in autumn it already knows has gone.

It places the whole endeavour to buy food for the starving millions in Ireland into the hands of a *single* Liverpudlian corn merchant, with his own warehouse, no less. A Mr Eric Erickson Mr. Erickson although trying his best is given strict instructions by the main Architect of this enterprise of mass starvation, to only bid for corn and cereals on the open market with rock bottom bids. In a time of European wide mass starvation and food famine, his silly bids only produce a trickle of food. All other countries even the small poor ones like Latvia buy food on the open market at market prices.

Death by design quickly follows on a monstrous scale. At the time Irish papers call it rightly... a *HOLOCAUST*! Millions die in excruciating pain over the next seven years in Ireland Across the rest of Europe it's just a few hundred thousand in total! The worst hit area by the mysterious bacillus was Belgium. It too had a mass population density, much more populous than Irelands, and it too was hit harder than Ireland by the fungus. Yet little Belgium fed most of its people successfully, just like the rest of Europe did. Only in Britain was the mass starvation process looked upon as a *golden opportunity to depopulate Ireland.*

American author Henry Thoreau from Concorde New England is taking in the fresh sea air of Cape Cod. An Irish famine ship has dashed upon the American rocks, and dead people litter the beaches. The New Englander natives are picking up the dead bodies and placing them in coffins with a white cloth to hide their bruised and battered naked bodies * Henry kicks over the ship's *rotten* timbers and Thoreau peers into one coffin into which the Americans, had lifted a young Irish girl. Her Irish body is swollen up and Thoreau is instantly attracted and drawn down into her eyes which were wide open. Her little body is battered and bruised by the rocks.

Thoreau sees in the young Irish girls eyes the story of Ireland and America, and the horror of her story in Ireland and how she got here, washed up on an American beach with the world closing in smoothly like water over her coffin. ...Washed up on an American beach like so much human flotsam, bobbing about aimlessly upon the waves, until her little bruised body was deposited upon New England's shores... poor little thing... Washed up and starved out.

So sad, so very sad but true... R.I.P.

*.Astonishingly the New Englanders managed to get a coffin for each corpse. And each corpse was removed with respect... Thank you... They made it to America. The land of the free... Dead on arrival!

...... And so, my dear friends we have come to the final part of our quest and journey. It is now time to depart, but I must say before I go that the real history of the revolution is fascinating, from an Irish perspective and I dearly hope it makes its way into the curriculum of every Irish school North and South. And into every American junior high.

America is a land of immigrants, no other country on this earth has been more welcoming to immigrants than America. It is built upon immigration from its very start!

America's foreign origins are English, Irish, Scottish, French, Spanish, and African then a whole swelter of old European peoples, from every corner and nook and cranny of old Europe. Asian and Spanish peoples dominated the west coast. Spanish the southern border and French the mid-west.

All Americans are immigrants from somewhere else. All that is except the *NATIVE AMERICANS*. All have made America their home, and what a good home it has been to generations of Americans of all hue's creeds and colours. All have contributed in their own way. *Ask not what America can do for you, but more importantly ask what you can do for America.* May it continue to be a shining beacon on the hill. A country that uniquely places the goal of human happiness as a stated governmental aim

So, there we have it, I hope you have enjoyed the trip down memory lane, and that I have given you something to chew on or given you a desire to dig some more, into the American Revolutions rich historical narrative soil. It's now time to go, and for you to put the book back on the shelf. Adios amigos, ciao baby. Until we meet again.

Christmas 1976, Princeton

Yes; C.N.N. was right; snow was general all over the east coast of America. It was falling softly upon the quiet leafy streets of Boston, the suburbs of Philadelphia, and on the soft, green well-tended fields of Long Island, and on into the waters of the Hudson, and further southwards, softly falling into the dark mutinous waves of Delaware bay.

It was falling too upon every part of a lonely New England churchyard, where an American Patriot lay, blanketing him snugly up in a quiet final cold embrace. It lay thickly, drifted on the crooked crosses and headstones, on the spears of the little gate, on the barren thorns.

The solitary student's inner soul and heart swooned softly, and slowly.

He was deep in thought in a veritable self-contained bubble of swirling snow about him, in his own drifting universe. Just as it had swirled about the river of time... years ago, surrounding a troop of desperate men on a desperate journey, in a life and death struggle of manly birth. The birth of his nation. He peered upwards towards the sky. It was as if he heard the snow falling faintly through the universe and faintly falling, like the descent of their last end, upon all the living and the patriot dead. He walked away slowly, deep in thought. The silent sentinel bullet holes on the college walls trickled down ice cool teardrops with fresh falling snow...... it was Christmas 1976 and a storm front was moving in across the Delaware, across Princeton and Trenton. Just as it had done, 200 years ago, blanketing ill shod freezing

American soldiers, not to far from where he stood. He trundled on thru the snow... quietly, lost in his own journey. Home......*So much water had flowed thru the mighty Delaware since that Christmas day in 1776, and it that short space of time so much had changed. Would Washington recognise his country? Was it worth fighting for? I think he would be very proud of its achievement's. So, so much water under the bridge, and that my friends is what we call history.*

Adaption of James Joyce's "The Dead"

A LIST, OF JUST SOME OF THE MORE PROMINENT PEOPLE WHO TESTIFIED, MANY UNDER OATH. MANY STATED IN BRITISH PARLIAMENTARY INQUIRIES DURING THE WAR AND AFTER THE WAR WAS LOST. THAT AMERICA AND ITS THIRTEEN COLONIES WAS LOST DUE TO IRISH STAMINA, MILITARY ACTIVITY, POLITICAL ACTIVITY AND IN SUPPLYING THE MAIN ELEMENT OF SOLDIERS IN ITS RANKS, SUPPLYING THE ARMY WITH FEED, GOODS, AND MATERIALS AND GIVING FULL SUPPORT TO THE REVOLUTIONARY CAUSE.... THEY ALL; EVERY LAST ONE OF THEM BLAMED THE LOSS OF AMERICA. FIRMLY AND SQUARLY UPON THE WORK OF THE IRISH PEOPLE.

Joseph Galloway, (member of the first Continental Congress. Friend of Benjamin Franklin.Loyalist to Crown. Aid to British General Howe and personally responsible for interrogating Patriotic prisoner.

Lord George Germain, (Secretary of state for America)

Lord Cornwallis, (British General American theatre of Operations)

Sir Guy Carlton, (Commander in Chief, British Forces America)

WHY WE FOUGHT

Major General Gray, (Commander in Chief British Forces America)

Major General Robertson, (British General, American Theatre of Operations)

Lord Dartmouth (Leading British politician with portfolio for America)

General Sir Henry Clinton, (British Commander in Chief, British Forces America)

Joshua Pell, (Loyalist War Diarist)

Ambrose Searle, (Private Secretary to British General William Howe)

If you have enjoyed this little journey around the American Revolution then please leave or write a review; from the site you bought the book from. Kind regards E G RUTLEDGE

Bibliography

IRELAND Gustave De Beaumont Harvard University Press 2007. A good book into Irelands economic/Social background *****

The Last Conquest of Ireland {Perhaps} John Mitchel pub. Books Ulster 1878Another good book on Ireland, and its Woes-- *****

How the Irish Won the American Revolution Phillip T. Tucker pub. Skyhorse 2015an essential read for further study into this fascinating subject as regards American colonial history*****

Irelands Important and Heroic Part in Americas Independence & Development by Rev. Frank L Reynolds. Pub. Leopold Classic Library 2016 reprint of old copy *****

The Three Battles at Trenton & Princeton by C.C. Haven 1871***

The Battles of Trenton & Princeton William S Stryker Riverside Press 1898 (Excellent book) *****

A People Numerous and Armed Pub. University Michigan Press 1990 ****

A Hidden Phase of American History (Irelands part in America's Struggle...) Michael Joseph O'Brien Reprint of 19th century book pub Hard Press 2014 *****

WHY WE FOUGHT

A Peoples History of the American Revolution Raphael Ray New Press 2011 ****

Paisanos The Forgotten Irish who changed the face of Latin America Tim Fanning Pub. Gill Dublin 2016***

History of the Protestant Reformation in England and Ireland William Cobbett pub. Tan Books North Carolina 2012 reprint 1896 By far the best book on this subject. By a true and honest proud English protestant. And sergeant major of the British Army served in the American war of Independence for Britain Highly accurate and precise a real eyeopener should be on the reading list of every secondary school in Britain******

Cobbett in Ireland (A warning to England) William Cobbett pub Lawrence Wishart 1984 ***

Lincoln and the Irish Niall O Dowd pub Skyhorse 2018 ***

The American Revolution Vol 3 reprint of 19ᵗʰ century book

George Trevelyan pub Forgotten Books 2019

A History of the War with America, France, Spain & Holland 1775-1783 pub1787 Author(unknown)

History of the American War Vol 1 Charles Stedman original 1794

Famine Fenians and Freedom 1830-1882 Richard Brown pub Authoring History 2011

Memoirs of a life chiefly passed in Pennsylvania within the last sixty years Alexander Graydon 1811 (free on Google books) Revolution picks up p/100+

Irish in the American Revolution and their early influence on the colonies James Haltigan 1908 *****

A Catholic History of North America by Thomas Darcy McGee 1885(A very prolific writer on American Colonisation)

A True History of the American Revolution Sidney George Fisher 1902 ***

Washington's Crossing by David Hackett Fischer 2006***

Washington's Immortals by Patrick O'Donnell 2017***

Who we are vol.1 1750s-1850s by Anton Chaitkin 2020****

How the Nation was won 1630-1754 (Americas untold story) by Graham Lowry 2003 ****

I have not read the rest of these books but I enclose them, because I came across the titles in my research and I would hope you may find them interesting.

George Bancroft's 10 vol; History of the U.S.A. 1834-1874 (period of writing)

A Pictorial Field Book of the Revolution vol 1&2 by Benson John Lossing (another prolific writer on subject)

*NOTE ABOUT THE ILLUSTRATIONS... I am well aware images do not accurately fit in to the narrative some images are of different battles and the Irish eviction images are 19th century not 16th, 17th or 18th century but they are there to visually aid the story that is all. I am well aware thru is not the standard English spelling, but hey languages like history evolve over time... I am well aware standard English does not allow one to begin a sentence with "And" but eh get over it,.. I am rebel writer

A NOTE ABOUT THE FRONT COVER This is a painting by an esteemed American Artist named Howard Pyle. It is titled "THE NATION MAKERS" 1906. In reality these people are. the real nation makers. They fought and, in many cases, died for it or were mutilated in the endeavour I really like how Mr. Pyle has debunked the snappy dressed "Chimney Corner Gang" version of the Revolutionary War. Instead, he goes with "rough reality". And all the better it is too, for it..... well done Howard.